THE HAMLYN BOOK OF

soft furnishings

THE HAMLYN BOOK OF

soft
furnishings

Essential advice and practical projects for decorating with fabrics

HAMLYN

contents

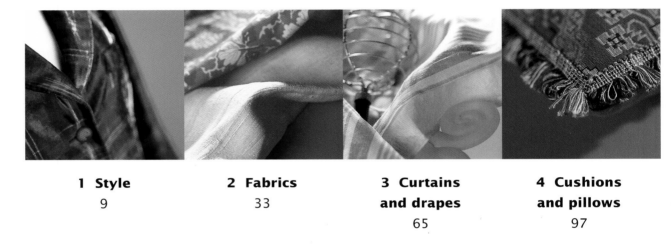
First published in Great Britain in 1997 by Hamlyn, an imprint of Reed International Books
Michelin House, 81 Fulham Road, London, SW3 6RB
and Auckland, Melbourne, Singapore and Toronto

Copyright © 1997 Reed International Books Limited

ISBN 0-600-58972-2

A CIP catalogue record for this book is available from the British Library

Publishing Director: Laura Bamford   Art Director: Keith Martin   Executive Editor: Simon Tuite   Executive Art Editor: Mark Stevens
Managing Editor: Lucinda Pearce-Higgins   Consultant Editor: Deborah Evans   Project Editor: Katie Cowan   Editor: Mary Lambert
Production Controller: Mark Walker   Design and Art Editing: Mark Richardson Design   Assistant Designer: Louise Griffiths
Studio Photographer: Debi Treloar   Location Photographers: Rupert Horrox, David Parmitter and Paul Ryan   Illustrator: Jane Hughes
Picture Researchers: Emily Hedges and Sally Claxton

Contributors: Denise Brock – *Accessories*; Deborah Evans – *The workshop*; Elizabeth Keevill – *Curtains and drapes, Linens*;
Heather Luke – *Style, Fabrics, Cushions and pillows*; Jenny Plucknett – *Soft seating and cover-ups*;
Catherine Woram – *Merging the indoors and outdoors*

Produced by Mandarin Offset
Printed in China

Introduction

A look round the fabric department of a large store, or a visit to a specialist shop, may leave you bewildered – with such a vast choice, how can you begin to decide which look suits your home and lifestyle? What is the best choice of fabric to re-cover a sofa, and which style of window dressing will fulfil all your needs in terms of colour, light and privacy?

The Hamlyn Book of Soft Furnishings brings you solutions, from building up a colour scheme to actually making the soft furnishings you have chosen. You will find pages of inspiration, clearly illustrated projects to follow through, and lots of practical hints and tips.

Soft furnishings are an important element of home style, being both practical and decorative. Fabrics can be used for essential items, such as curtains and blinds, upholstery, bed linen and table linen, as well as for more creative details, such as cushion covers, swags draped across windows or at bedheads, and accessories such as lighting or nursery equipment.

Whether you are new to sewing, or have several years' experience, **The Hamlyn Book of Soft Furnishings** shows you how to use fabric throughout your home. You will find general guidance on colour schemes and style, practical information about the best types of fabric for particular situations, and detailed step-by-step advice on measuring up and working out how much fabric you need for a particular project. All this information is followed up with a practical reference section on sewing techniques and measurements .

From the bedroom to the kitchen, and from the bathroom to the garden, soft furnishings add the last details in comfort and style. **The Hamlyn Book of Soft Furnishings** shows you how to achieve that style.

1 Style

Style

The details that make up a room's style include everything from the wall and floor finishes to the chosen ornaments or flower arrangement. Fabrics and soft furnishings need to be chosen to suit the overall design scheme, and can make a major style statement in any room.

To create our own style we need to acquire knowledge about flooring, fabrics, colours, textures, heating, lighting and furniture. How is it possible to make a home that is

elegant, neat and stylish, but still comfortable, friendly and welcoming?

By reading home style magazines and looking at manufacturer's brochures you can see how design schemes are put together in different styles of rooms. Then you can experiment with colour and furnishing schemes until you find the one to suit you. Try and work out whether you want the room to appear bright or dark, and then use sample paint pots to try out paint colours and buy large samples of wallpapers and furnishing fabrics to see how they will blend in. Always study the character and geographical aspect of your home before finally choosing decorative schemes.

By learning how to mix and match colours, patterns, textures and accessories, and following your own design instincts, you will soon create a happy and attractive mix in your home.

The simplicity of whitewashed walls and silky wooden boards overlaid with a crunchy rush mat creates a welcoming environment of space and light in this room, left. The natural elements of brick and stone are joined by carved woods and earthenware pots. Mattress cushions and tied pillows in taupe and white ticking provide rest for day or night, the only 'colour' in the room appears in the faded roses of an antique quilt. With plain decorating schemes, the emphasis can be placed on the room's furniture. Here, far left, the rattan furniture blends with the polished floorboards, and accentuates the pure white bedlinen. In striking contrast a colourful mixture of cushion fabrics sit together on the bed in this sun filled scene (inset).

1 Where to start

What exactly is style and how do we go about finding it? Style is putting together a cohesive interior design scheme in a room that is pleasing to all your senses. It is learning how to combine the use of colour with furniture, fabrics and accessories to achieve a well-balanced, coordinated look that suits your home.

It might not be possible to smell fabrics and colours but you can use wonderful colour tones which can evoke a sense of a perfume in a room. The whole scheme can then be enhanced by adding some seasonal fresh flowers with their own delicate perfume. A room furnished completely in calico and ticking, for example, would have a heavenly scent even in winter by just adding a few Regalia lilies.

You need to make a room work for you, but do not be put off if it is small, large or dark, or an awkward shape because you can transform it cosmetically. You can increase or reduce a room's size or bring more light in with the subtle use of colour. You can also conceal ugly features or corners by using attractive accessories.

Budget and effort

It is a popular misconception that money and style go hand in hand. Certainly, if you have plenty of money you can buy the expertise of interior designers, but even if you are on a low budget, you can create your own style within the limits you have set yourself, if you put enough time and effort into the project. Remember to spread your budget throughout the house, do not be tempted to spend it all on one room. If your funds are low, try clothing all of the windows in an inexpensive fabric such as calico or muslin and then introduce imaginative trimmings and hold-backs.

Look at home magazines and home store brochures and see which elements you like. Study their room sets and learn from them. If you have to compromise, do so on wallpapers, paints and accessories, but try to buy the best quality you can afford in sofas, side tables, soft furnishing fabrics and carpets, and rugs as these need to last and be hardwearing. Also choose colours that are not too fashionable, but which you know you can live with for some time.

No one is born with an innate sense of style, but everyone can acquire it. By reading style books and magazines, and absorbing different design schemes everywhere you go, you will soon find out what you like and dislike.

Developing your style

In time you will develop your own taste in interior decor. You might find you prefer a period look to your home rather than a more modern feel. Your taste in decoration will also be affected by travelling abroad. In fact, you may find you want to create a colonial living room, a Mediterranean bathroom or an oriental dining room in your home or follow one theme throughout.

Home making is an art, but do not get too carried away with elaborate room plans, think logically whether the plans will work in your home environment. Of course the most important visual aspects when you walk into a room are its colours, its fabrics and flooring. But ultimately it is your innate common sense that will tell you where to position furniture, and the best way to conceal something in a room such as an unattractive radiator, an ugly corner or an unsightly fireplace.

Above *Bright yellow walls bring sunshine into any room, whether during the day or night, summer or winter, which is especially welcome in cooler countries with greyer light. The strength of the yellow becomes the perfect foil for the polished floor, natural table and antique painted chairs, while antique toile de jouy covers extend the country element and provide all the colour and pattern necessary in this room.*

Following through a style

When planning the style in your home, you need to think about how it will follow through from room to room. Avoid using strong contrasts, because if you create a different colour and style in each room it can be uncomfortable and unsettling to live with. So try to coordinate the flow of colours through the rooms, keeping the flooring colours and surfaces as near in tone to each other as possible to make a good base from which you can work. Think about having wood flooring and using wood colours as they can be very restful.

Individual taste

Even if you decide to copy your room styles from a magazine, they will always have your taste and possessions reflected in them, whether it is a cherished accessory, a homemade patchwork bedspread in the bedroom, special cushion covers in a living room or re-covered dining chairs in the dining room.

Although your furnishings will reflect the changing needs and preferences of the other family members, ultimately the style and colour choices will completely and utterly reflect your character. As your most expen-

sive purchases will be the long-term furniture and soft furnishings, which must be sensible choices, all the other accessories that you choose can be less expensive, fashionable additions or ones that are chosen straight from the heart.

1 Influences and imagination

If you are looking for a starting point for a style to suit your home, step back and think about the particular interests and passions in your life. By doing this you can then build up a style around a theme: if you love gardening, a floral theme, or leafy green colours can set the style of a room. If you enjoy travel, you can have fun planning your room schemes around different countries. Think about developing a richly coloured Indian living room or maybe develop a sunny French kitchen. Alternatively, you can build a room scheme around a favourite collection of ornaments, choosing the room's paints, wallpapers and fabrics to blend in with the collection's colours. If classical music is an interest, use black and white as the main colours, and then add wood and chrome accessories.

Everyone is influenced by everything that goes on around them. Current fashions, friends and social life, and self awareness will all influence a person's taste and ultimate style. Money is useful, but not essential. Imagination, patience, determination and time are the main criteria for good design planning. Here are some suggestions for making style statements that are based on everyday life, and which are very easy to follow.

Above To compile your colour board, choose pieces which you like for colour and shape and then add items which seem to make the others come alive.

Far left Market stalls and food shop windows are rich sources for imaginative colour groupings. Whether mouth-watering patisserie or fresh vegetables and fruits, the colours of nature never fail to inspire.

Left The old back streets of any Mediterranean country town cannot fail to inspire. Faded soft wall paints and brightly coloured shutters, jostle for attention with cloths and blankets hanging from balconies.

Above *The formal layout and exactness of Elizabethan topiary gardens evoke a sense of order and controlled beauty which can be used as the benchmark for every design scheme, or they might simply inspire the way to place tiles in a floor or the form and scale required for a specific piece of sculpture.*

Above right *Nature is the most valuable source for tips on the perfect colour scheme. Tones of one colour, plus a generous dose of accent colour, are the order of the day here, as brilliant pink blooms from rosa Caroline Testoyt are the zest of life for a season in this all green garden.*

Right *Great masterpieces, such as this painting by J M W Turner, become timeless works of art not only for their content but for the artist's special use of colour. You might choose a single artist or picture, for all your inspiration, or you might decide to use a different one for each room in your home.*

1 Making an inspiration board

There has never been a better time for interior design. Numerous ranges of paints, both modern and traditional colours, wallpapers and a diverse collection of good-quality, affordable soft furnishing fabrics are now available. As there is so much choice it can often be hard to decide on a room's design scheme, so to help you make up your mind try compiling an inspiration board made up of the images and items that appeal to you.

Looking for inspiration

To find out what decorating styles you like, ask yourself some basic questions about design, collect ideas from magazines and brochures, and make an inspiration board. Keep revising what you have on the board as this will give you the confidence you need to create a scheme that is very special and unique.

Question checklist

- What are your favourite colours?
- What furnishings do you need to keep?
- How do you want to live in your home?
- How much entertaining do you do?
- How long do you intend to remain in your home?
- How much can you spend now, next year and the year after, including housekeeping and maintenance?

At the same time, there are some things that cannot be changed. When you are looking for ideas for a particular room, bear in mind its aspect (whether it is flooded with sun, or has a cooler light); the geographical location (do you live in a hot, Mediterranean-type climate, or a more temperate zone); the character of the house (is it a spacious suburban home, a city apartment or a lakeside chalet, for example).

Building the board

Use tear sheets from magazines to build up your scheme. You will never find a whole project to suit you, but pick out the most pleasing aspects. Take snippets of fabrics which attract you for colour and design, paint swatches, flower colours – in short, anything which is pleasurable to look at.

After a few weeks of collecting different items you will find a pattern emerging. You might find that texture dominates, that two particular colours really stand out, or that architectural form is the strong point. From this selection you will know whether you prefer random prints, stylized prints or no print at all. You will soon be able to decide whether you prefer a cluttered country look or a chic minimalist style.

Below *Making up your own inspiration board can be great fun and will really let you find out what colours, styles and textures you like. Build up the board gradually, adding fabrics, swatches and pictures to suit. Do not be afraid to change your mind and revise the look on the board accordingly.*

Choosing a design scheme

Once you have made up your inspiration board, have faith in your choice when you go out to buy your fabrics, paints and wallpapers.

• Have courage – even interior designers make mistakes. But your common sense will normally make sure these are never major ones.

• Look at your total budget and spread it evenly throughout your home. It is better to leave an empty space in a room rather than buying something that is out of style.

• Give your scheme time: interiors take a while to develop. You cannot wave a magic wand. Patience and tender care will allow your home to grow up with you.

• Remember to follow the character of your home. If it is a modern flat, with chrome and steel fixtures, do not try to make it look like a country cottage as it will just not work.

Now take out anything that bores you and make a priority list of the things that still interest you, so that you are now in a much better position to start your proper research. Visit different homes and department stores and look through the available fabric collections. Take pictures and samples that you can add to your board.

Soon you will be able to spot immediately anything that does not work and you will discover that precise colour matching is not important but that colour tones and values are.

If your choices appear to be limited, do not worry: a comfortable home revolves around very few colours. It is the variety of texture and accessories which create a room's atmosphere and personal style.

Look at your home's structure

Of course your inspiration board will be influenced to an extent by the home in which you live. Is it a country cottage with many old, traditional features, or is it a modern city apartment that needs the right contemporary furnishings? Does it have character already or do you need to create it? Remember that period fittings can be put back in. You can seek them out in second-hand shops or salvage yards.

Above *A love of antique fabrics and early prints is the style source for this pretty bedroom. Toile de jouy and hand-embroidered pillows sit against simple block checks, all of which have been chosen to blend with the antique hand-quilted bedcover and curtain fabric.*

Below *If your chosen starting point in a room is blue and white as here, experiment with tones of other colours to balance the effect. Soft reds and terracottas, furniture with polished wood and country tweed fabrics have been chosen to contrast the soft grey and Prussian blue colours.*

Classical style

1

By looking at the development of style in a historical context, we can learn how past trends and traditions in soft furnishings have brought about their look today. Architectural and interior design has come a long way from the classic carvings and columns of Egypt and Greece to the style of buildings that are our modern residences.

There are many different ways to arrange and decorate a home and this has always been the case. However, with each historical era there has been a particular fashion with soft furnishings, often set by the court of the time, which was then followed implicitly by the important and wealthy people. Often new ideas have been possible only because of technological improvements, but at other times craftsmen have been inspired to stretch beyond the designs of the day, to re-think and develop more complicated weaves and colours.

Perhaps one of the main differences today is that current trends are set by particular designers, whether it is with furniture, dress or interior designers, whereas in the past it was directed from the court of the time.

Ancient influences

The Egyptians gave us perhaps the first structured forms and the beginnings of elegance, both in the style of their palaces and how they dressed.

When the Greeks built the Parthenon in Athens they created a perfect balance of proportion and grace which has inspired the most elegant architecture ever since. Much later, in 1570, Italian architect Andrea Palladio published his works on architecture, and in this he revived, refined and domesticized the same principles the Greeks had used in villas outside Venice. This was the birth of Italian classicism.

Wall hangings

English Tudor and Elizabethan furniture was heavy, very solid in its contruction, and crudely carved. Heavy, elaborate jewel-coloured tapestries and wall hangings were commissioned to cover doorways and to hang all the way around beds to keep out any draughts. These rich fabrics were either decorated with embroidery, needlework or were painted. Even simple folk often had wool and linen hangings in their homes that were painted to look like tapestries.

Grand tapestries and hangings were mainly woven in Europe (although some were also made in England), and soon wealthy Italians and French decorated their windows elaborately with rich, heavy woven brocades and velvets.

Introducing soft furnishings

In 1670 a new craft which was to have a major effect on soft furnishings was born. After years of people sitting on hard wooden chairs, but always horse riding in comfort, a craftsman came up with the idea of applying saddlery techniques to the seats of chairs, and so the upholstered chair was produced. The craft was very crude in its techniques at first, but within the space of 30 years upholstery methods were refined and perfected

Left *One of the most visited sites in the world, the Parthenon in Athens, demonstrates truly perfect proportion and classical lines, which remain the inspiration for many modern architects and designers.*

Left *Louis XV of France introduced a rich, curvacious form of decoration known as rococco. In grand rooms draperies were designed for ornamental as well as functional use.*

(with the single exception of springing, these methods have remained largely unchanged to this day) and the upholsterer (or upholder as he was known) became a very important man.

Window curtains

At the same time, window curtains started to become an essential part of a room's decorative scheme. The single curtain had already been divided into two, but now elaborate pelmets and draperies were constructed to hide their fittings. Soft, ruched valances began to appear at the tops of windows and even pull-up curtains started to be seen. The cord and pulley mechanism gave the curtains the effect of a festoon blind.

The furnishings of the 17th century were also dominated by the French kings. Louis X1V's court set up the silk industry in Lyons and opulently used the silks, taffetas, ribbed silks, brocades and satins on hangings and state beds.

Rococo and classical style

From 1720, Louis XV of France introduced a new style called rococo that had a peculiar informality and a sense of fun. It affected both the interior and exterior of buildings and every item of furnishings – decorated textiles, plasterwork, furniture and ornaments. Taken up across Europe, this light style showed a new spirit of adventure.

England was less affected by rococo style but when Inigo Jones, England's first great post-Gothic architect, returned inspired from his Grand Tour of Europe, he decided to resurrect the work of Andrea Palladio, the designer of some wonderful classical villas outside Venice. Faithful imitations of these villas were now to be seen in the 1720s and 1730s in windswept and rain-soaked English shires. This new development of style also became a major influence in the British colonies on the East coast of America. America was now becoming a major consumer of European furnishings, especially those of England and France. Apparently English furniture was considered solid and practical, while the French was regarded as more stylish and ostentatious.

The master craftsmen and architects of the late18th century England now came into their own, eclipsing the French for a time. Perhaps unique in their international acclaim, Hepplewhite, Adam, Sheraton and Chippendale not only designed and produced furniture with perfectly designed proportions, but they also recorded the details of current furniture style in their handbooks. In Thomas Chippendale's *Directory for Gentleman and Cabinet Makers* printed in 1754, it can be seen how much the influence from Greece, Rome, China and the Gothic period contributed to the design of any piece of furniture.

1 European styles

Home making in the late 18th century was becoming big business – worldwide. Trading throughout Europe and Asia brought not only exotic furnishings, but made many people wealthy enough to buy them. Silks, lacquerwork, porcelain items, screens and fans – all suitable materials for interior decoration – were imported from the Far East. Chintzes also came from India, porcelain from Meissen in Germany, glassware from Bohemia and Italy, carpets and tapestries from France, wooden furniture from England and silk wallcoverings from Italy were all available for wealthy people to add elegance to their homes.

Toward the end of the 18th century a Neo-classical revival was embraced by all nations. French furnishings under Louis XVI became simpler with less detail and straighter lines. Furniture had simplified bows and garlands for decoration, but displayed tapered, fluted legs. At the same time in England, the Adam brothers were at the forefront of Georgian style, turning their hands to every aspect of interior and exterior decoration.

Moving into the 19th century

By the early 19th century, most windows had curtains or drapes, whether paired or pulled up as festoons. Cloths were more plentiful: silks and velvets were now being woven in London, Lyons and Venice, and simple country prints were produced on Indian cottons. Wallpapers and wall panels were also being printed. The upholsterers' skills were becoming well honed and the printing methods were becoming more advanced.

During the same period (1815–1848) the German speaking nations adopted the Biedermeier look, which did not have the fussiness and intricacy of the previous styles. It was a phrase that was coined in derision, however, as people mocked the new simple, inexpensive furniture. Bieder means 'everyday, plain' and Meier is a common German surname, so Biedermeier described not just a particular style of furniture but also a new way of life.

The Biedermeier look then spread to Sweden and the craftsmen there reinterpreted it and scaled it down to fit the smaller size of rooms. The more bulbous outlines of the German style turned into gentle curves and Swedish Biedermeier became a sophisticated period style. In fact, its neat proportions and simple design still suit almost every home today.

Victoriana

When Queen Victoria married Prince Albert in 1840 it was seen as a time of dramatic change in style between the early and late 19th century. The Victorians craved innovation and novelty in design. Furniture and curtains

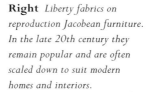

Right *Liberty fabrics on reproduction Jacobean furniture. In the late 20th century they remain popular and are often scaled down to suit modern homes and interiors.*

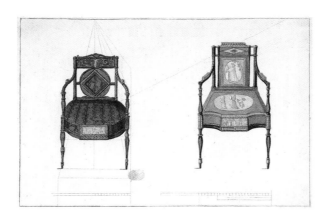

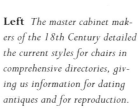

Left *The master cabinet makers of the 18th Century detailed the current styles for chairs in comprehensive directories, giving us information for dating antiques and for reproduction.*

New interior design

An interior decorator before the job title had been invented, Elsie de Wolfe (1865–1950), decided to break away from the Victorian stuffiness and laboured colours. She shocked people when she started to paint brown walls white, and used a palette of grey, soft blue, old rose and ivory colours. Her search for the ultimate in beauty and her decorating code – simplicity, suitability and proportion – are still the guidelines for modern interior decorators. Gradually, the upholsterer's power was transferred to the interior decorator. Women with panache and connections, such as Madeleine Gastaing, Syrie Maugham, Sister Parish, Sibyl Colefax and Nancy Lancaster, were joined by Billy Baldwin, Albert Hadley, John Fowler and Geoffrey Bennison – to name just a few leading lights of the 20th Century, who have also trained many of today's interior decorators.

were buttoned, fringed and tasselled; colours became richer and darker, fabrics heavier.

In the 1890s William Morris, John Ruskin and others formed a minority group known as the Arts and Crafts movement. The movement is still influential today, especially in their fabric designs. Their main aim was to bring back craftsmanship and natural forms, in architecture, furniture and simplistic fabric design. William Morris translated natural forms of images such as flowers into flat patterns and started a totally different style of fabric design.

The 20th century

In Germany the Bauhaus movement (1919–1948) was becoming firmly established, and produced some of the most original and innovative art, furniture design and architecture of the century.

During the 20th century a synthesis has been seen of all past styles, plus a new interest in design itself. This has resulted in simply styled furniture using materials such as chrome and steel, as well as traditional woods.

Daring colour schemes and different style ideas have now been developed. An all-white room design scheme was also seen for the very first time. Decorators created new landscapes whether combining painted furniture with floral chintzes or richly opulent silks with beautiful antiques.

The last 50 years

David Hicks and his designers have laid out rooms with great attention to symmetry and organized detail. They have used mostly plain colours in exciting combination with small geometric patterns for weaves and floorcoverings. This style has inspired many new designers worldwide.

A new revolution in home decorating also started to evolve. Stylish home decoration became available to all at budget prices. In Britain, Terence Conran started his Habitat chain of furnishing stores offering good design to everyone. Apart from British fabric and furniture designs, he sourced from Europe and as far afield as Asia.

Design today

At the forefront of contemporary design is Scandinavian furniture, which is crafted with much skill and care. It has become renowned for its clean lines and unadorned beauty. Italian and French furniture designers are also now producing a range of excellent contemporary furniture designs using woods, metals and leather.

1 International designers

Many of the room interiors that are seen in books and magazines are actually the work of professional designers, who are well paid to make decisions about style for their clients. These are the rooms that can give us inspiration for our own homes and set us thinking about the style that we would really like to achieve.

To a certain extent the work of all interior designers today is a distillation of ideas that are taken from past periods. Sometimes an individual idea is selected and extended; at other times 'period treatments', such as creating a room with Victorian style, are followed closely, with only the necessary adjustments being made to suit the 20th-century way of life. Whilst most people dislike the look of radiators and electrical sockets and normally attempt to disguise them as much as possible, few would choose to live without them.

Above *A delicately executed wall finish in three tones of cream is the perfect foil for these striking blue and white block check fabrics on the curtains and chair.*

Elements of style

One excellent way to begin to understand the mechanics of interior design is to dissect those rooms that you especially like and dislike in magazines. Take note of the rooms that seem to 'talk to you' and those which leave you feeling quite indifferent.

The photographs of rooms by well-known interior designers who have an international reputation illustrate how the elements of style can be drawn together in a cohesive way. You cannot expect any of them to suit your particular circumstances, and you do not have to like, unconditionally, everything you see in them, but they all have their own balance of elegance and simplicity which is appealing. Each room contains enough design ideas and inspired juxtapositioning of form and colour, to create that elusive element 'style', from which you can feed to create your own interpretation in your own home.

For example, Roger Banks Pye, at the helm of the British decorating company, Colefax and Fowler, has made himself master of the colours blue and white. Whether complemented with pure white and poignant saffron yellow, with muted creams, turquoise or walls bursting with rampant roses, each room features its own completely unique character. On the other hand, Swiss designer Mimmi O'Connell can transform a basic design scheme of stripes and checks with the flick of a paisley shawl, a pile of Fortuny cushions, a Chinese lamp or a lacquered chest. Her inspirational style can create wonderful flashes of colour and pools of texture.

Right *A truly international room by a truly international decorator. From a simple background of plain walls, accentuated by checks and stripes on the chairs, sofa and table, Mimmi O'Connell adds distinctive touches with the ironwork chandeliers and lampstand.*

Left *Decorating with a neutral colour demands very clever combinations of scale and proportion. With her intuitive, instinctive eye, Mimmi O'Connell selects exactly the right accessories, such as the Chinese urn, to balance the room. She also punctuates the whole scheme brilliantly with the ruched curtains and the checked red fabrics.*

1 Contemporary classic

*A*ny room scheme which contains cream and off-white fabrics will be restful, calming, light and warm to live in. The natural elements of terracotta tiles, wicker chairs, polished surfaces, limed wood, pottery and glass can provide both background and accessory colourings in soft brown and blue muted tones. By introducing one other colour into the scheme through the furniture, accessories or soft furnishings you can then add the interest which is necessary for a house to become a comfortable home.

Texture is the life blood of monochromatic scheming, as interesting weaves, mixed fabric weights and subtle patterns blend together in clever coordination. Here two examples are given of renowned European designers' interpretation of this type of scheming.

Left *The heavy painted beams and the diamond-patterned pelmet immediately show that this is a traditional Dutch house — the home of Marcel Wolterink. The tied slip covers on the sofas, the haphazardly drawn blinds, the slip-covered room divider — even the way in which the curtains are bunched onto the sill — create an informality of style, and reveal that this house is indeed a truly lived-in home. Details are the soul of the home, just as impossible perfection can be the stifling of style.*

A lived-in room

Marcel Wolterink is a celebrated Dutch florist, who has an amazing shop that is crammed full of the most exotic blooms, beautiful objets d'art which have come from all over the world and unusual antiques. His home characterizes perfectly the simple, edited elegance which also accompanies his design work. It is elegant without seeming too formal, and well lived in without having that strictly functional look.

Simplicity of style

On the other hand, the internationally renowned Greek designer John Stephanidis has a much gentler approach to style. Always clear and concise in his design, with just the right amount of softness, he has created some of the most classic room schemes of the latter half of the 20th century. The bedroom that he has designed here, with its simple bed posts and delicate hanging drapes, is in keeping with his ability to decorate within any given architectural style.

Far left *Although the bed is the largest item in the room, designed by John Stephanidis, this is not just a bedroom, so the drapes have been designed for all seasons. While the sun is shining and living is directed to the outdoors, these bed drapes are perfect with the colour concentrated to the inside, making the bed less important but no less inviting. As the cooler months approach and sunlight disappears, the drapes turn warm-side out, living is more indoors, and the bed takes a more prominent position in the room. The golden tones of the only printed fabric are picked up in the picture frames, baskets and limed wood.*

1 Innovation and inspiration

*J*ust occasionally an interior designer who is not afraid to challenge the style of the day and be innovative will stand out from all the rest. These are the leaders who encourage us to move on, to re-think accepted ways and ideas. As happens so often with fashion, a new idea is introduced by one designer, and is slow to gather ground, but once a foothold has been gained, very few people actually remember who it was who first introduced 'the new idea' in the first place.

American decorator John Saladino can always be relied upon to produce a room design that is controversial and excitingly different. This room is a masterpiece of classic design turned on its head, and bearing the true hall-marks of couture – enough but never too much.

All design schemes need at least one anchor point to provide solidity and to hold all of the other elements in place. Often there is a substantial item – whether a rug, sofa, fireplace or a painting – which a person is obliged to keep, and so this item becomes not only the starting point for the scheme but also the anchor. Where there is no natural anchor, this should be considered as a major and primary purchase. Often when a fireplace is absent and there is no means of ventilation, a false fireplace needs to be installed to provide the necessary focal point to a room.

Right *Extraordinary architecture called for a master hand: the uniqueness of this room is unquestionable, and the technical execution unsurpassed. There is inspired coordination of contemporary design with the period antiques – a classical Adam-style rug complements the crown mouldings and contrasts with an unusual unstructured wall finish. Fabric textiles in a classic mix of pinks, blues and greens have been re-interpreted as smooth chintz and rough linen. Silk damask and old leather sit hand in hand and side by side. Hues of vibrant pinks help to strengthen those visible in the carpet.*

Above *Here a large classical rug 'grounds' the room and has been used as a base for the furnishings, fabric colours and textures. Contemporary paintings provide secondary anchors, adding extra depth and dimension but are not attempting to compete with the main focal point.*

1 Colour and light

Coordinating the design of a total room scheme is an exacting task. Different influences and appeals come at you from all angles. Do not restrict yourself by thinking that one particular colour combination will have the same effect in every room. The balance of colour, the type of soft furnishings that are used and the use of accessories will all affect the room's final look.

The science of cause and effect proves irrefutably that nothing happens in isolation and that every experience will have a bearing on another. The phenomenal increase in travel possibilities over the last 20 years has had tremendous effect in the home. People now return with treasures and mementoes from trips – whether it is a Mexican sombrero, a piece of Madeiran lace, a handsome Venetian glass or an Indian wallhanging to decorate and adorn their homes.

Below *The British designer Stephen Ryans' hallmark of neo-classical minimalism is prevalent in this room, as he works with fabrics from French master colourist and designer Manuel Canovas, to show just how effective bold, sun-filled (yellows, reds, blues and greens) colours can be in a small space.*

More slowly, colours and styles have been modified and adapted to the home light. They have been used to introduce or incorporate an idea, another location, or a theme from a different culture. A Dufy print might be the jumping board for a room that is intended to immediately transport people to the South of France, a set of Chinese prints might give an oriental atmosphere to the colourings and furnishings of a guest bedroom.

In these two rooms that have similar colour schemes, the finished effect is quite different, reflecting the different locations and the styling of the rooms.

The summer cottage

Pink and yellow in soft hues have long been favourite colours to use in the drawing room, but these vibrating tones can also be used to evoke an altogether more lively atmosphere reminiscent of happy Mediterranean holidays and summer sun. The colours are immediately

Left *John Stephanidis; approach to interior design is firstly with an architect's eye, making sure that the proportion and detail in a room are both correct and simple. This converted cow shed in southwest England needs only a fresh coat of cream paint over the brick walls, as the fitted shutters confirm the rustic notion, allowing full light and clear view of the burgeoning garden situated beyond. Slip covers and hand-worked cushions are great decorating tricks to transform a room at will.*

Below *In this close-up of the John Stephanidis room, notice how the mauve flowers of the plant help to extend the sofa colour to the top half of the room and how well the geometric, styled and random needleworked cushions work together.*

welcoming and make a relaxing background for long evenings of animated discussion and hospitality. Simple styling and the use of flowers to emphasize the scheme help to create a fresh and relaxed atmosphere.

The city apartment

An unusual colour scheme to use for an inner city apartment, sunflower yellows and geranium pinks, can help to breathe a breath of fresh air into a living room. Whereas country rooms normally face outward to take best advantage of the surroundings, city rooms often need to look inward. Because of this, window treatments become important focal points and need to be as attractive to look at as they are functional. Roman blinds can show fabric to its best advantage and can look as smart fully raised in concertina pleats as they do fully lowered. They also give you full control of the light and the apartment's outlook.

1 Pattern on pattern

The English look is synonymous with an eclectic mixture of fabrics that are reminiscent of the annual flowering of an herbaceous garden. Flowers such as clematis and honeysuckle scramble together for space amongst roses and lilacs, peonies and daisies.

Beautifully coloured and printed fabric and wallpaper patterns can be mixed and matched to re-create the atmosphere of a garden or a florist's shop. Some of the best prints have a long history, but new and ever more appealing prints seem to be produced every year.

Below *A classic Bennison rose print in pink and green decorates this period room. And for decorating more contemporary rooms, think of this same rose design but in monochrome blues sitting against some white muslin curtains on a pale wood floor, or with contemporary textures in taupes and off-white colours.*

Above *These monochrome figurative prints from Liberty are mixed together to create an alternative English look.*

Soft, delicate prints

The tradition of Geoffrey Bennison lives on in his beautiful linen prints. Brilliantly drawn designs in soft colours printed onto oyster white or a wonderful tea-washed ground are reminiscent of a bygone age, but these prints have nevertheless found favour throughout the world. He produces soft and gentle fabrics which are easy to live with, but most importantly work well with so many other fabrics and furnishings. A chair covered in a Bennison print can be slotted into almost any room. It can almost be unnoticed yet add an undeniable quality. There is a Bennison fabric that can work with almost any eclectic room – whether it be a kelim, a Persian or crewel-worked rug or furnishings of chintzes, linens, weaves in rich and soft colours.

Clever combinations

Roger Banks Pye of Colefax and Fowler often builds on the relaxed effects of blue and white. He brings together floral prints and textures, checks, stripes and tones to create instant harmony. Touches of another colour – notably yellows and golds from the other side of the spectrum in a blue and white scheme – balance otherwise monochromatic schemes, and can be introduced in accessories such as picture frames, lamps and ornaments, rather than in the fabrics themselves.

Above *Roger Banks Pye's passion for blue and white has been well documented, and this exuberant mix of checks and tones is yet another brilliant creation in a room. His talent for blending old and new is clear – the fresh blue checks are a startling choice on the duvet of the period bed. They lift and enliven the antique crewel panels pinned to the wall and the dominant, traditional oil painting as no other fabric could. Large and small checks have been chosen meticulously to balance a sophisticated look and country style. To add a soft look, both the duvet and the cushions have been attractively finished with some informal ties.*

1 An artist's approach

Belgian artist and designer Isabella de Borchgrave produces the most wonderful hand-drawn and stencilled fabrics, perfect for all manner of soft furnishings. From a simple blue and white trellis to an exuberant rococo design, she combines the best of contemporary colours and ideas with the traditional structures, motifs and floral depictions which have recurred again and again throughout the history of fabric design. All the colours of a summer garden, contrasted with blue and white are an ever repeatable combination.

Below *Isabella de Borchgrave's ornate contemporary room includes a wonderful mix of blues: blue and white wine glasses highlight the colours in the tablecloth and drapes. The glass chandelier adds further style and an older elegance to the scheme.*

2 **Fabrics**

Fabrics

The starting point for creating beautiful soft furnishings is choosing the right fabric, whether it is wool, cotton, velvet or corduroy or perhaps silk. Colours, textures and patterns set the scene for any successful room scheme, but with the vast selection that is for sale, making a choice is not easy. You might be interested in soft spring florals, geometric-style prints or simple checks or stripes — take time to find out what is available, and build up your scheme with samples and swatches before starting a project.

The texture and colour of furnishing fabrics is very personal and can often be unrelated to the purpose for which a fabric will be chosen. Choose the fabrics that appeal to you, but always remember to check out how practical they are to wash or clean.

Soft furnishings need to last, so select them carefully. Start with the basics: curtains, chair covers and bedspreads, then indulge yourself by using current fashion colours and more costly fabrics for small details such as a lampshade or a cushion cover. Always buy the best quality material you can afford, especially for areas which get intense wear, such as sofa covers and window seats. If you are on a tight budget, look for utilitarian fabrics such as ticking, artists' canvas or denim. The fabrics you choose, and the details you add, will give your home a distinctive finish and style.

Draping fabrics, shawls and covers
over sofas and beds can bring a soft,
luxurious element into the home as the
true colour and weave can be seen in the
light and shadow (far left and above).
As a real treat for a special cushion or
chair, use richly coloured damasks and
lisérés (left). Below, stunning Fortuny
cushions hand painted in gold and
terracotta are perfectly balanced with
simple ticking in the same tones.

2 Colour

When choosing colours for soft furnishings, personal preferences are bound to prevail. Many interior decorators have their favourites, but there are no hard and fast rules. The success of a scheme is influenced by many different factors – from the structure and shape of the room itself to the personalities of the people using it.

The psychological effect of colour on people's mood is well documented, but the results are by no means conclusive enough to provide a rule book for the interior decorator. The best design solutions come from careful consideration of the effect of colour on a particular personality and in a particular room. For instance, most of us cannot face very bright colours anywhere first thing in the morning; also in a dining room, blues may seem too cold, unless they are enriched with warmer golden hues and a secluded sitting room is comfortable when it is decorated with soft pinks, creams and apricots, but a family room needs stronger, more rumbustious colours.

Light and climate

Colour choice also depends greatly on geographical location and climate, which determine the quality and amount of light in a room. Clear, light colours are great for sunny Mediterranean climates and tropical areas. Grey, white and soft blues look cool and calm in Scandinavia and parts of North America, but can be drab and uncomfortable in more southerly parts. Some of the deep, rich shades of terracotta and forest green are the perfect accompaniment for a country cottage, but they might appear oppressive when used in the Middle East or Southern States. The jewel-like colours of India, Malaysia, Indonesia and China or the bright, acid colours of Southern California need sub-tropical light to re-create the same atmosphere.

You need to bear in mind that fabrics will be seen in both natural and artificial light. In most situations, colours can seem warmer in artificial light, although halogen lamps tend to provide pools of cooler light. And of course, light also becomes affected by the other colours in the room, so when making a final choice, take generous swatches of fabric home and look at them in the appropriate setting before you make that final decision to buy.

Warm and cold

Everyone's likes and dislikes of colour come from experience and associations. While our tastes and horizons may be broadened with travel – or just by looking at other people's homes in magazines – a person's instinctive preferences will change little throughout life. Rely on using your long-term favourite colours in your home's main areas, but look at new ways of using them. Some of the very best rooms have yellow walls, whether traditional Georgian, Victorian or contemporary.

Above *Perennial favourites, blue and white never fail to please. Crisp white cottons and simple gingham checks, joined by deep blues and stencilled prints, translate equally well into bedroom, kitchen or country sitting room schemes.*

Below *Greens and whites, forever restful, help to bring the outside in. Add a touch of yellow for spring and geranium pink for the summer to make rooms for all seasons.*

Left *Blankets and rugs in window-pane checks, plaids and traditional Welsh weaves are inspired choices to create instant curtains, tablecloths and also sofa covers.*

While colour theories suggest that blue is a cold and unfriendly colour, some people are happy to live with the cool, tranquil tones of blues, greys and white.

Each colour has its warm and cold side, its friendly and less friendly associations. There are certain blues which bring to mind a stormy sea or winter swimming, while others suggest the brilliance of a summer sun and clear skies, or the cheerfulness of a mass of bluebells in a spring woodland.

Highlights and contrasts

When developing a room scheme, take care not to coordinate colours so closely that the result is dull. A room decorated with tones of green and white can look very flat if you do not mix strong enough depths of colour. Add highlights of golden yellow or fuchsia, or introduce related tones of blue and lilac, in small accessories such as lined baskets, decorative edgings – even in flower arrangements. Whites and creams are a practical choice for bed linen, but may be too bland to decorate the whole room. Break the monotones gently with pastel pinks or clear blues and violets, or add a touch of drama with red and green plaids, navy blue or warm terracottas and tans.

Fashion influences

Tastes and trends change over the years, and the options for colour choice seem to be ever increasing. For hundreds of years, colours were restricted to those produced from natural dyestuffs, but by the 18th century, fabric manufacturers had an intense colour palette to work with, which included acid greens, clear blues and florid pinks. The colours may appear brash and bright to our eyes in artificial light, but when seen by candlelight, draped at shuttered windows, these hues offered great depth and warmth. By the end of the last century, dark, sombre colours in heavy, deep weaves were fashionable in both Europe and North America, but during the early 20th century, Elsie de Wolfe and other innovative decorators championed a new freedom as they painted brown rooms white or introduced pretty prints and pastel colourings.

Interior fabrics and style have always been closely related to the fashion of the time. If you are looking for new colour ideas, start by looking at the clothes that are appearing on the catwalks. Recently, natural colours have been strongly promoted, in the form of muslins, unbleached linens, natural silks, calico, ticking and canvas, draped, tied and stitched as never before. Orange and lime, brown and tan, or animal-skin prints might be the popular colours for another year.

Left *Rain or shine, summer or winter, warm yellow provides a happy background colour in a room. Here crunchy textures and a strong navy blue add cooling elements to the scheme.*

Below *Glowing tones of red and orange are ideal choices for strong splashes of colour that can be used to bring a whole colour scheme to life.*

2 Texture and weave

The texture of a fabric, which is determined by the way in which it is woven, adds an extra dimension to a room scheme. By mixing different textures and tones, particularly in monochromatic schemes, you can add depth and interest to a room's overall look.

If you prefer to use a fabric that has a woven texture rather than a printed pattern, it may be a sign that you subscribe (consciously or subconsciously) to the 'less is more' school of interior decoration. Minimalist design, a style which has long been popular among those with a passion for the bare bones of architectural detail, is great to look at but can be difficult to attain and maintain within the exuberance of home or family life. Plain fabric furnishings provide a gentle, harmonious background to everyday clutter, but are dangerous to use in a situation where some spills and a high level or wear and tear are unavoidable. Textured and colour-woven fabrics help to give some relief and shading, can disguise unsightly marks, and may provide a way of mixing colours without adding any pattern.

Fabric structure

Any woven cloth is a variation of three basic weaving techniques: plain weave, satin and twill. All have warp threads, running down the length of the fabric. In a plain weave, the same weight of fibre is used for the weft threads, running across the width of the fabric, picking up alternate warp threads. In a twill weave, the weft runs under one warp thread and over two, producing a diagonal rib. In satin weave, only a few warp threads are picked up in the weave, creating a smoother surface.

During the weaving process, yarn can be looped to make towelling and bouclé fabrics, or the looped pile

can be cut to make velvet, and corduroy. These deeply piled textures take in light but also reflect light from the crevices as the fabric moves. You only have to run your hand over a piece of velvet, or to hang it upside down to see how the colour is affected by the angle of light as it falls on the pile.

Subtle patterns can be introduced with special weaving techniques, such as dobby weave, producing small, regular patterns on the cloth, bringing texture without adding colour contrasts. Fine white damask, and heavier damask upholstery fabrics are another way of adding texture to a room without introducing extra colours.

You can also create a depth of texture in a scheme by using fabrics woven from different yarns – rough silks and loosely woven linens have a different feel to plain polished cottons and soft cotton lawn. Many contemporary fabrics rely on the mix of interesting yarns. Thick and thin yarns might be woven together, either separated on warp and weft threads or programmed to create bands or a random pattern of texture. Chenille might combine lycra and cotton, or a wool bouclé surface may well be woven onto a cotton ground.

Colour and light

Some of the most interesting non-textured fabrics are woven with different colours on warp and weft. This effect is highlighted if the fibres used are silk as this can create shot silk taffetas in myriad colour combinations, which are as light as gossamer or as heavy as upholstery

Above *Pleating and quilting techniques add depth and interest to the plainest fabrics as shadows and light play against the grain. Sheer curtaining can be used most effectively to screen an ugly view, while still allowing the maximum, but softest, light into the room.*

Left *Chenille weaves have become very popular as velvets have become less so in the last few years. Soft and fluid to handle, chenille weaves make excellent drapes, cloths and cushions.*

Left *These neutral fabrics show clearly how weave structure can affect the texture of the cloth. The feel of the cloth is also characterized by the type of yarn that is used.*

Below *Crunchy cotton upholstery is trimmed with robust bullion fringe; a strong plaid is softened with gathered corners and an elegant, muted damask cloth is draped in between.*

fabric. The play of light on the material is delightful as conditions change throughout the day, or as you move around the room and catch the light from a different angle. A silk woven with green and red will sometimes appear to be green and sometimes red. If the fabric is draped over a piece of furniture, the light will reflect both colours from the surface and also from deep within the folds.

Textured fabrics all need some light to show off all their subtleties. A textured weave which looks flat when placed on the top of a table can look stunning as it drapes to the floor and catches the light in its folds. Strong light may bleach out any detail from the surface, while soft, cool light highlights the texture and brings out the soft shadows.

Gaufraging

This method is used to imprint a design directly into a finished plain woven cloth. Rollers carved with any design, from classical scrolls to a small geometric motif, are heat pressed onto the fabric as it is unrolled. The pile of velvet or cotton toile bends to accommodate the roller and the design is then permanently etched in place. Light reflects from a surface print as it would from a deeply woven damask.

2 Pattern

Patterns may be printed directly onto fabric, or woven into the fabric during manufacture. There is a vast range of beautifully printed patterns available – some are old established classics, while others are produced in response to fashionable trends. Very often, a pattern can be the starting point for a complete colour scheme, with the colours in the pattern providing the colour palette for paints, plain fabrics and other accessories.

When you look around a fabric showroom, you are bound to find yourself attracted to some patterns more than others. You might like the soft spring colours of a floral print coordinated with a striped fabric, or be more attracted to a rich, Navaho Indian style print, with geometric blocks of colour. Only you can decide on the style and colour combination that appeals to you. While there are no hard and fast rules to design, there are plenty of guidelines, and it is worth knowing something of how patterns are produced, and why some are more expensive than others.

Printed patterns

Silk screens and wood blocks are the traditional methods of printing patterns onto fabric, and modern machine prints are a development of these processes. A fresh screen or block is used for each colour, and each

time a 'layer' of the pattern is applied the block has to be carefully aligned so that it does not overlap the previous 'layer'. The more colours that are used, and the more complex the design, the more expensive the fabric will end up being.

Fabrics which have intricate, beautifully designed patterns benefit most from being used flat. They are best as tablecloths, cushions, screens or blinds, where the true beauty of the design can be enjoyed. No matter how much you like a pattern, you must be critical where you position it in a room, always combining it with other colours and patterns that will enhance it.

Woven patterns

The simplest woven patterns are checks and stripes, with a carefully balanced mix of colours running down and across the fabric. More sophisticated woven patterns may be textured designs, in a single colour, such as the dobby weave and damasks (see pages 38–39). However, the same weaving process can involve two or more colours, to create fabrics with a woven pattern. More intricate patterns depend on a variety of thread sizes and colours to make what are known as jacquard weaves. Jacquards, damasks, dobby and other patterned weaves have been radically transformed with the introduction of contemporary ideas and modern technology. Prints are now available over jacquards, stripes or geometric designs and damask all on one cloth. Metallic

Above *The colours from a flowing floral pattern can be repeated on coordinating cushions, a section of the main pattern can even be sewn onto some of the cushions.*

Left *Country charm is exemplified on this sofa and cushions as soft tones of pinks and whites combine to include naive embroidery motifs, hand-woven lace, and toile de jouy prints of country life and simple scenes.*

Far-flung
fabrics

Simple weaves and
geometric prints have
become synonymous with
the rustic style of early
North American settlers.

Traditional European prints and weaves take their
influence from the fabrics and patterns brought home
by 18th and 19th century voyagers.

Look for inspiration in the textures and colours of Gujerati fabrics (left and far left) or the brilliant embroidery yarns of the Mayan Indians (below).

Simple geometric pattern and natural colours are the trademark of Navago Indian weaves.

Woven and embroidered patterns in brilliant colours give texture to the fabrics of South American Indians.

Intricately woven or elaborately dyed fabrics in vibrant colours characterize the textiles of Asia — from India to the Far East.

Natural dyes give a subtle variation in depth of colour as you can see in this silk yarn used for Bhuddist robes (right). Richly coloured carpets come to life under the strong Morroccan sun (below).

Your own patterns

You can also apply pattern yourself to the surface of a completed cloth – by hand or machine – in the form of embroidery, canvaswork and appliqué. Look out for shopbought kits for canvaswork cushion covers – some are real works of art. You can also develop your own patterns, picking up motifs from other elements in a room. For example, you can trace patterns from china to use as a guide for embroidering table linen, or you can cut out elements from a printed fabric to use to make appliqué designs.

Right *A strong modern pattern on a bedspread can become the focal point in a plainly decorated room with natural, polished wooden surfaces.*

threads and synthetic fibres offer adventurous pattern and texture possibilities as the cloth is woven.

Choosing and buying patterns

One of the fun elements of designing and decorating a room comes when you have to choose the mix of patterns and colours. There are few rules to follow, so to a certain extent you must follow your instincts, but consider factors such as scale, colour tone and content. Usually, you need to use smaller patterns for smaller items, as the overall effect may be lost if you only use part of the pattern in a project. Experiment with mixing and matching: try tartan and toile, ticking and roses, stripes and checks, or stars and stripes. There must, however, be a common link – perhaps an all-over floral print in blues and pinks, combined with a blue ticking stripe, or a gold star print linked with a muslin that has a gold thread running through it.

If you do not have the confidence to mix and match patterns, follow the suggestions of the manufacturers who plan their ranges with common colour themes and motifs that are easy to combine.

Patterned fabrics almost always have pattern repeats to take into account when you are measuring and making up a soft furnishing item. A large repeat can be uneconomical, so consider making coordinating items for the same room to use up the fabric remnants. Small geometric prints are fairly easy to accommodate on most furnishings, as are all-over patterns. A print with a central pattern will be less economical for covers, as the dominant pattern should be centralized on the seats, backs, arms and on each cushion.

Below *The difference in these fabric patterns shows how important it is to consider the pattern repeat when you are measuring and making a soft furnishing item.*

2 Choosing the right fabric

Once you know the colour balance, texture and pattern that you like in a soft furnishing fabric, try to make sure that your choice is right for the project in hand. Fabrics are not cheap, make your decision carefully so that your soft furnishings look good and last well.

Fabrics will invariably be chosen to satisfy three main criteria: practicality, suitability and personal appeal. From a practical standpoint you need to decide: does a fabric feel good to sit on, is the colour tone right, will it fade in sunlight, will it look as good in all weathers, will it launder well and does it fit the budget? How the fabric suits the situation is equally important: does it drape well, stretch too much or too little, crease too easily, and is the pattern easy to work with? Only you can say

whether you are more comfortable with fresh cottons, scrunchy linens or printed, plain and heavy-weave fabrics. You should also decide whether you prefer a sunny room, or do you prefer it more shaded.

The starting point

The most expensive purchases in any room are the covers and curtains, so think about the practicality and suitability of materials before considering the final colour and pattern.

• Loose cover fabrics need to be heavy enough to withstand pets and boisterous family wear for many years, but be light enough to stitch with a normal sewing machine. They should be washable and not show every mark, and be colourful enough to be interesting.

• Curtains and drapes may need to be laundered regularly, so choose washable fabrics for kitchens and bathrooms, for example. However, heavily-lined and interlined curtains in dining rooms and living rooms only need cleaning annually, but dust or vacuum them in situ regularly.

• The piped edges of cushions and covers wear quickly, so check that the quality of fabric used is at least as good as the main fabric. You could use the same fabric, or a contrasting colour from the same range.

• Bed linen, tablecloths and napkins must be strong enough to withstand regular washing at high temperatures. The chosen fabric must also feel good and ideally be easy-care for minimal ironing.

• Heavy bedcovers are often too bulky to wash in a domestic machine. If covers are to be dry cleaned, you can use non-washable interlinings, but for laundering you should always choose a washable, probably synthetic, interlining.

• For small decorative accessories, such as a display cushion or a bedroom chair cover that will have little wear, fabrics can be chosen for their actual beauty rather than practicality.

Personal preferences

Once you have found a suitable fabric range, your final decision rests on your reaction to the fabric. Your personal lifestyle will determine whether you will choose the perfect colour in a lightweight fabric, or whether

Above *A lavish plaid in strong tones of lilac and yellow grounded with black proves an imaginative complement to the intricate and unusual chair with its needlework cover next to it.*

Left *Soft, drapy muslin, whether simple white butter muslin or coloured extravagantly as here, is stunning for light, airy window treatments and bed canopies, where fabric substance and durability are not major factors.*

yellow or grey in a large piece, and large patterns are completely lost on small fabric clippings. If you cannot obtain large samples, buy at least ½yd (½m) of any selected materials to check at home. No colour will be the same in all lights – or even in different parts of the same room – so do not expect to get an exact match. Look for hues and tones which blend with other fabrics in the room.

Check curtain fabrics with the light behind them, not in front – unless you have windows on opposite or adjacent walls, the light will always be behind the fabric.

Most woven cloths need light thrown onto them to bring out their pattern. Hang and drape your samples where they will be used, and look at them through the day. They might look quite different in the morning and afternoon, and artificial light can bring further changes.

you sacrifice an exact tone in line with some more practical considerations.

Even with the huge selection of textiles available, it is very rarely that you find every criteria met in one fabric. If you do not want to sacrifice your fabric choice, you may be able to introduce other elements for a workable solution. For example, if you like pale fabrics on armchairs, but know that this would not be suitable for your home life, consider a second set of covers or throws to indulge your preference in the summer months, but give the seating a more practical finish during the winter, when everyone spends a lot of time indoors.

With window dressing, if you love the open, airy effect of muslins, silks and organdie, but are worried about draughts and screening at night, combine the drapes with blinds or heavier outer curtains.

Making the final choice

It is almost impossible for even experienced decorators to choose a fabric from a small swatch. Even a colour as simple as ivory might take on definite hues of pink,

Left *Always take as large a sample of fabric as possible home with you before making a major purchase so that you can test the colour and strength of design in the room. Drape, fold or spread the fabric in the position you expect to see it.*

43

2 Where to begin

Building up a colour scheme is difficult if you do not have a starting point. The purpose a room will be used for, matching existing furnishings, and personal influences all provide useful pointers to the finished scheme.

It is most unlikely that there is anyone with no starting point when it comes to home furnishing. You may have definite colour preferences, an inherited piece of furniture or existing walls and flooring to work around. Alternatively, you could base your scheme on favourite accessories: a rug purchased on holiday, a painting, a bargain cushion, a set of china, or a decorative plate.

Starting points

The type of home you have – its architectural style and location – are fixed. A country cottage may suggest rough linens, stencilled prints and crunchy weaves, but you may need to hang heavy drapes to keep out draughts. A smart town house or apartment demands a neater finish and more elegant fabrics incorporating chintzes, stripes and tailored details. You may also want to choose a colour scheme to warm up a room, or you may want to choose a scheme that appears cool, even on the hottest summer's day.

How the room is used will also affect your choice of colours. A hallway should provide a warm, inviting welcome; bedrooms generally look good with a soft relaxing scheme of pastels; a sunny conservatory needs to reflect the natural, fresh tones of the garden beyond. Before planning the colour scheme, you should also plan the layout of the room, deciding where the tables and beds will be situated, how many chairs and sofas there are, and whether the room will be used mainly in one season or all year round. Professional decorators will also plan the lighting at this stage, checking that there are enough switches and sockets included before decorating the room.

If you are not re-styling a room completely you may have to work around existing floor finishes and wall colours. Natural wood, tile and stone finishes are easy to coordinate with different colours, but carpets may suggest a particular balance: a dingy brown carpet can be livened up with green and cream colours; a soft green

carpet may work best with a scheme including pinks or peaches. Plain wall colours are easier to work around than heavily patterned papers, but if you want to retain existing wallpaper, this should be the starting point for planning the rest of your scheme.

If you have a free hand with the colour scheme, you may want to build it around your favourite possessions: for example, a collection of blue and white plates might suggest white walls and fabrics in blue and white prints, checks and stripes. Add a touch of warm sunflower yellow to complement the blue and bring the room to life. Alternatively, use the blue and white as the basis for a related colour scheme in tones of mint green or lavender blue.

Building the scheme

When it comes to details, start first by choosing the colours for the walls and floors. Natural tones and

Above It is not always appropriate to re-cover a favourite chair from childhood that is battered and torn. However, this one, when placed with an eclectic mix of oriental rugs, time-honoured chintz, special prints and objets d'art works well as the overall effect is one of comfort and homeliness.

Left *Striking yellow walls enhance a lifelong collection of blue and white china, while cloths, napkins and tea towels in varying tone, size and geometric design mingle unobtrusively to soften the whole look.*

Below *The ethnic style and period chosen for your design scheme will be a major influence on your choice of fabric. Here the sandy coloured walls, bamboo furniture, rush matting and carved wooden screen have an oriental feel, complemented by the ikat weave fabric.*

finishes for floors are easier to build on than strong, definite colours. Remember that the finish must be practical as well as looking attractive. Wall colours are particularly important as they are dominating and they are one of the first aspects that you notice when you first enter the room.

Once you have decided on a wall colour, the other major items can be chosen: firstly curtains and covers, followed by the smaller items – blinds, cushions and occasional chairs. Finally, you can add special individual touches with your choice of accessories – tablecloths, screens, lampshades and scatter cushions.

If you really have no colour in mind, and do not feel confident to choose a mixture of plain colours, first find the perfect fabric for a major element of the room, such as the curtains or covers, then pick out colours from the fabric to create the other aspects of the scheme. The background colour of the fabric will help you choose the wall colour, and other colours in the pattern can be matched with cushions, piping and other details.

45

2 The effect of light

The major considerations as you begin to choose the soft furnishing fabrics for any house or room are geographical location, general aspect and the available light. The climate you live in will dictate a particular atmosphere, and the aspect of the room and the size of windows will affect the amount of sunshine and type of light that comes into the room.

In the northern hemisphere, a north facing room will always receive a colder light than one facing any other aspect. This cool, north light is much favoured by artists, because it is soft and even. Strong sunshine deadens colours and bleaches them, so special care must be taken in choosing the type and colour of fabric.

The amount of light received into any room can be modified: you can add climbers to drape themselves around the window, or remove some plants from windowsills to allow more light to filter through. But the aspect and climate cannot be changed.

Cool rooms

If you are decorating a cool room with soft light you may choose to capitalize on this by using shades of white with fresh blues, or tones of grey and ivory. Whether or not you then introduce a splash of highlight colour in the form of lampshades, a painting, a cloth or a floor rug is purely a personal decision. If you choose to bring in an accent with the accessories, the difference of effect between warm sunflower yellow or geranium pink, or tones of lilac or lime green, will create the individuality in a room.

The plus side of decorating in this manner – building a neutral structure with highlight accessories, is that the difficult decisions can be left until last. Fabric samples, a scarf or a napkin can be used to test the effects of adding different colours to the basic scheme.

Rooms in cool climates, which have little sunshine, may be warmed up with dark fabrics which absorb light and retain heat. If your room is inherently dark, you will never be able to make it light, and using whites and pastels can just make the room look cold and empty. Instead, take advantage of richly coloured, densely woven fabrics. Sensuous damasks and velvets in deep reds of all tones and hues go well with deep greens or blues. Furnish the room with darkly toned woods, or richly painted, lacquered and gilded pieces. You can then use artificial light to create intimacy and pools of light, making the most of shadow and light reflections on textiles. Warm colours and rich fabrics create intimate 'womb-like' rooms for relaxing, reading, studying and listening to music.

Sunny spaces

A room filled with sunlight is always a joy. If you have this type of room, the furnishing fabrics, floor and wall colours can be kept light and airy. Unfortunately, sunlight can also be an irritation, especially if you need to read or write near the window. Wood furniture and floor rugs should be positioned away from sunlight. In hot climates, where staying cool is the ultimate aim, look for white, light fabrics that will reflect the light and help to keep the inside of rooms cool.

Blocking the light totally by closing blinds or pulling heavy curtains is unnecessary. Bleached or unbleached

Above *The cool, light tones, simple fabrics and interior design ideas borrowed from Scandinavia can be re-interpreted throughout the world if a room has an open northerly aspect. Whites and off-whites that might glare under bright sunlight, come alive with the soft shadows of clear light that emanates from the north.*

Left *Inexpensive fabrics such as muslin, cotton, calico and linen scrim, in a raw state or bleached, make effective and unobtrusive draw curtains to filter rather than keep out any bright sunlight.*

Above *Permanent or semi-permanent sheer curtains at a window are enhanced when the light can pick up a pretty woven or lightly printed design.*

Below *These gathered and pleated, woven wool ochre wall drapes react to shadows and reflect what little light is received into a naturally dark room.*

linen scrims, muslin and calico drapes all make good lightweight draw curtains which diffuse the light enough to allow protection for furniture, and enough shade from the sun to work comfortably.

There is also scope for using shades and shutters to restrict light. Venetian blinds (traditionally made of wood) are infinitely adjustable and throw pleasing patterns across the floor and walls. Lightweight internal or external shutters are extremely effective for keeping out the sun. They can be painted in interesting colours, and look good hung with fine muslin for complete protection from glare. Fine muslin blinds will filter the sunshine, but can be rolled away on duller days when you want to let in more light.

Some fabrics, especially silk, are prone to fail if over-exposed to bright sunlight. Some colours, notably blues and reds, are also more susceptible to fading than others, and natural dyes will fade faster than modern chemical dyes. Both these potential problems can be avoided by adding fine cotton or linen material under the curtains, or alternatively by buying or making some good-quality linings.

2 Colour and tone

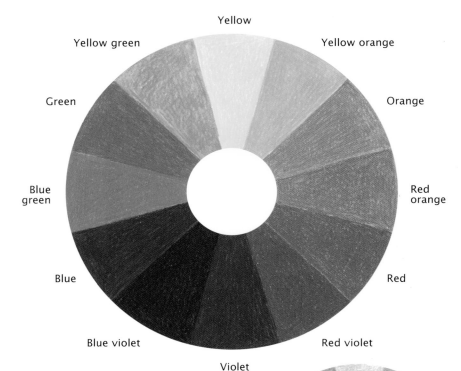

The theory of colour and how colours relate to each other within the colour wheel may not at first appear to be relevant to the making of soft furnishings. However, a basic knowledge of the origins of each colour and how they relate to each other will certainly be of great benefit when you are combining colours in a room scheme.

Every colour you see is a combination of the three primary colours: red, yellow and blue, with white and black. You do not need to know which colours harmonize and which contrast. Any colours can work together, so it is not so much which colours to use, but how colours and their tones can be made to work.

The full spectrum of primary and secondary colours can be shown on a colour wheel. Combining two primaries creates a secondary colour, and adding the third primary colour creates a tertiary colour. Tertiary colours may have a more natural feel, but often lack the cleanness of primary and secondary colours.

While mixing colours together creates a new colour, adding white or black creates different tones of a colour. Again, mixing black with a colour to create a darker tone may make the colour muddy. If you want dark colours, choose those based on primary or secondary colours that have naturally dark tones – red or purple, for example.

Tones and hues

So we arrive at precise terms to describe colours.

• The hue of a colour denotes the balance of the colours which combine to make it. For example, a shade of turquoise might be made up of 50 percent blue and 50 percent green, while a golden orange colour might be made up of a combination of 70 percent yellow and 30 percent red.

• The tone of a colour explains the amount of white which has been added to lighten it, or the amount of black that has been added to produce a darker shade. All colour schemes need a good balance of both tones and hues. You can choose closely related colours to create harmonious blends, or alternatively pick and choose a few colours from around the colour wheel to create several different contrasts.

Above *Yellow, red and blue are the primary colours. Mixing two primaries creates a secondary colour. The exact hue of a secondary colour depends on the balance of the two primary colours used.*

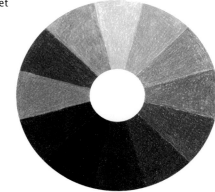

Basic schemes

The three basic categories of a colour scheme are:

• Monochromatic: This is where a variety of textures and designs are chosen in shades of one colour, for example, a stunning blue scheme could be created.

• Related: Here combinations of tones and hues of two colours which lie next to each other on the colour wheel are selected – for example, yellow and green.

• Complementary: This scheme is achieved with the addition of another colour that lies on the opposite side of the wheel, for example, blue and orange for the bottom left and top right of this colour wheel.

Most rooms are, in practice, a combination of these basic schemes, with the hues and tones of colours being sensitively balanced to suit the particular atmosphere and decorative style that is required by the people in question.

Above *The same colour wheel shown in black and white demonstrates how some colours (e.g. yellow) have naturally light tones, while others (such as blue violet) have naturally dark tones.*

A room scheme incorporating only yellows and blues, for example, would be described as a related colour scheme, and in itself may appear rather dull and flat. However, the addition of a bookcase full of books with different coloured spines, a colourful rug or some plants and flowers would mean that complementary colours had been added to bring the room to life.

Right *Looking at a room in black and white highlights matching tones, rather than the coordinated hues. Curtains, quilt and wooden furnishings have the same tone, as do the floor and walls, while the upholstery fabric strikes a balance between lighter and darker tones.*

Above *The simplest, but often the most effective way to build a colour scheme, is to use just two colours or one colour and a neutral one. A pink striped paper was the starting point for this scheme, then the same colour combination was picked up in the upholstery fabric. Stronger colours and patterns form carefully considered blocks of colour on the quilt and curtains. The walls, floor and bedspread ensure that the overall impression remains light and airy, while wood and leather accessories give balanced depth.*

2 Colour emphasis

A *simple way to begin to understand the variety of colour and tone available is to look at a 'neutral' colour board. Then you can go on to look at colours and tones, and see how the balance of tone affects the look of a room. Of course, patterns and prints will also have a strong role to play in most schemes.*

To make a neutral colour board, start with fabrics in neutral shades and of natural fibre content. Samples of wood, straw, bricks, slate, terracotta and even metal provide a structure for the scheme, then you can include textures and weaves, using materials such as voile, muslin, wool, silk, linen and velvet to provide extra interest and warmth. The finished board – using mainly inexpensive materials – is so inspiring that you may feel that you do not want to add further colour!

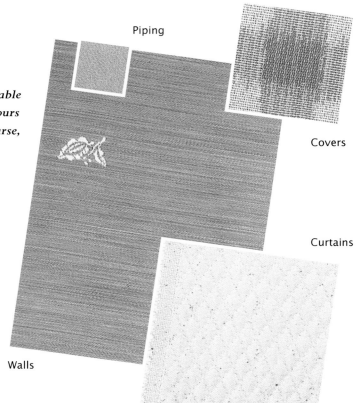

Piping

Covers

Curtains

Walls

Above *Dark walls create warmth, but a large block of a paler tone for the curtains, relieves the heavy tones in this scheme (left). A pattern may be very dominant if used on large areas such as walls (centre). Large blocks of closely related colours will soften the pattern. Pale tones for the walls can be livened up with touches of darker colours and patterns on drapes and furnishings (right).*

Left *The range of colour and tone that can be found in a collection of 'neutral' materials is in fact so great that you might well find that the addition of any other colour is superfluous.*

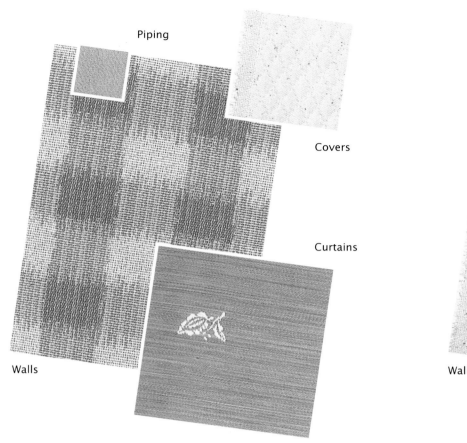

Piping

Covers

Curtains

Walls

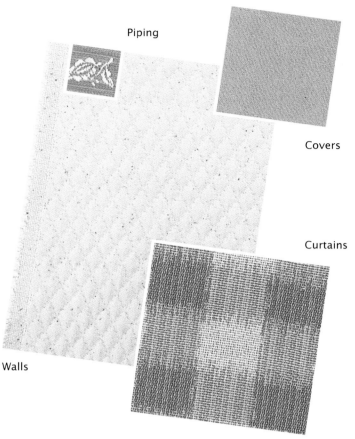

Piping

Covers

Curtains

Walls

Balance of colour

To understand the relationship of fabrics within the room, build up simple colour schemes using just one basic colour and a neutral colour, then add in the related and/or complementary hues.

Making a colour scheme

• Keep the walls, curtains and covers in tones of white. The floor might be another white tone, or a natural surface such as wood or terracotta tiles, or possibly a neutral cream carpet or seagrass.

• A second colour, in the form of one chair and a couple of cushions, introduces another dimension, but can look uncomfortable by itself.

• Adding more of this second colour with other accessories such as rugs and lampshades, all in varied tones, weaves and textures, settles this second colour into the room scheme.

Depth of tone

The balance of a room can be very affected by the depth of colour used for specific areas. Using three tones of one colour and a neutral colour explains this.

Using patterns

You can build very successful room schemes with only a limited range of plain colours, as long as due care is taken to ensure the right variety of tone and texture. However, personal preference, special ornament collections and other focal interests usually ensure that at least one other colour is present, and that at least one item will contain some form of pattern. Most schemes benefit from the introduction of pattern, even if it is just one needlepoint cushion or a painted lampshade, because it adds a touch of informality.

When choosing and mixing patterns, consider the scale of the main design, the balance of colours and also the background design. Classical designs of floral motifs on either strong or loosely defined striped grounds work well with small prints and small jacquard weaves. You can mix and match patterns as long as there are elements that still relate to each other. For example, a colour which is in both designs, similar mixes of colour tones and hues, or different types of design which somehow manage to balance and complement each other.

2 Colour scheming

Once you have decided on the function of a room, the fun part of decorating can begin. Collecting fabric and wallpaper swatches, looking for ideas and building up a colour board, is the basis for creating a successful room scheme.

The shape and size of a room, the climate that affects it, the aspect and the light, together with your own feelings about the atmosphere you want to create will all influence your final colour scheme. You may find inspiration in books and magazines, or maybe fall in love with a scheme in a fabric catalogue, but you still need to create a colour board to see how you can use paints and fabrics in your particular room, to bring about the look you want to create.

Start by drawing a plan of the room (preferably to scale on squared paper), marking in the positions of pieces of furniture. If you have to retain existing finishes anywhere, look for samples that match the colour and texture of the items you have to work around. Paste them in place on your room plan, to show the bare bones of your scheme. Then start to collect swatches of fabric, paint chips and magazine cuttings in the colours you particularly like, and position them in varying intensities on your basic plan to create the finished room

Right *A personal collection of articles in natural materials: soft brown colours, dark woods, bleached grass, pottery, white candles and wrought iron all blend together in an interesting interplay of colour and texture.*

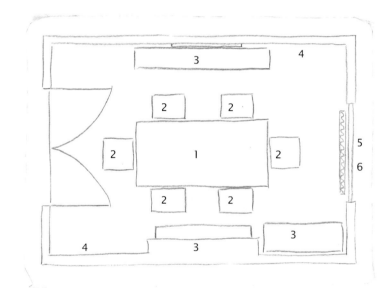

Left and Above *Draw a sample plan of your room to scale and cut out pieces of paper to represent the furniture — include both those pieces you already have and any you might wish to acquire. Place your selected pieces of fabric, wall-covering and paint swatches or crayon colours over the planned areas. You will quickly be able to see the overall effect and then you can have the opportunity to move colours around and to adjust the depths and tones until you are satisfied with the final look.*

plan in miniature. Each colour needs to be tried out in varying tones and textures, until you feel comfortable with the finished result. Test the colour balance by changing larger and smaller swatches around in relation to the different areas of use, and you will be surprised at how accurate a representation of the finished room you can start to achieve.

It is also important to look at these basic colour boards and samples in the room. Each part of the world has its own type of light, and colours can appear completely different even a few miles apart.

All the time you are building up your scheme, consider other items in the room. Lighting fixtures, pictures, ornaments and crockery need to blend in so that they do not look out of place in the finished scheme.

The final choice

Editing a decorative scheme is perhaps the hardest lesson to learn, as so often the heart will rule the head where favourite colours and treasured possessions are concerned. With careful planning and selective use of colour, you can include everything you want, but still maintain a cohesive design.

If you are still uncertain about which combinations of colours and patterns to use, perhaps the easiest way to decorate is to start with tones of a single colour, balanced by a neutral tone. Leave the accent colours and finishing touches until the room is almost complete. With the major items such as flooring, walls, covers and curtains in place, you can either add extra furnishings in the form of cushions, tie-backs and so on, or just simply accessorize the room to suit the mood or occasion. Try introducing strongly coloured china or ornaments, or add attractive floral arrangements to suit the season.

Above *Quiet elegance is assured when just two colour tones are used for the furnishing fabrics. Even though three different prints have been used, the subtle colouring and the simplicity of each design brings perfect harmony.*

2 Walling and tenting

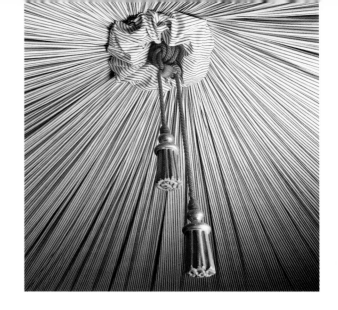

*U*sing fabric to cover walls has always been a decorating possibility, particularly for the wealthy. It can also be a practical solution for uneven walls, but first consider the cost and practicality before you embark on a project.

Over the last couple of centuries, walls in exclusive homes have been finished with a range of fabrics. Silk damasks have been pinned to walls and then finished with gilded filets for drawing rooms and chintz panels for bedrooms. Centuries ago tapestries were commissioned for the same purpose and when the owner moved castle or went to another property, the wallcovering went too.

Practically, a fabric wallcovering can hide a multitude of irregularities. It can disguise uneven brickwork, failing plaster, a disused window or doorway, and it also provides excellent soundproofing. Although the walls behind can be poor in quality they must be sound in structure as any dampness or draughts that get through will soon discolour and rot the stretched fabric. Sensually, fabric on walls radiates warmth, deadens sound, is soft to touch and provides an interesting texture, whether lit by day or artificial light.

Pleated or gathered, flat or in panels, the fabric will need to be stable in all temperatures – beware of any fabric which responds even slightly to humidity or you risk having walls that are taut one day and then sagging the next. Cost is also an important factor to bear in mind when large wall areas are involved, so look for tightly woven cotton, linen or felt. Try to find fabric which is extra wide so that few joins are needed and any necessary seams can mostly be disguised in corners or be insignificant against doorways.

Tented ceilings might be used to suit a specific function. You might want to tent a dining area within a large reception hall, use it to lower a ceiling, to soften a long corridor or to add character to a boxy room.

Covering walls

Walling fabric is usually attached to flat battens, which are fitted around the perimeters of every wall and opening. Staples or upholstery tacks are used to hold the fabric in place and a border of upholstery gimp or ribbon will be glued over the fixings and raw edges to provide a neat finish. To soften or deaden the sound, polyester wadding, thin foam or cotton interlining can also be fitted in between the battens.

Left *Mattress ticking has been used to tent this large ceiling with dramatic effect.*

Right *Attaching fabric to walls helps to soften a room's atmosphere and also disguises uneven areas. Large patterns are extremely effective when seen flat, and perhaps even more so when the fabric is gathered on the same wall.*

Left *Ugly wardrobe doors have been transformed with the addition of wooden mouldings to the lower sections. Warm crewel work fabric has then been stretched over the higher portions to lighten the effect and to provide soundproofing. For continuity, the sections of wall between the doors have also been covered in the same material.*

There are also special fixing systems that are available at specialist shops, which enable you to fit the fabric and remove it for cleaning when necessary. In some rooms, it may be more appropriate to fit the fabric to plastic-covered spring curtain wires, fitted around the ceiling and baseboards (skirting) of a room. By stitching a simple cased heading at the top of the fabric, it can be gathered directly onto the wires and then can be easily removed for cleaning.

Any pictures, shelves or coat hooks have to be mounted on battens fitted behind the fabric to keep the fixtures level with the fabric. Whether fabric is pleated or stretched flat, the grain should be kept straight and a plumb line used at each corner. Some careful measuring might also be necessary to define a straight line at the ceiling or floor to give a horizontal to line up the fabric grain accurately.

Stripes and definite patterns can be difficult to control, and plain fabric will show up any errors or marks. Any mistake in lining up the drops of fabric will be compounded with a strong, geometric fabric, and very uneven walls may make the task impossible, whereas a bubble, crease or pull can usually be stretched out of an all-over print, whether two-toned or multi-coloured.

2 Linen and cotton

Linen and cotton are strong, practical fibres, which are either finely spun and woven into firm, smooth cloth or roughly spun and loosely woven to create a softer effect.

Linen, the fabric of intimacy, has been popular for centuries and is arguably the king of fabrics. It is so durable that linen sheets, cloths and covers can become heirlooms – it is also so fine that the best under garments and night clothes are made from it. Because it is harvested from sustainable sources, it can be enjoyed by everyone, although it is not always a cheap option.

Practical considerations

Linen can be washed frequently and at very high temperatures – it is hygienic, healthy and does not cause skin irritations. It also readily absorbs humidity making it the ideal fibre to use for bed clothes. As linen is

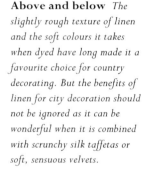

Above and below *The slightly rough texture of linen and the soft colours it takes when dyed have long made it a favourite choice for country decorating. But the benefits of linen for city decoration should not be ignored as it can be wonderful when it is combined with scrunchy silk taffetas or soft, sensuous velvets.*

stronger wet than dry, linen glass cloths are useful in the kitchen and other household objects such as slip covers, tablecloths and napkins can also be safely washed again and again.

Interesting weaves are limited only because linen looks so good plain woven and can be elegantly fine or rough and rustic. Hopsacks, herringbone and damask weaves are also available. Linen takes dyes well but the colour never penetrates right through to the inner core so any colour will eventually wear away with the course of time.

Perhaps the only real drawback to using linen for everything is that it is prone to creasing and demands a time and care to keep it looking pristine. Cotton, silk and wool are all woven with linen, to combine the best of their natural properties. Linen and cotton are extremely hardwearing, while linen and silk make a luxurious fabric. Crease-resistant finishes and a general acceptance of the 'creased' look have combined to make linen one of the most popular furnishing fabrics in the last few years.

In spite of its penchant for creasing, linen is ideal to work with as it finger-presses accurately and will stretch and pull well for slip covers. When it is unlined, linen looks fantastic with the light shining through and, when heavily interlined it drapes well. Linen can be pressed at the highest temperatures and curtains can be steamed once hung.

Choosing cotton

If linen is king then cotton is definitely the most versatile of fabrics. It can be woven plain or in infinite pattern combinations from simple hopsack to heavy damasks.

The best cotton is harvested from crops grown in the South Sea Islands where the filaments are long and fine, followed by Egyptian, American and Indian crops. Once the flowers have died away, the soft hairy fibres come from the boll, a downy white casing for the seeds. Twisted and spun to a soft strong thread, the cotton is then woven on looms into tabby, satin or twill cloths, or many different variations.

Cotton textures

Towelling, corduroy and velvet are just a few of the deeper pile cotton fabrics that are suitable for tenting canvas. Cotton may be knitted, felted, brushed or mercerized, and combines effortlessly with linen, wool, silk, rayon, lycra and many other synthetic fibres.

Organdie and organza, muslin and calico, twill and drill, poplin and lawn, canvas and duck, knitted and crocheted, hopsack and basket weave, herringbone and seersucker, satin and sateen, corduroy and ottoman, faille and taffeta, damask and liséré, ticking and gingham, velvet, towelling, piqué and matelasse, are some of the furnishing fabrics you will come across.

There is a colour, weave and weight of cotton that is suitable for every household use from curtains, slip covers, squabs, window seats and scatter cushions to tablecloths, bedcovers, sheets and pillows, towels, awnings and deck chairs.

Cotton can be easily dyed in delicate pastels or deep, strong colours and will also accept other finishes such as glazing, fire proofing, plasticizing, waterproofing and stain-resistant treatments. Cotton is also stronger wet than dry, and can be washed extensively making it the most popular less costly alternative to linen for bed-clothes, table linen, slip covers, curtains and cushions.

Mix and match

Of course, cotton and linen can be happily mixed with each other or with other fibres. Linen union is a linen/cotton mix which is practical and more economical than pure linen. It is ideal for making loose covers. Polyester/cotton mixtures are easy-care fabrics that are ideal for bed and table linens. They demand only minimal ironing, but do not have the same luxurious feel of 100 percent natural fibres.

Above *Gingham-inspired fresh country checks, deck chair stripes in soft colours and the plain delicate hues of pink and green, display the versatility of cotton as a furnishing fabric.*

Right *Cotton gingham is perhaps the most basic fabric of all and is arguably one of the most used and well-loved of all time. It can look fresh and jolly on its own or, as here, can be a good companion to a fun print.*

2 Wool and silk

Wool and silk are produced from two completely different types of animals – sheep and moths. Both are then woven into truly luxurious fabrics that have many practical as well as decorative uses in soft furnishings.

The primary source of wool is sheep. This is a wonderful provision of nature as each sheep in whatever climate needs to have its fleece removed at least once a year! The hair from long-haired goats and rabbits also produces other wool known as mohair and cashmere and angora.

Properties and uses

The natural properties of wool are what you would expect, bearing in mind the fleece's original purpose, which was to repel water, then supply warmth by trapping air in order not to conduct heat. The cloth woven with wool returns to shape easily after laundering, retains a springy bounce, but can also be encouraged to mould into shape when pressed with a hot iron and a damp cloth. Wool carpeting might show marks more readily than some other fibres, but it will release all dirt easily when cleaned and the natural colour and springiness will be immediately restored for far longer than any other carpeting.

Think about using wool plaids, tweeds, twills and suiting for chair and sofa covers, bedcovers and heavy curtains. Fine wool challis can make romantic bed curtains, sofa cushions, window drapes, decorative tablecloths, lampshades and sumptuous walling. Wool accepts colour easily and can be dyed to any shade from the deepest green to the softest oyster.

Care needs to be taken when washing, as wool is liable to shrink and felt up if the water is too hot. Also, if it is roughly handled, the scales which run along each fibre can open out and tangle up. Wool is relatively expensive to buy, but it mixes well with other fibres such as cotton, which helps to keep its price down. Wool can be susceptible to moths and needs to be cleaned thoroughly before leaving in the closet, or in an empty house for any length of time.

Left *Wool takes colour easily, and can be dyed to any shade as this glorious rich tartan and strong plain coloured cloth shows.*

Below *Red, sand and jade wool chenile cover this elegant hall seat while Baronial style banners in matching colour ranges decorate the painted wood panelled wall.*

Origins of silk

Silk originated in the Chinese province of Shantung and for a long time the production and source of silk was a well-kept secret. Later it was farmed in Italy and Prussia and the silk was woven into fantastically beautiful fabrics in Venice, London and Lyons. Nowadays the most affordable furnishing silks come from Asia, India and Thailand.

The coarser silks – wild silk, natural silk and Tussah – come from wild silk moths which lay their eggs in oak trees. The caterpillars feed on the oak leaves to produce a thread which is grey-brown in colour, and because the moth eats itself out of its cocoon, the fine threads are broken and short. Slubs result as the pieces are joined in the spinning and small pieces of leaf and other impurities are also woven in, which gives the silk its very distinctive character.

Farmed silk worms are fed on mulberry leaves to produce a whiter thread and the filaments are reeled off whilst the cocoons are still intact to produce a long thread with fewer joins and irregularities.

Above *The fibre content of these fabrics will, to an extent, dictate their use. These silks could be used for elegant curtains and drapes or to upholster a small ornate chair or sofa.*

Practical considerations

Although silk takes dye very easily there are often variations within a length of fabric as the natural fibre colours accept more or less dye. Silk does not conduct heat so it will remain warm in winter and cool in summer. The fibre is strong, resilient and absorbent, but can be weak when wet, requiring careful laundering. If you want to check whether a fabric is real or imitation silk, hold a piece in your hand and real silk will quickly take on your body temperature. Care needs to be taken when stitching silk so that it does not ride and pucker. Accurate and plentiful pinning and basting will help to hold the two layers together. Seams can also be slightly wetted and finger pressed.

Silk is vulnerable to sun rot and fading, and the extent depends on the type, its construction and the method of dying. Protective under curtains will allow silk curtains to last for many years. Always allow extra allowance in the turn-back in case it is needed. Two-ply silk can be a fabric that is as fine as gossamer, while six-ply silk is very durable and can compete with the strongest of upholstery fabrics.

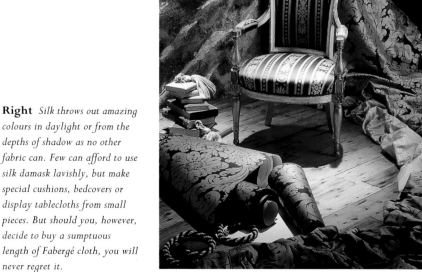

Right *Silk throws out amazing colours in daylight or from the depths of shadow as no other fabric can. Few can afford to use silk damask lavishly, but make special cushions, bedcovers or display tablecloths from small pieces. But should you, however, decide to buy a sumptuous length of Fabergé cloth, you will never regret it.*

2 Traditional prints

There are some printed fabrics whose long-lasting appeal has ensured that production has been continuous for many years. Traditional methods and distinctive design are the ingredients of classic prints.

The English look, which is renowned worldwide, owes special acknowledgement to the floral cotton prints which were imported from China with tea leaves and spices. Typically, these fabrics carried intricately drawn designs of flora and fauna and the celebrated tree of life design, printed onto plain cotton which was often glazed. London printers started to copy these ideas and developed more meandering designs with European flowers. They joined a pretty design with ribbons, or frequently added a light pattern to the background, often including a bird of paradise – or rather a designer's interpretation of these exotic birds. The background colours tended to be tones of ivory, Chinese yellow, Sung green or porcelain blue.

French developments

Also from the East, but this time from India, came calico as a basic cotton cloth from Calcutta. It is often printed with small geometric designs known as 'les Indiennes'. Imported into Marseilles, the French loved these printed calicoes and adapted the ideas by designing their own small floral and geometric prints, learning how to carve the designs onto hand blocks. They also learnt how to mix the typical vibrant blue, saffron yellow and tomato red dyes, printing onto the same imported calico base cloth. The original pear wood block designs are still used today and colour recipes are used by French companies in Provence and are often now referred to as Provençal prints.

Almost a century later in northern France (at Jouy en Josas, near Versailles) talented artists and carvers were employed to depict scenes from everyday life onto copperplate. Only the highest standards and best craftsmen were employed as rustic scenes of everyday life – children playing, a working mill scene, hunting and farming, classical figures and motifs – were carefully detailed and shaded. The characteristic of toile de Jouy (as these fabrics are now called) is that only one print colour is used on a light calico-coloured ground. The intricate tones and shading are a direct result of the superb craftsmanship employed.

Right *English prints on linen or cotton, highly decorated with roses, pansies, peonies and every flower from an English garden in summer are adored the world over. Whether a room is festooned with many different floral prints or just a single rosy cushion placed on a white sofa, a feeling of homeliness and comfort is exuded.*

Right *This range of printed fabric shows the variety of patterns that are available today. Although this selection is traditional in feel, they do not necessarily dictate the use of antiques or period style furnishings in the rest of the room.*

The British tradition

In the late nineteenth century William Morris and A W N Pugin both designed fabrics and wallpapers which are still available up to two centuries later. William Morris warned against the excess of industrialization and standardization, and devoted his drawing to the themes of nature, reproducing daisies, strawberries, willow leaves, acanthus leaves, birds and fruit and foliage from his own garden as accurately as possible, but in simple stylized form. These characteristic printed designs are still in demand throughout the world and are today printed by Sandersons in England. Pugin's Gothic revival designs with formal stylized patterns of trefoils, thistles and classical ornament are still being produced for period buildings.

Vanessa Bell and Duncan Grant, who were part of the infamous Bloomsbury set in the early 20th century carried on the example of William Morris, by doing free exuberant and colourful prints to decorate household objects. The contemporary designer, Laura Ashley, reproduced some of the most usable designs. At the same time, the French artist Raoul Dufy turned his talents to textile design, producing light-hearted fun prints, many of which are still available.

Manufacturers such as Warners, Greef, Charles Hammond, Colefax and Fowler and Courtaulds have enormous libraries of traditional designs, many of which have been printed and reprinted, coloured and re-coloured for decades. Classic in interpretation and colouring, many so-called 'new' designs are, in fact, copies of old ones which have been found in old boxes, attics and trunks.

Right *Classical motifs have been drawn and re-drawn over the years but the design team, Timney Fowler of London has perfected the art. By using black and white, gold and black, strong or muted tones, they produce elaborate or simple designs to satisfy every personal taste.*

2 Furnishing with finished fabrics

*S*ometimes fabrics which have already been made up and destined for one life can be put to another use to make attractive covers, throws, drapes, blinds, curtains and cushions.

With just a little imagination and confidence many inexpensive household materials can provide interesting and instant soft furnishings.

Decorators' dust sheets are made from hardwearing cotton drill, cost very little, and once they are laundered make wonderful raw materials to be stitched into loose covers or curtains. Antique kelims and cotton bedcovers can also make attractive practical impromptu sofa covers and tablecloths. By gathering the top of wonderfully coloured Indian bedcovers you can convert them into curtains and exotic bed drapes.

Tartan and plaid fringed blankets can be clipped over wood or metal poles. If they are too long, fold the top over and stitch to make an attached pelmet. Jolly checked kitchen tablecloths can make informal curtains for small windows; napkins can be stitched together to make bright summer duvet covers and teacloths can be

Below *In this stylish room setting a wool shawl has been used as a diagonal tablecloth, while crewel work has been framed to create original wall decoration.*

transformed into window blinds or cushions. Silk paisley shawls, woollen wraps or country quilts can be casually thrown over saggy armchairs to cover areas of wear or to disguise an ugly fabric beneath. Scarves, shawls and wraps can also make attractive and interesting top cloths on display tables. They can look pretty folded at the end of a bed, or tied up to make unusual cushion covers. Embroidered crewel work throws and bedcovers might be used for inexpensive bed drapes, walling and informal sofa covers.

Most of us, at some time or another, inherit or buy an old sofa or chair, and then find it is too expensive to re-cover them. Colourful patterned rugs or large ethnic blankets make perfect throw-over coverings, which can also be utilized in another space later on.

Below *Here, heavy chenille cloths have been shaped to fit the seats of two chairs and the excess fabric has been snipped away, allowing the back to drape onto the floor. For an upholstered chair, the excess could be fitted down into the tuck-in areas between the arms, back and seat.*

Above *Household items such as tablecloths, napkins and even bedding can be utilized throughout the home — here two tea towels have been pierced with eyelets to slip over simple brass hooks in front of a window.*

Below *A padded appliquéed bedspread with a floral appliqué motif is used as a tablecloth in this pretty garden room.*

2 Know your fabrics

FABRIC/FIBRE	DURABILITY	DRAPE	USES	CARE
Cotton	Strong, but hardwearing. Weakened by strong sunlight. Different weights are available from light muslin to thick canvas.	Good, but creases easily unless mixed with a synthetic fibre.	All areas of soft furnishings from fine muslin for sheers and lampshades to heavy deck chair canvas.	Always washable, but check if pre-shrunk from manufacturer's instructions. Can be machine or hand washed at hot (60°C) (2) without special finish or hand hot (50°C) (4) with special finishes. Also dry cleanable.
Linen	Very strong and hardwearing, but stronger when wet. Weakened by sunlight.	Fair, but creases very readily in 100% form. Can be blended with other fibres.	Curtains, loose covers and household linens.	As above. Try to minimize creasing to aid ironing – always iron damp. Refit loose covers when damp so they stretch to fit.
Wool	Fairly strong, but weaker when wet.	Very good, sheds creases easily. When mixed with other fibres the fabric is less expensive.	Mainly upholstery.	Check manufacturer's instructions. Washable in machine or by hand at warm 40° (7). Take care not to stretch when wet. Iron on wrong side with a steam iron.
Silk	Fairly strong. Weakened by strong sunlight; strength reduced by weighting.	Very good, sheds creases easily.	Curtains, cushions, lampshades. Ideal for luxurious accessories.	Check with manufacturer's instructions. Dry cleaning is generally recommended, but can be washed cool at 30°C (8) with care. Steam iron on cool.
Viscose	Fairly strong, but weaker when wet. Weakened by sunlight.	Good. Blends well with cotton and wool; inexpensive fabric.	Used in all areas of soft furnishing; usually in a blended form.	Hand or machine wash at warm 40°C (7). Take care not to stretch when wet. Iron with a warm iron.
Polyester	Very strong. Good resistance to sunlight.	Good in its lighter forms. Blends well with cotton, wool and silk; inexpensive fabric.	Used in most areas of soft furnishings and in household textiles; often blended with cotton or linen.	Refer to manufacturer's instructions for care, especially with the blended forms incorporating wool. For pure polyester, wash hand-hot at 50°C (4). Steam iron on warm.
Acetate	Fairly weak and weaker when wet. Weakened by sunlight.	Fair. Improved when mixed with other materials. Inexpensive fabric.	Limited use as not very durable. Good for curtains and upholstery fabrics.	Requires careful attention and handling. Wash cool at 30°C (8).

Note: Use machine wash powders/liquid (suitable for coloured washes) or soap flakes for washing by hand. White cotton and linen can be soaked in a solution of biological pre-wash powder.

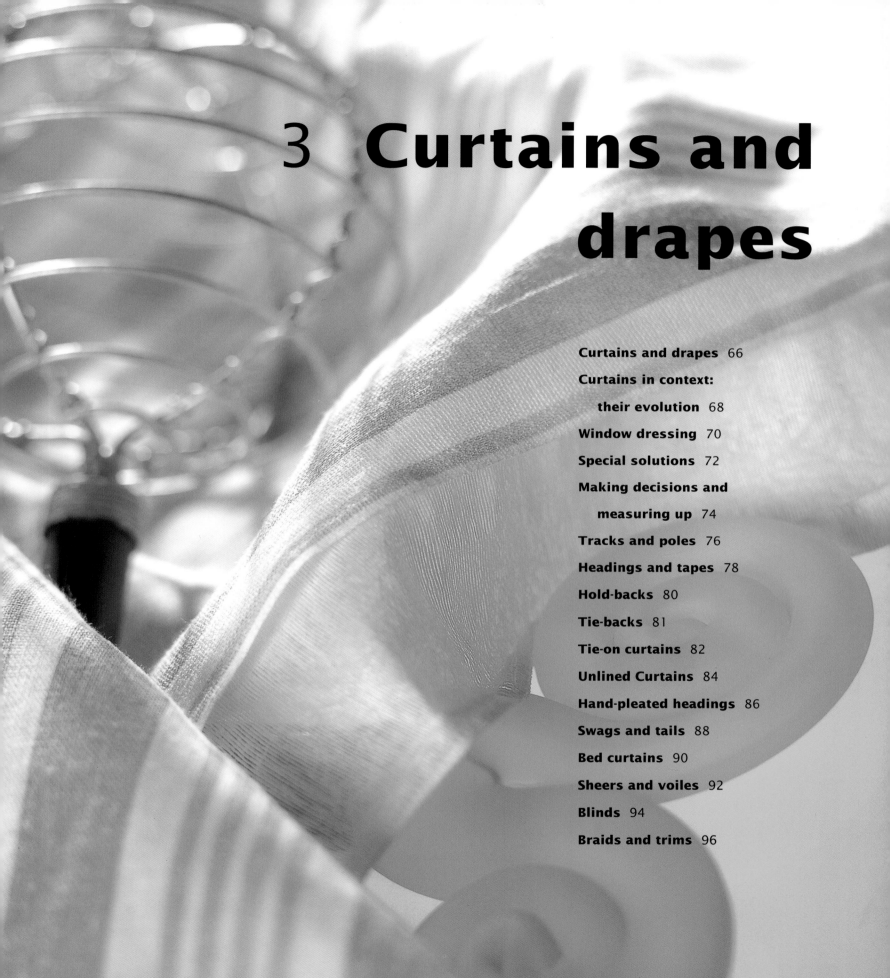

3 Curtains and drapes

Curtains and drapes

*W*indows are said to be the eyes of a house – they give light and vitality to a room. A room can just seem so lifeless and dreary when it has no natural light. So it is important to make the most of the windows in your home, but you need to get the right balance between allowing as much light to flood in as possible, dressing them in a way that complements the style of the windows as well as the whole room, and gaining any necessary privacy.

It sounds like a tall order, but it isn't really. The secret is to take things slowly. Look at pictures for inspiration in magazines and brochures and start a scrapbook with pictures that appeal to you. Look around the shops and collect samples of fabric you like: there are beautiful laces and voiles in the shops at the moment or, if you are on a tight budget, you can choose generous amounts of muslin to create romantic, billowing curtains that belie their inexpensive origins.

Choose from the fabulous ranges of curtain fabrics that are available. There are bold, vibrant patterns, discreet neutrals, subtle designs in plain colours and more formal fabrics. Also think about blinds. They can look stylish, are very economical with fabric, and can be combined with sheer fabric curtains for extra privacy.

Curtains and drapes come in a huge variety of styles, fabrics and designs: when you are choosing a window treatment for a room the problem is often that there is too much choice rather than too little. What is most important is to find the look that fits best into the setting, whether modern or traditional, and to select a fabric which suits your needs practically too.

3 Curtains in context: their evolution

Window curtains, suprisingly, do not have a long history. In fact curtains as we know them have only been around for about 300 years. Even in medieval times glazed windows were rare except amongst the rich. For everyone else wind-eyes, as they were known, were small, narrow holes to let out smoke and fumes and let in a little light and air. They may have been covered with oiled or waxed paper and horn or wooden shutters, but no curtains.

The medieval period was the great age of the tapestry. The cold, clammy walls of castles and palaces were hung with these finely woven scenes of hunting or mythical stories. The nobility lavished large sums of money on these tapestries not only because of status, but because they could be transported to their owners' other residences. Drapes were often used around beds, to partition off parts of rooms for privacy, and to keep out draughts. Curtains were even hung in doorways but windows at this time were always left bare.

Movable drapes

By the late 15th century much of this movement between residences had stopped. Bed curtains were becoming more elaborate but it was not until well into the 16th century that window curtains, made of one piece of material suspended from an iron rod, with rings or ties to hold them in place, started to appear.

The evolving style

In the 17th century curtains and drapes became more noticeable among the rich gentry, and were particularly in evidence at the French court of Versailles. An increased interest in harmony and symmetry resulted in the first attempts to 'dress' windows, but generally elsewhere curtains were still utilitarian. They were usually of fine fabric and acted as sun blinds rather than draught excluders. To keep out draughts, special mats were hooked into place in the window recesses at night.

In Britain, window curtains were rarely used until the late 17th century, and then only in rich homes. By the end of the 17th century curtains were arranged in pairs as part of a more symmetrical approach to interiors, and a new curtain was also introduced into wealthy homes. This pulled upward on cords to form a swag at the top of the window. In modest homes, curtains were made of dark wool cloth.

Rococo and classical influences

The 18th century began with a period of new refinement. In France this was the lighter Rococo style which arose as a reaction to the gilded Baroque style of the French court in the previous century. In Britain it was the Georgian era, which brought elegant classical influences. The use of curtains became widespread for the first time, either as a pair or the pull-up variety.

Above *Halftester beds were fitted with curtains designed to shield the occupant from draughts, while still allowing the air to circulate. Halftester bed heads are simple to make, yet they are a very effective and attractive way to dress a bed.*

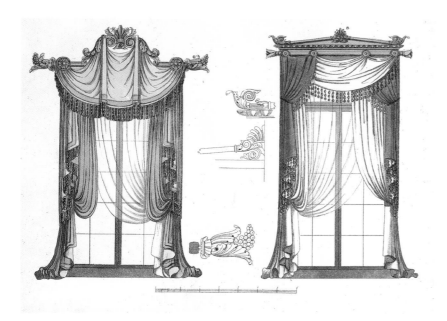

Above *This engraving from the early 19th century combines many fashionable elements of the day. Swags with fringes and floor length tails hang from ornamental brass poles with elaborate finials.*

Right *Drapes were used in doorways to keep out draughts long before curtains were used at windows. Heavy fabrics which feature traditional, tapestry-style designs are the most suitable to use in this type of period setting.*

Bed curtains were still lavish and sumptuous and were available in many expensive fabrics, such as cotton chintzes from India, damasks and velvets from Italy, and pretty woven silks from France. Blinds began to be used at this time too, both the roller and Venetian styles. Toward the end of the century Italian-strung curtains came into fashion. These were fitted with cords at the back which drew the curtains up away from each other diagonally when they were opened.

Regency style
The early 19th century was influenced by the French Empire style – the Regency period in England. Windows were dressed in layers: heavy drapery was thrown over ornamental poles to form a swag-style pelmet which was then combined with colourful silk or wool curtains. Behind them lace or muslin under-curtains were often placed, plus a blind. In the 1840s these fancy swag pelmets were often replaced by the lambrequin – a rigid pelmet cut into an ornamental shape which could reach right down the window cutting out light.

The Industrial Revolution
For the first time curtains were generally available as the Industrial Revolution had allowed home furnishings to be mass produced. The very cluttered window treatments of the Victorians were first seen in the 1860s, becoming very popular by the 1870s. Windows were dressed with large brass poles, swags, tails, dress curtains, tie-backs, lambrequins and lace curtains, all embellished with lavish braiding and accessories, which tended to make the rooms look gloomy. This style waned toward the end of the 1890s, when tastes were influenced by influential Arts and Crafts designers such as William Morris and C F A Voysey who preferred the pure and simple approach.

New fibres and dyes
By the 1920s the Victorian influence had faded and new developments in fibres and dyes led to the introduction of easy-care fabrics. Exciting new printed designs were produced and there was a much simpler approach to window treatments.

Curtains are still inspired by past styles and there have been recent revivals of elaborate window treatments with swags, tails and decorative poles, but they have been toned down to suit today's modest homes. Many more styles and fabrics are available than ever, but it can make choosing curtains difficult. So always try and decide on a curtain treatment that both complements the style of your home and which is also practical for all your daily needs.

3 Window dressing

Window treatments should always be devised as part of the overall room scheme. This means looking at the colours, style, patterns and period of the room and its decor, and choosing fabrics and a treatment which work well in that setting. However attractive you may think some fabric is in the shop, or however appealing a window treatment looks in a magazine, if it does not relate to the rest of the room it is intended for, then the results will be disappointing. For inspiration, look at coordinated ranges of fabrics that allow you to make blinds, pelmets, tie-backs, voile drapes and other accessories in colours and patterns to match your chosen curtain fabric.

New room schemes

Alternatively, of course, if you are starting from scratch with your room scheme, you can have much more freedom and leeway in choosing your decor as you can make the window treatment the focal point and take your inspiration for the rest of the room scheme from this. If you choose a multi-coloured fabric, for example, you can pick out the colour of the carpet, wallpaper and paint colours from it. Mix-while-you-wait paint ranges will allow you to find a near-perfect colour match.

The details of your window treatment also need careful consideration. You need to consider: do you want tie-backs, or to edge the curtains with braid or a contrast trim? Also, would you like to add rosettes, for example, on tie-backs? To gain inspiration, look in this book, in magazines and in hotels, restaurants and other people's homes. Collect any cuttings of your favourite fabrics and keep any pictures that appeal from magazines. You can make an inspiration board (see pages 16–17) and then take a miniature version with you when you go out shopping.

Left Coordinating ranges of fabrics and wallpapers make for easy colour scheming. The roller blind and window seat cushion have been made with fabric from the same range as the curtains and pelmet, while bands of fabric cut from the blind have been used as an edging. The wallpaper blends with the green in the curtains. The overall effect is perfect for this room where the large window is a dramatic focal point.

Above The colour and style of this window treatment has been carefully chosen to complement the character and decor of the room. The black iron pole is in keeping with the displayed accessories, the tassel complements the lampshade's colour, and the voile curtains give a diffused light that is perfect in an all-white room.

Above *When you plan a co-ordinated look for your curtains and blinds it is important that you get the accessories right. Here, gold and blue tassel and cord tie-backs have been chosen to blend in with the overall colour scheme.*

Left *Room schemes work best if they are conceived as a whole, with themes from the window treatment continuing in the rest of the room. Here the curtains and sofa are covered in the same fabric, the walls are painted in a toning background colour, and the braid, tassels and wallpaper border are in a matching shade of plum.*

Below *Details are a very important part of window treatments, especially if you are choosing a more formal look. Here braid, trims and rosettes have been chosen to complement this draped valance with matching curtains.*

Choosing fabrics

When you find a fabric that you like, ask if you can borrow a large swatch from the store to try out in the actual room. Many retailers are prepared to lend them. They may ask for a deposit, which is only reasonable. If they will not lend, consider buying a metre or so of fabric anyway. Light can play tricks on fabrics – especially artificial light – and the way it looks in the shop is unlikely to be the way it will appear in your home.

Always take plenty of time when you are choosing fabric. Do not try and rush the process. The money and time invested in creating window treatments can be considerable so it is important to be sure that you are going to be happy with the results. Fabric usually needs to be used generously for the best effect, and of course, the more you buy the more it will cost, so it is important that you are sure that you have chosen the right materials for your needs before you spend your money.

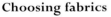

3 Special solutions

*S*ome windows only need a very simple approach to display them at their best, especially if the windows themselves are particularly attractive. Designs, such as arch top windows, pointed Gothic windows or pretty leaded cottage casements, only need a restrained treatment in order to show them off to their best effect.

Curtain styles

Café curtains, which only cover the lower part of the window, are a good choice for interesting windows — they might have a pointed or arched shape, for example. These type of curtains are ideal where you need some privacy, such as a kitchen window which overlooks a street. Voile also works well with unusual window shapes, as it can be used with special touch-and-close curtain tape and can be fitted around the actual arch itself. Alternatively, voile can be hung from a pole above the window, allowing you to see the shape of the window through the fabric. Of course, at night anyone outside will be able to see in when you have a light on, so this treatment will only work in the right situation.

Right *Roller blinds are an ideal alternative on windows where there is no space on either side to draw curtains back into, or for recessed windows that need to be screened but not insulated.*

Blinds

Using blinds is a good idea if you want an uncluttered look, as most types will lift up out of the way to leave the window clear. Windows where there is no space on either side to draw the curtain back into, such as dormer windows or windows that fully occupy alcoves, are also a perfect candidate for blinds. Roman and roller blinds in particular are not difficult to make yourself and have the advantage of being very economical with fabric.

Plain windows

Of course some windows do not need any coverage at all. If privacy is not an issue, because you are not over-looked by anyone and you have a particularly interesting window, then just leave it bare. Windows with stained glass are also best left uncovered if you are to display them to their full advantage. Of course, you can always decide to have an ordinary window pane replaced with stained glass. This can be particularly useful with windows that are positioned awkwardly, such as those high up in stairwells.

Left *Arch-top windows are lovely architectural features but fixing curtains can prove difficult. The best solution is to use a fixed heading in the arch as here — attached with easy to fix touch-and-close fastening and special tape. A simple swag has then been added at picture rail height as a theatrical touch.*

Rich silk taffeta looks best draped and tied, so that the light catches on the folds (above). A tailored blind (below) trimmed with gold cord, provides privacy so that the curtains do not have to be disturbed at night.

A ready-made tasselled cord (above and below right) gives a distinctive touch to your curtains. Use elaborately woven cords with luxurious fabrics, or simpler styles with plain cottons and linens (below).

A deep shaped lambrequin adds importance to lined curtains in this bedroom (above). The curtain fabric matches the paper, while a simpler fabric from the same range is used for the pelmet. Generously gathered plain and printed fabrics are draped at windows, bed head and across storage spaces. Extra emphasis is created by using a contrast border (right).

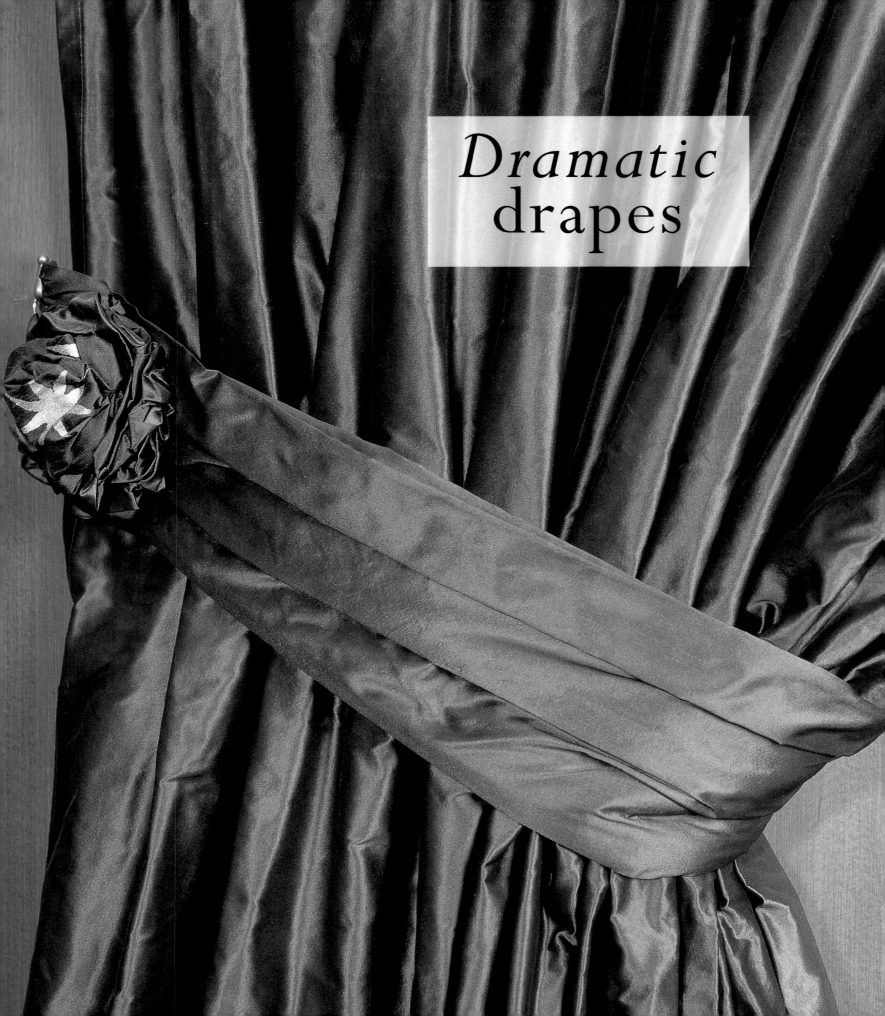

Dramatic
drapes

Curtains can be as simple
or elaborate as you want to
make them. At one end of
the scale, tie plain, unlined
cotton drapes with a bootlace
(left); at the other end of the
scale, trim intricate swags
and tails with bullion
fringing (right). Or make
a colour statement with a
broad band of contrasting
fabric (above).

Plain cotton voile suspended from a simple metal rod makes an elegant screen in an open-plan hallway (above). An equally simple treatment — white cotton stretched on fine rods — gives a minimalist effect at an attic window (right). Rustic windows also deserve a simple treatment: these unlined and ungathered gingham curtains are hung from a bamboo pole fixed above the window (top right).

Simple elements — white muslin draped from a wooden hoop — create a hazy effect at this simple window seat.

Left *Dramatic window treatments with swags and tails can also be informal and fun. This arrangement is striking in grey and yellow without detracting from the unusual shaped room and its pretty Georgian sash window.*

Above *To make the most of the light in this airy living room, the owners have chosen unlined curtains with a simple cased heading. Anything heavier or more complicated would detract from the fresh, summery theme of the room's decor.*

The natural light in a room is also an important factor to take into account when you choose a window treatment. If the room is airy with plenty of natural light, then it can be very effective to allow the sunshine to stream in through voiles and unlined cotton. On the other hand, the same sort of room can be given a more formal treatment and not lose out on too much light even if the drapes partially obscure the windows.

If a room is not well lit, perhaps there are trees or a wall outside the window or maybe it faces north, then you should ideally choose a treatment in a pale-coloured fabric that is arranged in such a way that it does not block out too much light. You can also pick a colour scheme for the whole room that reflects as much light into the room as possible.

Right *This circular window is a stunning feature in its own right and any attempt to cover it with curtains or blinds would be a mistake. The sill makes a perfect home for personal collections such as these shells and pebbles brought home from seaside walks.*

3 Making decisions and measuring up

Before *you can start to make your curtains, you need to buy the fabric, and in order to work out how much to buy, you must have your track in position and measure up. So you need to make some decisions. As long as you work logically through the process, you will find all the details soon fall into place.*

Decisions to make

There is so much choice today with window treatments that it can be very difficult to know where to start. Work through this checklist first to help you decide.

• Do you want to hide an ugly view or is your home overlooked? Try using sheers and blinds; a multi-layered look will give flexibility (see pages 92–93).
• Do you want to make the most of a lovely outlook? If so, keep the treatment simple, especially if privacy is not an issue, and make sure you can draw curtains well back from the window.
• Will you need to open and close the curtains or blinds frequently? This can be particularly troublesome with inward-opening casement windows. So choose corded track or a very simple treatment.
• Is it important to keep light out or heat in? Heavier fabric and thermal or black-out linings, or even interlining (see pages 86–87) are good in this situation.
• Are the proportions of the window satisfactory or do you want to disguise them in some way? This can be suprisingly simple to do with the right treatment (see page 77).

Measuring up

Measuring up is probably the most important part of curtain making. It sounds complicated but if you follow the steps methodically it is quite simple. Use a calculator for speed and accuracy.

• The finished width
To find out what the finished width of the curtains should be, measure from one end of the track or pole (excluding finials) to the other (see pages 76–77). If you have a track with an overlap arm you need to measure that too and add it onto the measurement.

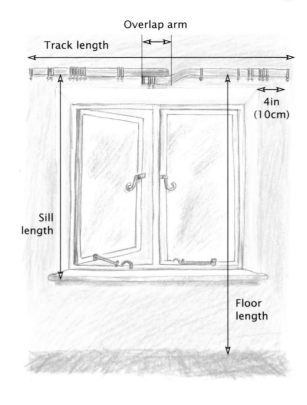

Casement window with a track system

Overlap arm
Track length
4in (10cm)
Sill length
Floor length

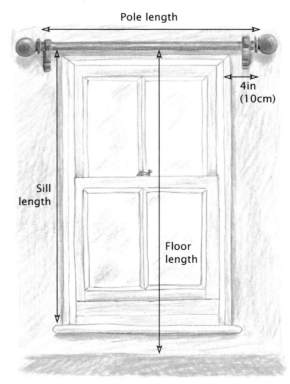

Sash window with a traditional curtain pole

Pole length
4in (10cm)
Sill length
Floor length

Curtain length

• *Curtains can hang to the sill, a little below the sill, or to the floor*

• *For a more formal treatment or a larger room, opt for floor-length curtains*

• *Sill-length curtains or just below sill-length curtains are best for small rooms such as guest bedrooms, kitchens and bathrooms.*

• Overall fabric width

Decide on how full your curtains need to be; even when drawn, they should still appear gathered. Choose your heading (see pages 78–79) as this will affect the fullness of the curtains. You then need to multiply your finished width by the amount needed for fullness (see pages 78–79). This will give you your overall fabric width.

• The number of widths

To get fabric this wide you will probably need to join fabric widths. Divide your overall fabric width by the fabric's width. Round up or down to the nearest whole number. This will give the number of widths needed. If it comes to an odd number and you are having two curtains, you need to cut one width in half and sew one piece onto each curtain.

• Overall fabric drop

Decide how long you want your curtains to be. Measure from the bottom of the track or curtain rings to where you want the bottom of the finished curtains to come. You need to do this in several places just to check whether your window and floor are even. To this measurement then add around 9in (22cm) for turnings and hems at the top and bottom (the exact amount will depend on the curtains you are making, so remember to check all the instructions first (see pages 82–93). This is your overall fabric drop measurement.

• Total fabric requirement

When you have arrived at your overall fabric drop measurement, multiply this by the number of widths that are needed. This final amount will then give you your total fabric requirement for the curtain project that you are planning.

• Allowing for patterns

With patterned fabrics you have to match the design when joining widths. Add the pattern repeat size onto each width or your fabric drop measurment. Find out the pattern repeat from the manufacturer – this is sometimes printed on the selvedge. If the pattern is half drop you will have to add one and a half times this measurement to the overall fabric drop measurement. Position bold motifs at the bottom of a curtain, so you do not cut off any pattern (right). Always check that the pattern matches across all widths before cutting out (far right).

Left *Cottage windows, especially with deep reveals like this one, can be tricky to dress. As with dormer windows, curtains can be unsuccessful as they cannot be drawn away from the window on either side. A simple blind would be a good choice here – or you could leave it bare to show off the view and the rustic simplicity of the window.*

Summary of calculations

Set out your calculations like this:

• Length of track or pole + any overlap
   = finished curtain width

• Finished curtain width × fullness
   = overall fabric width

• Overall fabric width ÷ width of chosen fabric
   = number of widths

• Fabric drop measurement + allowance for turnings + any extra for pattern repeats
   = overall fabric drop measurement

• Overall fabric drop measurement × number of widths
   = total fabric amount

Note: work in either inches or centimetres. Divide the total fabric amount by 36 to give the number of yards (if you are working in inches) or by 100 to give the number of metres (if you are working in centimetres).

3 Tracks and poles

Tracks and poles can play a very important part in the overall look of window treaments, so you need to put almost as much time into choosing them as you do your fabric. Many decorative poles are now available, and there are now some very inspiring designs available in cast iron, wood and brass.

Poles usually have decorative ends on them called finials. These come in a stunning range of shapes and materials – metal ones shaped like arrowheads, wooden ones carved like pineapples and even frosted glass spirals in acidic colours. So if you opt for this sort of decorative pole, make sure it fits with your room style and curtains. But whereas you might choose a pole so that it can be seen, a track is usually chosen to be as discreet as possible. With some designs, the track is completely hidden by the curtains when they are drawn. Others consist of very plain track with the curtains hanging below. Sometimes it is possible to stick wallpaper or paint onto the surface of track to camouflage it. Alternatively, conceal the track with a valance or pelmet.

Choosing tracks

Some tracks come ready-corded, so that you never need to touch the curtains but can open and close them by pulling a cord at one side. Cord tensioners are available which keep the cord tidy and out of the way. Automatic systems are also available which allow you to set times for the curtains to open and close; this can be very useful for security if you are away from home a lot.

With a track system you can have an overlap in the middle of the curtains. You can also buy multi-layer track, which allows you to hang sheer curtains and even a valance, all from the same brackets. There is also a halfway measure between track and poles, which is really track disguised behind a false pole-shaped front. This offers some of the advantages of track, but this type is limited to a few traditional styles.

Above *Poles do not have the same range of features as tracks, which can be corded, electronically operated or multi-layered so that you can hang a valance and sheers on the same brackets as your curtains. However, the advantage with poles is that they are very decorative to look at, so that unlike tracks you do not have to conceal them with pelmets or valances.*

Left *Poles can be a stunning feature in their own right. Here, a shapely hand-forged metal pole is given a gold tassel as a stunning finishing touch.*

Weight considerations

What you also need to think about is how strong you need your pole or track to be, especially if you wish to hang heavy drapes. Poles vary in thickness and metal tracks tend to be stronger than plastic. Manufacturers usually state on the packaging what weight their products will hold. Obviously tracks and poles are only as strong as their fixings, so also make sure they are firmly fitted in place and regularly supported along their length (see The Workshop pages 218–221).

Awkward windows

If you have bay windows in your home the easiest choice is track as there are products which you can bend around corners and curves. Make sure the track is designed for this before you buy – not all track is suitable. If you prefer to have poles you can buy adjustable corner fittings to allow you to link wooden poles. Some companies will make you iron poles to order, but be sure to measure up accurately. If someone from the company will measure up for you then you are covered if the pole does not fit.

Sizing up

Before you buy your pole or track you need to know its length as this will also govern your curtains' width. Poles and tracks need to extend beyond the window on either side to allow the curtains to be drawn out of the way, otherwise they will obscure the view and cut out light.

Disguising oddly-shaped windows

If your windows are not quite the shape you would like them to be there is a lot you can do to alter the visual effect.

- Short windows will look taller if you fix the track or pole much higher than usual and make curtains that reach down to the floor.
- Tall windows will look shorter if you position the track as low as possible and add a deep pelmet or valance.
- Wide windows look narrower if the track or pole is as short as possible and the curtains are permanently joined at the top and draped open with hold-backs or tie-backs.
- Narrow windows will look wider if the track or pole extends well to either side and is hung with generous, full-length curtains.

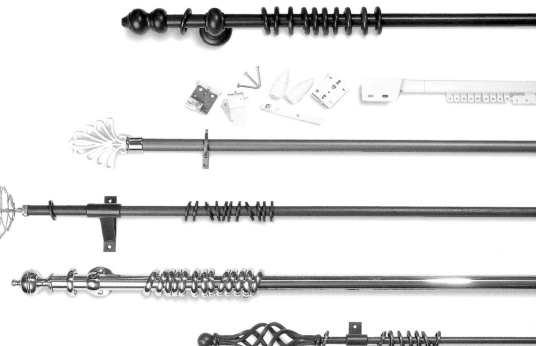

Above *Tracks and poles now come in an enormous range of metals, woods and plastics, and are available in many different shapes, sizes and materials, so you are bound to find one to complement your chosen window treatment. Also make sure that as well as looking good, your track or pole suits your needs from a practical point of view.*

Right *Some tracks and poles can be adapted to fit around bay windows. Poles can be made to measure or they can be fitted with adjustable corner brackets, while some tracks are designed so that they can be bent around corners.*

3 Headings and tapes

*A*fter choosing the width of your track or pole, you also need to decide on the fullness of your curtains before you can calculate the fabric needed. Even when they are drawn, with most curtain styles the fabric should still look full – not flat. This fullness is achieved by sewing special tape onto the top of the back of the curtains and drawing up the pull-cords to gather the fabric into pleats. Alternatively, curtains can be gathered without tape, by folding and sewing the pleats into place by hand. This is more time consuming but can give a very classy, tailored effect (see pages 86–87).

Buying headings and tapes

Curtain tapes come in many varieties, giving all sorts of effects. The simplest of all is standard tape, which is 1in (2.5cm) deep and gives a straightforward gathered effect. Pencil pleats are deeper and more regular, and are usually around 3in (7.5cm) deep. Fancier headings such as triple pleats, goblet pleats and lattice pleats require even deeper headings. These different headings give varying amounts of fullness to the curtains, ranging from half as full again as ungathered fabric for standard tape to three times as full for some pencil pleats.

Curtains should look generous but not too full. Take into account the fabric you are choosing: heavy fabric does not need to be as full as finer fabric in order to look good, while lined (and especially interlined) curtains will also not need to be as full as their unlined counterparts.

Very occasionally, however, you may want curtains to be ungathered. Informal effects where fabric is tied onto poles and bunched up with casual folds can look good in certain settings, or you may wish to hang flat panels of lace or fabric over glazed doors or small windows.

Choosing fabric

• Never skimp on fabric to save money. Tight curtains look mean however attractive the fabric. Just choose something less expensive and buy more fabric.
• Always buy the best-quality fabric you can afford.
• You will normally be making curtains as part of a room scheme so choose the design and colour to suit the other furnishings. Take paint, carpet, wallpaper and other fabric samples with you when you go shopping.
• Ask if you can borrow a large sample of fabric to take home with you. It is amazing how different colours can look in your own home.

Above *A cased heading does not require tapes or any complicated sewing. The two parallel rows of stitching create a slot which you slide onto a curtain pole without rings. The curtains are best held open with a tie-back or hold-back.*

Left *This pinch pleat heading is simple yet elegant for these semi-formal curtains. The track has been disguised by a strip of fabric to match the curtains. A coordinating Roman blind and a sheer complete the treatment.*

Right *Sheer and semi-sheer curtains can look good with a pleated heading and rope tie-backs. For extra privacy, a blind can be added for night-time use.*

Left Curtains can be fixed onto shaped pelmets with self-adhesive touch-and-close fastening and special curtain tape.

- Fabrics with large patterns can be very wasteful of fabric as you have to buy extra to match up the repeats (see pages 74–75). Matching up repeats can also be difficult, so avoid large patterns if you are on a tight budget or you are new to curtain-making.
- Check the fabric will drape nicely. There is little you can do to make stiff fabric drape well, but you can always add extra body to lighter-weight fabric by lining or even interlining it (see pages 86–87).

Heading tapes

Front		Back
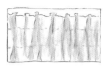		

Simple gathered heading

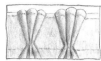		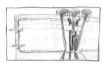

Triple pinch pleating

Pencil pleating

		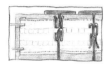

Box pleating

		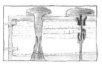

Goblet pleating

Detachable lining tape

Draw-cord tidy

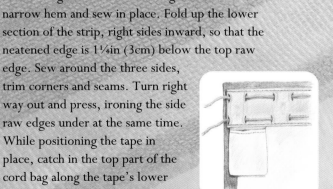

Do not cut the drawcords after gathering the heading, or you will not be able to flatten this for cleaning. Make a small bag for each curtain to hold the draw cords of the curtain tape. Cut a rectangle of lining fabric 3½in (9cm) wide by 8¼in (20.5cm) long. Turn the bottom edge under to the wrong side to form a narrow hem and sew in place. Fold up the lower section of the strip, right sides inward, so that the neatened edge is 1¼in (3cm) below the top raw edge. Sew around the three sides, trim corners and seams. Turn right way out and press, ironing the side raw edges under at the same time. While positioning the tape in place, catch in the top part of the cord bag along the tape's lower edge. Tie cords and put in bag.

3 Hold-backs

*H*old-backs and tie-backs have become popular recently because they give an attractive, stylish line to curtains when they are drawn back.

Hold-backs are rigid, are usually made from wood or metal, and are either in the form of a disc or decorative shape on the end of a short rod which you drape the curtain over. Some are like large hooks which you tuck the curtain behind.

If you have chosen a decorative pole for your curtain you may be able to buy matching hold-backs. Otherwise, look for designs that complement your room's style. Some hold-backs are rather formal while others have more novelty value.

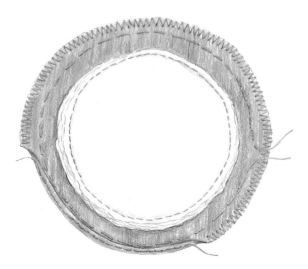

Covering a hold-back

If you cannot find a hold-back that you like, you can easily cover a plain, circular wooden one yourself. If you want to use your curtain fabric, the hold-back might get a bit lost, so try using a coordinating or contrasting fabric.

Preparing the fabric

Measure the diameter of the hold-back disc and double it. Cut out a circle of this diameter from paper or thin card and use it as a template to cut a circle of fabric for each hold-back. Neaten the raw edges of the circles either by overlocking or making a small turning. Then run a strong gathering thread near the edge of the circle. If you would like a slightly more padded look to your hold-back, cut a circle of wadding about 1½in (4cm) smaller in diameter than your fabric circle and centre it on the wrong side of the fabric. Baste in place close to the edge of the wadding.

Covering the hold-back

Place the fabric over the wooden hold-back and pull up the gathers to fit around the rod at the back and fasten off the ends of the thread securely. You can wind seam binding around the back to hold the gathers in place, adding a few stitches to hold the binding, if preferred. You can add a motif to the front, such as a starfish or carved wooden shape. Fix it in place with strong adhesive such as epoxy resin.

Above *A hold-back is an elegant way of drawing back curtains during the day, particularly if you have chosen a traditional or rather dramatic window treatment.*

Left *For a modern look a simple hold-back can be covered in bright fabric that contrasts with your curtain, such as this rather vibrant blue and pink colour combination.*

Tie-backs

*L*ike hold-backs, tie-backs are practical as they
allow you to pull the curtains well back out of the
window's way to gain the maximum amount of light,
and they are also decorative. Tie-backs are either
corded tassels that loop around the curtains, or fabric
tie-backs. They are usually fixed onto hooks close to
the curtain's edge furthest from the window. As some
hooks can be a bit utilitarian, more ornate hooks are
available from curtain accessory manufacturers.
The base of the tie-back should be about two-thirds
of the way down the window, so try to position the
hook accordingly.

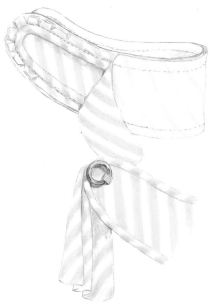

Making fabric tie-backs

Fabric tie-backs are simple to make. This tie-back style
is the traditional crescent-shape and has optional piping.

Measuring up and cutting out

Measure around the drawn-back curtain with a tape
measure. Adjust drape, then add 2in (5cm). Cut a
rectangle to this length and 4–6in (10–15cm) deep from
thin card then fold in half from right to left. Curve edges
and unfold. Check the effect and adjust if necessary.
Cut one interfacing shape for each tie-back. Add a ⅝in
(1.5cm) seam allowance all round the pattern and use it
to cut two fabric pieces for each tie-back.

Adding interfacing and piping

Centre interfacing, adhesive side down, on wrong side
of one fabric piece and press in place. To pipe tie-backs,
make up covered piping for each (see pages 210–211)
then pin and baste it around the seam allowance with
raw edges matching. Snip the seam allowances to make
the piping lie flat on the curves.

Finishing the tie-back

Pin, then baste the other fabric piece onto the tie-back,
right sides together. Machine close to piping, leaving a
gap for turning right sides out. Trim and clip seams; turn
to right side; press. Slipstitch opening for the tail, line a
semicircle of fabric and attach to outer edge of tie-backs.
Sew a curtain ring on back of tie-backs to hang.

Above *You do not have to
restrict yourself to one tie-back
or hold-back for a curtain. Here
two tassels are used to hold a
door curtain out of the way,
transforming the curtain into an
interestingly shaped feature.*

Left *A fabric tie-back is simple
to make, either in a matching
fabric or one that coordinates
with your curtains. A lined,
semi-circular tail can be hung
from the tie-back hook for extra
detail, if preferred.*

3 Tie-on curtains

Curtains with a bound edge in a contrasting colour look stylish but informal, and are also easy to make. It is very simple to line this type of curtain, should you wish to: you just work with two thicknesses of fabric rather than one. You can choose a coordinating fabric for the lining, but not one that is so strongly patterned or coloured that it will show through to the front. Also use coordinating fabric for the ties, but make sure that all the fabrics are of a similar weight and content: coordinates chosen from the same range are ideal.

Right *The top edge of curtains with ties can be left ungathered or gathered for a fuller look. You can also make the ties wider and more decorative if you wish, as shown here.*

Left *A coordinating plain bound edge makes a stylish finish for these patterned drapes. Ties along the top are threaded through curtain rings, but could be tied around a pole.*

Suggested fabrics
Plain, printed and colour woven cotton. Avoid bold designs or heavy fabrics.

Materials
Curtain fabric • Lining fabric (optional – same quantity as curtain fabric) • Coordinating fabric for binding and ties • Scissors and sewing equipment (see The workshop, pages 200–201) • Mediumweight iron-on dressmaker's interfacing – sufficient to cut strips 2in (5cm) deep by the total width of the curtains (you will need to butt up strips to join them) • Matching sewing thread • Curtain pole

Measuring up
Measure up the window, from pole to finished length. You do not need to allow extra for hems or side turnings, unless you have to join curtain lengths (see The workshop, pages 204–205). You may have to allow extra for facings if your curtains are unlined (see below). The lining, if it is used, needs to be exactly the same size as the fabric.

Cutting out
Cut the curtain fabric and lining fabric to size, if using (see pages 74–75). To line the curtains, make any joins using ⅝in (1.5cm) flat seams and press them open. If your curtains are to be unlined, use flat fell seams (see The workshop, page 205). Cut four pieces of binding, 2½in (6.5cm) wide, for each curtain: two pieces the

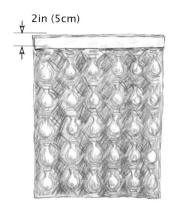

2in (5cm)

length of the curtains, and two pieces the same as the width plus 1¼in (3cm). Work out how many ties you need: position them every 8in (20cm) to come across the curtain's width. Make up 18in (46cm) long ties from fabric strips 2½in (6cm) wide (see The workshop, page 217).

Applying the interfacing
Lay out the curtain fabric face down and iron on strips of interfacing at the top following the manufacturer's instructions carefully. Butt up the strips to join them where necessary.

Positioning the lining
Lay the lining fabric, if used, on top of the curtain fabric, wrong sides together and all raw edges level. Pin, then baste close to the edges (or use a large machine stitch). Then turn over your curtain fabric so it is right side up.

Binding the edges
Press the binding fabric pieces in half lengthwise, open them up, then press the raw edges in to meet the centre line. Lay the long binding strips (with right sides facing) along the long raw edges of the curtain fabric, with raw edges level at the side, top and bottom. Machine along the first fold in the binding – ⅝in (1.5cm) in from the edge. Fold the binding around the seam allowance to the back of the curtain, tuck in the pressed fold and slipstitch in place, catching into the back of the machining to hide the stitches. If the heading is faced, slipstitch the lower edge of the facing in place.

Finishing the binding
Repeat along the top and bottom edges, but let the binding extend ⅝in (1.5cm) on either side. After machining the binding in place, fold these extended pieces in so that when you fold the binding to the back they are enclosed. Slipstitch these corners closed.

Adding the ties
Press the made-up ties, tuck in raw edges and oversew. Fold each tie in half widthwise and sew in place at 8in (20cm) intervals along the top, bound edge. Tie onto the pole with a bow.

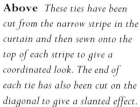

Above *These ties have been cut from the narrow stripe in the curtain and then sewn onto the top of each stripe to give a coordinated look. The end of each tie has also been cut on the diagonal to give a slanted effect.*

Right *Loops are an alternative to ties, and need to be placed onto the pole before hanging. Unlike ties there is no room for adjustment, so make sure that the curtains and loops are the right length before hanging.*

Tips
● When buying fabric for binding, make sure it is equal in length to one of the curtain drops, otherwise you will have to join the strips.
● Try using curtain tape instead of tabs or ties. Ideal tape for this is standard (narrow) tape (see pages 78–79). You will need to make your curtains 2in (5cm) longer to allow for a top turning.

3 Unlined curtains

Unlined curtains have less body than lined curtains, so they do not hang so well, but they are easier to make, wash or clean, making them ideal to use in kitchens, bathrooms and children's rooms. If you find that they let in too much light or you want to protect them from fading, you can always add a pair of detachable linings.

Suggested fabrics
Chintz, colour-woven cotton, gingham, floral prints.

Materials
Curtain fabric • Scissors and sewing equipment (see The workshop, pages 200–201) • Matching sewing thread • Pencil pleat tape – as long as the curtain fabric width plus 8in (20cm) for turnings • Curtain hooks to suit the tape

Right *Kitchen curtains are best left unlined, as are these gingham café curtains. The steamy atmosphere of most kitchens means that window coverings need frequent washing and this is easiest if drapes are unlined or alternatively have a detachable lining.*

Below left *While some people prefer their bedroom to be as dark as possible, others like to be woken up by sunlight streaming in through the window. If the latter is your choice, then unlined curtains are your best option.*

Cutting out
Measure up the window and calculate the fabric needed (see pages 74–75); this heading needs 2½ times the width; add 6¼in (15.5cm) to each length for turnings. If joining fabric in an unlined curtain, use ⅝in (1.5cm) flat fell seams (see the Workshop, page 205).

Finishing the edges
Turn in the long side edges of the lengths ⅜in (1cm) to the wrong side then turn ⅝in (1.5cm) again and machine in place.

Making the hem
Press under the bottom edge 3in (7.5cm) to the wrong side, then press another 3in (7.5cm) to form a double hem. Press. To mitre the corners, unfold the hem once and fold in the corner at an angle, from where the last hem meets the side edge to a point ⅜in (1cm) in along the bottom edge. Press in place and then fold the hem back again. Oversew the mitre and hand stitch the hem neatly in place.

Neatening the top edge
Turn under a ¼in (6mm) single hem to the wrong side along top edge. Press, pin and baste in place.

Preparing the tape
Cut a piece of pencil pleat tape 4in (10cm) longer than the width of each finished curtain. At the end of each piece of tape that will be at the centre of the window (you will usually have a left- and a right-hand curtain), pull a 1½in (4cm) piece of each cord through to the back and knot. Trim tape to ⅝in (1.5cm) of the knot and press this end to the wrong side.

Making a pair of detachable linings

Detachable linings are simple to make, and they can be made at a later date. You also only need 1½ times the track's width, so they are economical on fabric. Choose from ordinary, thermal or blackout lining.

Measuring up

The fabric needed depends whether you hang the lining on the same hooks as the curtains, or use special combined hooks and gliders. If you use the same hooks as the curtain, each lining fabric length needs to be 3in (7.5cm) longer than the curtains. With combined hooks and gliders lining fabric lengths need to be 2in (5cm) longer than the curtains.

Making hems

Turn under hem allowances around sides and across the lower edge as for unlined curtains. Cut lining tape for each curtain, each 4in (10cm) longer than fabric widths. Knot cords at centre edge of each tape (see Finishing the curtain, below left). Pin the lining tape onto the top of the linings, with the raw edge of the lining fabric between the 'skirts' of the tape and the knotted ends at the centre edges of each lining, with the tape extending ⅜in (1cm) beyond the centre edge. Check that lining will not hang down below the curtain's hem and adjust length at top, if necessary.

Positioning the tape

Baste tape in place, making sure you catch the back skirt of the tape. Turn centre tape overhangs to the wrong side to form a double ³⁄₁₆in (5mm) hem which should conceal the knots, and baste in place. On the tape's outer edges pull cords free, to the front of the tape, for about 2in (5cm). Trim tape to form ⅜in (1cm) overhangs, neaten as for the centre tape ends except the cords must be free at the front of the tape, then baste in place. Machine along bottom of tape, close to edge, catching in the other side of the skirt, then machine down the short ends, leaving cords free. Remove basting.

Hanging the linings

Gather up linings and insert hooks to hang lining with wrong side of the curtains and the wrong side of the lining facing (if your track has combined gliders and hooks).

Positioning the tape

Ensure the tape is the correct way up then position the knotted ends of the tape at the centre edges of the curtains with the tape's top edge ⅛in (3mm) below the top of the curtain. Pin in place. At the outer edges of each curtain pull cords through to the front of the tape and trim to ⅝in (1.5cm) beyond the curtain edge; tuck under. Baste tape in place then machine along both long edges, close to the edge and avoiding cords. Both stitching rows should be in the same direction to avoid puckering. Machine across both short ends of the tape, leaving cords free.

Finishing the curtain

Draw up the cords from the outer edges of the curtain, pleating the tape evenly until it is the right width. Tie the cords together and then tuck them into the cord bag (see pages 78–79), or alternatively wind them around a cord tidy. Do not cut them off as you will need to pull the curtains flat when they need cleaning. To finish, insert hooks in the tape about every 3in (7.5cm) and hang on pole or track.

Above Although more elaborate bed coronets are usually lined, less formal ones can be made from unlined fabric, provided it looks the same on both sides. Plain and woven designs are the best choice for fabrics.

3 Hand-pleated headings

*L*ining curtains always improves their look.
*It helps them to hang better and to last longer
as lining protects the main fabric from dirt, fading
and window condensation. This project shows you the
professional approach to lining, where the two layers
of fabric are locked together to improve the drape.
A hand-pleated heading gives an additionally classy
look. Use a large work area to lay the curtains out on
when you lock-stitch the lining in place.*

Suggested fabrics

Choose good-quality, luxurious fabrics; use cotton
sateen in a neutral or dark colour for the linings.

Materials

Curtain fabric (see pages 82–83) • Lining fabric (see
pages 82–83) • Scissors and sewing equipment (see The
workshop, pages 200–201) • Lead curtain penny-
weights (discs) • Matching sewing thread • Vanishing
marker or tailor's chalk • Heavy-weight iron-on dressmaker's interfacing or 4in (10cm) deep buckram strips
• Curtain or pin hooks

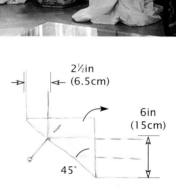

Right *Important windows
deserve the hand-pleated treatment. Intricately sewn goblet
headings ensure a perfect drape
at these tall windows.*

Below *Make the most of
hand-pleated headings by
fitting them so that the
heading is shown off to its best
advantage, with the leading
edges meeting in the middle.
Use tie-backs to let in the light.*

Measuring up and cutting out

Measure, cut and join fabric widths, allowing two times
fullness; add 5in (12.5cm) to width for turnings and
14in (35cm) to length. Repeat for lining but make 14in
(35cm) shorter and 5in (13cm) narrower.

Pressing the side and lower hem

Turn in side seams of curtain fabric 2½in (6.5cm) and
press. Turn up bottom hem 6in (15cm) and press. Open
out fold and press in half again to make a 3in (7.5cm)
double hem. Unfold side edge and hem and fold corner
back toward the fabric's centre at 45°. To fold at correct
point, insert a pin where the side fold and the top hem
fold meet.

Attaching weights

Cover each penny-weight with a small rectangle of
lining fabric, turn in raw edges and oversew, then hand
stitch covered weights to the hem allowance.

Stitching the hems

Herringbone stitch (see The workshop page 207)
the side seams in place with 2in (5cm) stitches and
matching sewing thread. Slipstitch hem and mitres.

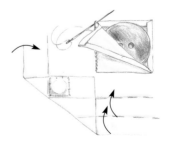

2½in
(6.5cm)

6in
(15cm)

45°

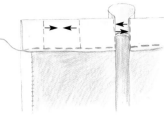

Marking the pleats

To calculate goblet pleats, measure curtain's width and halve it. Take away 2in (5cm) then divide remainder into even widths of 4–6in (10–12.5 cm). The number of even widths equals the pleats. The size of the width is the width of the pleat. To find gap width between pleats take half width measurement of curtain as before, take away 2in (5cm) and divide by pleats minus one. Using tailor's chalk on wrong side of fabric, mark a right-angled line to top edge, 2in (5cm) in from each side; it should run from basting to fabric's top. Then mark a pleat width and a gap width, alternating the two across top of fabric.

Stitching pleats and adding hooks

Bring each pair of pleat lines together on back of curtain to form a pleat on right side. Stitch pleat together on the right side, from top to bottom of the stiffening. Pinch up base of pleat, along basting line to form gathered base of goblet. Stitch in place. Open out top of pleat and oversew back top edge to the top of the curtain, ½in (12mm) either side of the centre line. Sew a curtain hook on the wrong side of each pleat or insert pin hooks, close to top of curtain.

Below *Hand-sewn pleats are particularly effective heading a valance fitted above a window. Matching curtains can be made with ordinary pencil-pleat tape.*

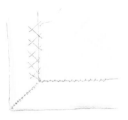

Adding the lining

Mark parallel lines down the length of the curtain 12–15in (30–37.5 cm) apart. Lay lining on top of curtain, wrong sides together and raw edges level with the curtain's side and bottom edges. Pin lining down centre then fold back against pins and lockstitch (see The workshop page 209) lining to the curtain fabric, beginning at the top and ending 4in (10cm) from the curtain hem's bottom. Repeat along next marked line to one side of centre and continue, working from the centre in both directions, until all is lockstitched.

Finishing the lining

Make ¾in (2cm) turnings toward wrong side along lining's side seams, and do a turn of 2in (5cm) along bottom edge. Press, pin and slipstitch in place.

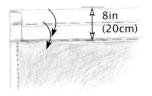

8in (20cm)

Making the heading

Turn down 8in (20cm) from main fabric's top edge, press then open. Trim lining level with this fold, then iron interfacing strips 4in (10cm) deep across the top flap of curtain so that the bottom edge is level with the pressed fold. If using buckram, herringbone stitch it in place. Fold top edge of curtain fabric over stiffening and fold again along pressed fold for a double hem. Baste across curtain along bottom edge of stiffening; slipstitch ends.

3 Swags and tails

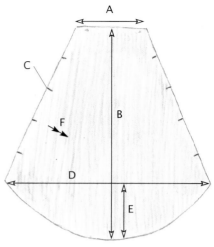

S wags and tails give a much more formal look to curtains than a conventional pelmet. This treatment is best on larger windows as, not only is it meant to look grand, but it does reduce the light coming through the window. Swags and tails are usually teamed with lined curtains with a pencil pleat heading. You can decorate the edges of swags and tails with braid or fringing (see page 96). As the size of swags and tails depends on a window's proportions, you will have to make your own pattern. You will also need to fit a pelmet shelf with angle brackets (see The workshop pages 220–221) so that the swags and tails can be fitted above it. If your window is wide you may need more than one swag, in which case they should overlap by 4–6in (10–15cm).

A *16in (40cm) narrower than pelmet*

B *2½ x finished length*

C *Pleat points*

D *8in (20cm) longer than pelmet*

E *¼ x pattern length*

F *Straight grain of fabric*

Suggested fabrics

Use good-quality curtain fabric that will drape well. Since the swag is cut on the diagonal, very bold designs or checks and stripes may not be suitable. The lining will show, so choose it carefully to coordinate or contrast with your room scheme.

Materials

Curtain fabric for the swags and tails • Coordinating or contrasting lining fabric • Tape measure • Paper and pencil for making patterns • Scissors and sewing equipment (see The workshop, pages 200–201) • Spare fabric for testing out pattern • Drawing pins • Matching sewing thread • Self-adhesive touch-and-close fastening or a staple gun

Making a pattern for the swag

Measure up the window and make a scale drawing, then sketch in the finished effect needed. The swag should drape no more than one-sixth way down the window. The inner length of the tails should be about the same as the finished centre depth of the swag, while the outer tail should come about half to two-thirds of the way down the window. Draw up your swag pattern. The top edge should be about 16in (40cm) narrower than the shelf width (the swag ends need to be hidden under the tails) and the lower edge about 8in (20cm) longer than the shelf, although this will depend on the window proportions and the drape wanted. For your lower edge measurement, hold a tape measure down in a loop from one corner of the shelf to the other until you like the effect. The pattern length for the swag should be two and a half times the finished length to allow for pleats, and the widest point (the lower edge measurement) three quarters of the way down the pattern. Round off bottom quarter to form an even curve. Mark an even number of points down the sloping sides of the pattern, spaced every 4–6in (10–15cm).

Testing the pattern

Cut a trial piece from your spare fabric, turning the pattern through 45° to cut the shape on the bias. Pleat the side edges, bringing the lowest point to the one above, then that point to the one above that and so on. Pin pleats in place then fix swag to the pelmet board temporarily with drawing pins. Adjust pleats if necessary.

Cutting out

When you have the effect you want, add a ⅝in (1.5cm) seam allowance all round and cut one swag from the curtain fabric and one from the lining – both on the bias.

Left *An alternative way of hanging tails is to fix them to the return of the curtain pelmet rather than extending them around to the front. This method gives a slightly less formal effect.*

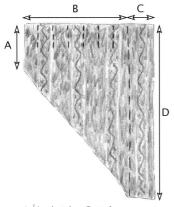

Making the swag

Place them right sides together and sew around all edges, leaving a top gap for turning. Trim seams, clip curves and corners and turn right sides out and press. Slipstitch the opening closed. Machine the 'sew' half of the touch-and-close tape along the back top edge of the swag. Pleat swag as before. Stick adhesive side of the touch-and-close fastening to the top of the pelmet board and press swag in place. (If using a staple gun, hold swag in place with drawing pins temporarily.) When satisfied, tack then machine down each sloping edge to hold pleats in place. Press or staple swag in position.

Making a pattern for the tails

Make this pattern, following the proportions in Making a pattern for the swag. Decide on the desired finished width and triple it, then add a return of 4in (10cm) – the depth of the pelmet from front to back.

Testing the pattern

Cut a left- and a right-hand tail on the straight grain from your trial fabric. Pleat the sloping section and pin in place. Fix to pelmet with drawing pins, with the return sections along the ends of the pelmet. The tails should hide the ends of the swag.

Cutting out

When satisfied with the shape of the tails and the pleating, add a ⅝in (1.5cm) seam allowance all round plus 4in (10cm) at the top for fixing to pelmet. Cut out a left and a right tail from curtain fabric, on the straight grain, reversing the pattern to cut the second piece. Then cut a left and a right lining in the same way.

A ⅙ x height of window

B 3 x finished width

C 4in (10cm)

D ⅔ x height of window

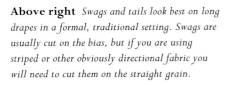

Making the tails

Place each curtain fabric piece with its lining, right sides together, and sew and turn right sides out as for the swag. Pleat up tails and pin pleats in place and position on pelmet board to check. If satisfactory, machine along the top edge to hold pleats in place. Sew touch-and-close fastening to the top back edges of the tails and stick other strip to the top of the pelmet board as before. Press tails in place on pelmet board.

Above right *Swags and tails look best on long drapes in a formal, traditional setting. Swags are usually cut on the bias, but if you are using striped or other obviously directional fabric you will need to cut them on the straight grain.*

Right *Two-tone swags can be made by sewing a strip of the curtain fabric along the bottom edge of a coordinating plain fabric swag, as shown here. These curtains cleverly conceal a large clothes hanging area in this attic bedroom.*

3 Bed curtains

*You can decorate a bed head with many devices –
from simple wall hangings to elaborate coronets
and half testers. Making drapes is similar to curtains,
but the fixture you choose will dictate the heading
and lining.*

Historical influences

Bed curtains were used for privacy and to keep out
draughts long before curtains were hung at windows. In
medieval and Tudor times wool drapes kept out prying
eyes in a time when there were no corridors.

By the 18th century four-poster beds were going out
of fashion and instead beds were given decorative drapes
which hung from the ceiling or wall. The Victorians
briefly reintroduced the four-poster but decided that it
was not healthy to enclose the bed with curtains, so they
chose the half tester instead. This was a canopy over the
head end of the bed only, designed to keep out draughts.
Now the four-poster is undergoing another revival and
decorative bed drapes are currently very fashionable.

Contemporary styles

The easiest way to add style and interest to a bed is to
display a rug, patchwork quilt or fabric hanging behind
the bed head. Another simple approach is to drape
muslin, mosquito-net style, from a ceiling hook above
the bed. Alternatively, you can fit a coronet on the wall
above the bed head. This is a small semi-circular pelmet
from which you hang drapes. These need to be lined,
preferably with a contrasting fabric, and are supported
on either side of the bedhead with hold-backs. Half
testers are similar to coronets, but the pelmet, often
decorative, is rectangular. The drapes again are lined.

Dressing four-poster beds is dictated to some extent
by the bed's style. With a modern design drape some
muslin over the canopy. Or go for dress curtains at each
corner, a canopy (a piece of fabric that ties to the top of the
frame), tie-backs if you wish and a matching bed valance
and comforter. Bound-edge curtains (see pages 82–83)
look good on contemporary four-poster beds.

Traditional four-posters can have the complete look:
full lined curtains with braid and fringed edges, sumptuous tie-backs, a canopy and pelmet, matching bed valance,
contrasting light curtains, plus coordinating bedding.

Right *A panel of fabric
suspended from the ceiling and
wall on wooden curtain poles
makes an exotic-looking canopy
from simple, inexpensive
components. Triangular fabric
sections with tassels help to give
the finishing touch.*

Below *Sheer and translucent
fabrics are ideal for bed hangings. A simple metal, wooden
or bamboo hoop supports the
fabric. Look in Indian sari shops
for unusual voiles.*

Hanging a rug or quilt above a bed

• You can hang a patchwork quilt or embroidered tapestry above a bed head, but if it is old check that it is sturdy enough to take the strain. Keep valuable pieces out of sunlight and do not hang indefinitely. Rest them periodically for the amount of time that they have been hanging.

• Quilts can be fixed to the wall with curtain pincer clips hung onto a row of hooks or nails. Use plenty to spread the weight and protect the quilt edge from damage by the teeth of the clip by protecting it with a small piece of matching fabric. Alternatively, use touch-and-close fastening. Buy a piece of 2in (5cm) deep tape slightly shorter than the width of the quilt. Sew the fuzzy part by hand just below the top edge of the quilt. Staple the opposite component to a batten just shorter than the width of the quilt and screw to the wall.

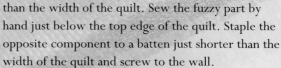

• Rugs such as kelims can be hung on a length of carpet gripper, used for fitting wall-to-wall carpets. Cut a piece slightly narrower than the rug and screw to wall with the pins pointing toward the ceiling. Press rug onto the gripper working from the centre outward.

• Alternatively, make a fabric sleeve from cotton, slightly narrower than the rug and hand sew it just below the top edge. Do not sew the sleeve flat, allow it to balloon out slightly for inserting the batten or pole. Ensure the batten is strong enough to take the weight, and that it extends beyond the rug. Support both ends on brackets. Wider and heavier pieces need short sleeving pieces with gaps between, these allow the pole to be supported at intervals on wall hooks. Here the pole does not have to extend beyond the rug. This is also suitable for displaying quilts and hangings.

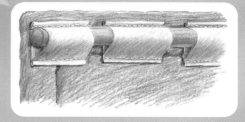

Above *An elegant coronet transforms a bed into a stunning centrepiece. The curtains are finished with a scalloped trim, a bound top edge and a pretty rosette. Formal coronet curtains are usually lined with a contrasting fabric.*

Left *A halftester canopy is easy to make. It is simply a curtain hung from a decorative pelmet shelf, which has been fitted with a gathered valance. The shelf here is quite shallow, but you can make a deeper one from front to back, if preferred.*

3 Sheers and voiles

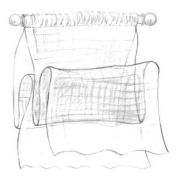

Sheer fabrics have become a very important part of window treatments. They are no longer just for privacy; laces and voiles can look romantic or stylish as they billow in the breeze on a summer's day, and most furnishing fabric manufacturers now offer coordinating sheers as part of their ranges.

Sheers come in many textures, designs and fabric types and in a variety of colours and effects, and can play a stunning part in a multi-layered look. For period-style rooms, off-white cotton lace can be bought in wonderful authentic Victorian designs.

Double sheers

These overlapping voile curtains are easy to make and can either be used on their own if the window is not overlooked, or teamed with a blind or conventional curtains for privacy. All turnings must be neat and straight as they will be seen through the fabric.

Suggested fabrics

The fabric must be reversible and the design must be the same in both directions. Also, look for fabric with a neat selvedge that will not need hemming.

Materials

• Voile, lace or other sheer fabric (see below for quantities needed) • Scissors and sewing equipment (see The workshop, pages 200–201 • Matching sewing thread • Expanding net pole for fitting curtains inside window recess, or a fitted curtain pole (see pages 76–77) minus the rings if they are to be fitted outside (fully described in the project)

Measuring up and calculating fabric

Measure up for the curtains (see pages 74–75) allowing twice the width of the pole for fullness. For recess fitting, double the length of the window and add 3in (7.5cm) for hems. If the curtains are to be hung outside the recess, decide how long you want them to be then measure from the top of the pole to the bottom of the intended drop, double this then add a further 3in (7.5cm for hems).

Right *These simple double sheer curtains use swathes of inexpensive fabric in a lightly woven check to create a luxurious and romantic effect.*

Fitting the drapes

Fold the fabric in half widthwise, drape around the pole and pin underneath. The casing must be deep enough to allow you to slide the pole in easily, but not so deep that it will look baggy.

Making the casing

Measure the depth of the casing, remove the fabric, measure up again so that you are sure the casing is straight, baste and then sew in position.

Making the hems

Thread the curtain pole, if using, through the casing and check the curtains' length. Then fold up a double hem on each fabric length, making sure that the two parts of the hem are the same depth, otherwise the raw edge will be visible. Make sure the hem is straight too, as this is also seen from the right side. Both hems must be folded toward the window side of the fabric. Machine or hand sew the hems.

Hanging the curtains

Hang the curtains (or fit on net pole, if using), then fit hold-backs or tie-backs two-thirds way down the sides (see pages 80–81) and drape the front piece of fabric over the left hand one and the back piece of fabric over the right.

Decorative ideas
- You can make tie-backs from patterned fabric and add a border strip of the same fabric along the bottom edges of the curtains to coordinate.
- If you use plain sheers, you can add a trim of lace or fringing along the hem and along the centre edges when the curtains are drawn back.

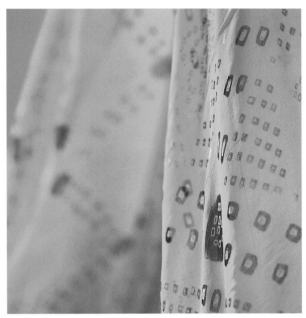

Sheer tips
- At night, when the lights are on in a room, sheer fabrics offer no privacy, so if you are overlooked combine them with blinds or conventional curtains.
- You can buy special transparent curtain tape for sheer fabrics, and also special lightweight track or expanding poles give a much more professional look than the old-fashioned stretch wires.
- Avoid making joins in sheer fabrics. You can hang widths next to each other without sewing as the fullness of the curtains will usually disguise the overlap. If you have to join sheers use flat fell seams (see The workshop, page 205).
- Use sharp scissors when cutting sheer fabric and a fine, sharp needle in your sewing machine to avoid snagging.

Above left *Sheer fabrics allow a beautiful diffused light into a room and make a stunning window covering, provided privacy and draughts are not a problem. In winter you can always add a blind or change them for warmer curtains.*

Above right *Sheers do not just mean a plain white fabric. There is a big choice of coloured and printed voiles and semi-translucent fabrics available, some of which come with matching curtain fabric.*

Left *Voiles and sheers can be combined with other window coverings for a more intimate look. Here, the fabric has been used with wooden shutters but you can also use roller, Roman or Venetian blinds.*

3 Blinds

Blinds look neat and stylish and are economical on fabric. They work well as part of a layered look and are great for showing off bold patterns because when the blinds are lowered the fabric lies flat. Blinds may sound a little complicated to make but there is really no window finish quite as easy as a simple roller blind. This Roman blind has dowels to ensure that the blind folds up neatly when raised and needs to be fixed to a batten; for fitting instructions see page 219.

Making a Roman blind

Roman blinds are the most elegant of the flat-faced blinds, and complement almost any decorative scheme.

Suggested fabrics

Good-quality fabrics, with firm, straight weave. Any pattern that is used must be printed squarely on the fabric grain.

Materials

Main fabric • Suitable lining fabric • Tape measure • Scissors and sewing equipment (see The workshop, pages 200–201) • Matching sewing thread • Pencil or dressmaking marker • Several strips of fine dowelling 1¼in (3cm) less than blind's width • A wooden lath

Below *A Roman blind in a colourful, modern fabric can make an eyecatching feature in a bathroom that combines both old and new styles.*

¾in (2cm) shorter than finished blind width • Small brass or nylon blind rings – two or more for each dowel •A staple gun and staples or small flat-topped nails and a hammer • Small screw-eyes • Fine nylon blind cord • A wooden or nylon blind acorn • Basic DIY toolkit (see The workshop, page 223) • Small angle irons and screws or masonry screws and rawlplugs • Cleat

Measuring up and cutting out

For hanging a blind inside the window recess, measure the width of the recess in several places and deduct ⅜in (1cm) from the smallest measurement for clearance. This is the blind's finished width. If the blind is to hang outside the recess or on a flush-fitting window (ie surface-mounted), measure the window's width, adding 2in (5cm) for finished blind width. Then add 3½in (9cm) to the blind's width (for turnings) for your fabric width. Measure from top of window to sill for blind's finished length. Add 5in (12.5 cm) for turnings and hems. Add an extra 2in (5cm) if surface-mounting your blind. Cut fabric to this length and as wide as your fabric width. Cut lining to same length as the top fabric and the same width less 4¾in (12cm). Add extra lining for dowel casings.

Making up the blind

Lay top fabric on lining with right sides together and edges level top and bottom. Pin side seams with raw edges level. Machine together with a ⅝in (1.5cm) seam. Press seam open and turn tube of fabric right side out. Working with lining uppermost, press outside edges so an equal margin of top fabric shows on either side. Baste down and across centres to hold the layers together.

Finishing the lower edge

Turn fabric and lining under ½in (12mm) along bottom edge, toward lining, and press. Turn under another 2¾in (7cm) for a casing. Machine close to fold.

Above *A roller blind makes a neat and cheerful covering for a kitchen's glazed door, without cutting out too much light.*

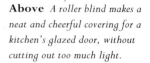

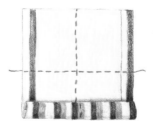

Making dowel casings

Cut some pieces of lining fabric the same width as your finished blind width and 2in (5cm) deep. These are to hold the dowels and the number depends on the blind's length: you will need one every 8–10in (20–25cm). Mark lengthwise along centre line of each lining strip with a pencil or dressmaking marker. Press in ⅜in (1cm) along long edges and short ends. Temporarily mark a line across back of your blind for each dowel (for fine fabrics). Space lines evenly down blind with an even gap top and bottom. Pin a lining strip to every line on your blind, matching up marked lines with ⅜in (1cm) in from blind edges.

Fitting the dowels

Machine each strip in place along line. Fold each strip in half along centre line and slipstitch by hand or machine close to folded long edges. Slide a dowel into each of the pockets and slipstitch both ends. Slide lath into bottom casing and stitch ends. Remove basting. Sew two rings to each dowel pocket, ¾in (2cm) in from the sides of the blind. Unless blind is narrow, add one or more vertical rows in between. Space out evenly, about 10–12in (25–30cm) apart.

Finishing the top edge

Fold 1¾in (4.5cm) of top of blind over wide side of batten. Fix with staple gun or small, flat-topped nails. Ensure the blind is square on the batten to hang straight.

Cording the blind

Fix a screw eye into the underside of batten above each row of rings. To calculate cord needed, double blind's length, add distance between left- and right-hand rows of rings and multiply by number of vertical rows of rings. Cut cord into equal lengths, one for each vertical row of rings. Decide which side of the window to hang pull-cord. Thread each cord vertically through each row of rings and then through the screw eye at top of row. Tie cord to bottom ring of each vertical row, thread each cord through previous screw eyes to the eye at the end where the pull cord is to be. Gather up cords hanging at side, trim to same length and thread on acorn. Knot cords just above sill and pull acorn down to cover knot.

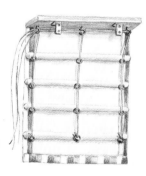

Fixing the blind in place

Fix blind on window frame using angle irons or screw through batten upward into the reveal. Fix cleat to wall or in reveal. When blind is raised, wind cord around cleat.

Above *London blinds and balloon blinds are variations on the roman blind. This elaborate pull-up blind is based on the type often used in Georgian times and is perfect for town houses of this period.*

Joining fabric widths

If your main or lining fabrics are too narrow for the window, join lengths together. Add 1¼in (3cm) to your fabric width for every join. Make any joins either in the centre or equally spaced to either side of the centre point, taking a ⅝in (1.5cm) seam. Match any repeats — you may need some extra fabric for this (see The workshop, page 203). Press seams open.

Left *Assembling roller blinds is easy when using a kit. The kits are available with every component. Apply stiffener to untreated fabric, following the manufacturer's instructions.*

3 Braids and trims

Braids and trims, which have recently made a big come-back, can add something special to curtains and blinds. Trims should coordinate and enhance a window feature, not dominate. Avoid heavy or skimpy fabric edgings, and if you are going to use them around curves make sure they are flexible. More soft furnishing manufacturers are bringing out ranges of cord, gimp, ready-covered piping, bullion fringing and bobble trim to coordinate with their fabrics. These beautiful new designs and colourways are very different from the heavy, dusty looking Victorian braids and trims. However, trims can be expensive, especially if handmade, so work out what is needed before buying.

Below *Big tassels and cords give a bold, theatrical look to curtains when they are used as tie-backs.*

Right *Braids and trims are back in fashion and manufacturers are producing stunning ranges of designs to coordinate with their furnishing fabric ranges.*

Applying braid and trims

Braids and trims need to be applied carefully to achieve the best effect. Use these instructions to find out how to apply them in the neatest and most attractive way.

Attaching cord

Sew cord onto the edge of curtains, pelmets, tie-backs and drapes by taking an invisible stitch along the folded edge of the curtain, then along the inside of the cord and back along the curtain edge.

Fixing braid

Braid is usually sewn close to the finished edges of curtains, swags, tails, pelmets and blinds. Alternatively, it can be inset from the edge to create a strong border. Sew braid down both sides by hand or machine. Some braids will be flattened by machining, while others are too bulky to get under the presser foot at all, so experiment with an off-cut of braid and material first. If machine sewing is acceptable, sew both sides in the same direction to avoid puckering. Mitre corners of braid and baste in place before topstitching. If hand sewing, use tiny invisible slipstitches. Turn cut ends of braid in ¼in (6mm) before sewing to stop them unravelling.

Adding fringing

Covered piping and some fringing can be sandwiched on the inside edge of seams where the lining is the same size as the main fabric – such as with swags and tails – while sewing. Baste braid in place to right side of the fabric along seam line, but do not catch fringing in the stitching. As with piping (see The workshop, page 210–211), when right side out the piping or fringing is on the outside edge.

4 Cushions and pillows

Cushions and pillows

Furnishing accessories play a major part in everyone's home. They are as vital to living rooms as scarves, gloves, hats and belts are to complete a wardrobe. Whether you use a single striking colour or a mix of colours to pull all the others together, each accessory is chosen to make a particular

statement. Other soft furnishings such as rugs and curtains help to create a room's style, but cushions are an important accessory as they can be made as large colourful floor cushions for children or for extra seating, or they can be made smaller and grouped together on a plain sofa to make a striking focal point. They are easy to make, can be easily moved around, and are inexpensive so that the covers can be changed every season. They can be made in versatile cottons and linens or, to make a room special, in more sumptuous velvets or damasks.

You can also customize cushions by adding trimmings, piping, buttons or beads to complement your furniture or the room's decorative style. Once you have acquired more skills you can make bolsters or boxed cushions to revamp an old sofa. Pillows can also be made to suit your bedroom style: coloured borders can tone in with a duvet cover or by adding frills or lace you can give a soft, romantic appeal.

Pattern and texture play an important part in the choice of soft furnishings as shown in the eclectic mix of these coordinating cushions, below left. Classic navy blue and white striped fabric can look stunning against a pure white background, above. A daring and dramatic contemporary picture, bright yellow pumpkin cushions and a stool cover make striking accent points to a neutral scheme, left. Exquisite tapestry and classic check cushions can perfectly complement a traditional chintz sofa, far left.

4 Setting the style

S *catter cushions are decorative, practical and versatile. They can be placed in colourful piles in children's playrooms, one can be given prominence in an elegant chair or they can be massed on a squashy sofa. Leave cushions plain or embellish them with fringes, tassels, cords and buttons to suit your style.*

Materials and textures

When you make cushions yourself, the choice and use of different materials, textures, patterns, details and colour combinations ensure that no one else will ever have your furnishing style.

Cushions can be carefully planned to give just the right balance of size, shape, position, colour and texture to create a certain impact on their own, or two cushions might be designed to work together on a plain background. Blending colour, tone or fabric style will become instinctive as you get to know the colours which you most enjoy.

Durable fabrics

Always choose fabric which will wear and clean well. If possible always buy fabrics made from natural fibres and, if washable, wash all cover fabrics before making up. Loose covers and seat cushions especially should be machine washable.

Some fabrics which are not normally used for soft furnishings or cushions are available from other sources. Look for some unbleached linen, denim, artists' canvas, fine woven jute, gingham, woven rugs and kelims or mattress tickings.

Colour schemes

Neutral and all white rooms may be 'traditional' or 'contemporary' in style and the colours and design of the accessories can emphasize or detract from the period or modern look. A single cushion in shocking pink can make a huge impact on an all-white room; a cushion with a small white and pale lilac print makes little impact, but can help lead the way for other patterns and colours.

Monochromatic room schemes can be interesting to put together and very restful to live with. Use different textures, and lighter and darker tones to gain variety. A colour scheme with cushions and covers in colours that combine pale brown, light and golden yellows will never be boring if you pay attention to fabric textures. Find samples of matt linen, shot silk, crunchy-textured woven wool, fine cottons and self-patterned jacquards and pin them together to make a simple colour board. Then select which fabrics you want for cushions and which for covers. If you want to extend the colour palette more with soft pinks and apricots or with strong reds and greens, find small pieces of coloured fabric, paint charts or magazine cuttings and add to the first colours to see what can be accomplished within a small colour span.

Cushion styles

The shapes and sizes of pillows that can be used on a bed are endless. Large round bolsters, huge square pillows, frilled, bordered, tasselled and fringed pillows and embroidered or heart-shaped pillows all combine well with a bed's traditional shape.

Comfortable 'bedheads' can be made with slim box cushions; fit them to a pole behind the bed or hang them by ribbons tied to small decorative coat hooks. Alternatively, you can make two quilted and stuffed large bordered pillows to prop up against a less comfortable wooden or cane headboard.

Left *An oversized squashy bolster and double seat cushions soften the angular shape of the sofa, while the bold striped pattern helps to reinforce the room's strong formality.*

Above *Plain off-white and taupe fabrics, in checks and stripes, are anchored with a strong swirl design which is re-invented in the curtains with the colours reversed.*

Left *This cushion covered in leopard skin, the luxury fashion fabric of the season, perfectly accessorizes this simple and elegant white scheme.*

Seating styles

Cushions can be piled on the floor for additional seating. Make large scatter cushions in mixed, washable fabrics or stripy box cushions and scatter cushions to place outside on the sun terrace or deck. For a touch of elegance, make three or four box cushions in richly coloured damasks, add cords and tasselled corners, and pile in a corner of an elegant living room.

Seat cushions are mostly made with a firm inner pad, to soften a hard surface and to give support. Buttoning and piping in a deep tone against the main fabric will give seat cushions a strong identity. This more tailored look works well with metal and wooden chairs, and on window seats.

Less formal chair styles, such as wicker chairs and soft sofas will need softer cushions. More feminine fabrics and lighter colours and self toning piping can look good. Detailed ties and ruching can be appropriate with less formal treatments.

Decorative Finishes

Cords, braids, tassels and fringes add style and elegance to any cushions or pillows, whether in a Fortuny silk or a piece of kelim carpet. Look out for special antique or antique-style trimmings with beads and toggles. Simple ric-rac braid or soft patterned Tyrolean woven braids can blend well with country fabrics.

Stencilled designs and appliqué motifs can liven up a plain fabric. Pick up a motif from a fabric or wallpaper border, or use a classical stencil such as an everlasting Greek key motif, or design a specific stencil such as a bowl of fruit.

Above *Classic motifs printed in a black and white fabric on these cushions sit well together, while a red velvet patterned cushion adds further texture.*

4 Trimmings

Buttons and bows, ribbons and braids, cords and piping, frills and fringes can all add a distinctive touch to your cushions. Buy them ready-made or make them up from other fabrics to coordinate with other furnishings. Use them to add bold accents, to create ornamentation, or to add a soft country touch.

When planning soft furnishings, think about the details of selecting fabrics and building up colour schemes. If you cannot find ready-made piping and braids to match your fabric, make up your own binding or frills and ties. Build up a colour board of fabric swatches and samples – you can even try out the effects with offcuts of fabric, making up your own details to trim your covers.

Trimmings fall into two main categories: they may be topstitched to the front panel of a cushion cover or inserted in the seams around the edge. Trimmings for topstitching include woven braids, ribbons, fine cords, and lace – you can even cut fabric strips to stitch across the front of a cover. For example, a chunky wool fan-edged braid stitched to woven horsehair immediately makes a rather stiff fabric appear softer and more interesting; while ric-rac braid on a bordered cushion gives a cheerful touch to a child's bedroom. Topstitched trims are usually added to the cushion's front panel before it is made up (see The workshop, page 211), or they may be used to accentuate a topstitched seam line on a flat-bordered cover.

Around a cushion's seam lines, you can add crisp piping, gathered frills, lace or broderie anglaise. Mix and match trimmings, emphasizing a frilled pillow with piping, or adding a softer touch by combining a narrow, gathered lace trim with a frill of crisp, floral chintz.

Bought trimmings are available in many styles and colours. Specialist companies will even make anything to order – from simple walling braid to elaborate period tasselled fringes. You can also find fantastic antique braids and fringes in bric-a-brac shops.

Buttons can form the closure to an envelope-style cover, but can also be trimmings. Cover special button forms (see The workshop, page 217) in fabric to match piping on a boxed cushion, for example, or add buttons and tassels in wood or bone and soft silk to trim a flat-bordered cushion. Rosettes, too, can add extra detail.

Left *While the colours of the naive curtain print have all been picked up in this bold plaid cushion, the pink fan-edged trimming was chosen especially to identify one particular flower's colour.*

Left *Chenille ruched fringing contrasts with the cushion's texture while emphasizing the lime green colour from an eclectic mix of plaids and checks.*

Left *Blue and white checks and stripes are trimmed with a crisp cotton border in similar coordinating tones.*

Left *Use your imagination and needlework skills to make your own cushion trimmings. Here, left-over tapestry wools have been cleverly worked to make a looped fringe.*

Making a rosette

Measurements

Size of rosette 4in (10cm) (finished diameter)

Suggested fabrics

Corded silk, glazed cotton or folded ribbon. This trim is not suited to heavy fabrics.

Materials

Strip of fabric 16 × 5in (40 × 12.5cm) (four times the finished diameter by twice the radius, plus seam allowance) ● Scissors and sewing equipment (see The workshop, pages 200–201) ● Matching sewing thread ● Covered button, if required

Making up the rosette

Fold fabric in half, right sides together and with raw edges matching. Taking a ½in (12mm) seam, stitch along the open edge. Trim seam allowance and press seam flat, centring the seam. Turn right side out. Press. Fold and press a ½in (12mm) turning at the open raw edge and then slipstitch to opposite end to make a ring.

Gathering the rosette

Make a line of gathering stitch along one folded edge of the rosette, ¼in (6mm) in from the fold line. Then gather up the thread tightly, flattening out the fabric to form a rosette. Secure all the gathering threads with some backstitches. Trim the rosette with a covered button, if required.

Above *Fluffy bobbles complement the crunchy cotton throw and bring an interesting informality to the bold striped fabric and classic arrangement of the rest of the room.*

Above right *Professionally made tassels add a distinctive finish to a ruched bolster.*

Making a tassel

Measurements

Size of tassel 2in (5cm) long.

Suggested yarn

Any yarn, from knitting wools to stranded embroidery cotton.

Materials

1 piece of stiff card, 4in (10cm) square ● Yarn ● Bodkin ● Scissors

Making up the tassel

Fold card in half. Wind yarn around card until you have the desired thickness for the tassel. Cut several strands of yarn about 8in (20cm) long. Twist them together, then use a bodkin to thread them under the strands of tassel on one side of the card. Tie ends, then pull the knot under the threads of tassel. Tie a knot in the loops of thread, tightening it against the tassel. Cut strands of tassel at the opposite side to the knot.

Binding the tassel

Leaving the end of yarn hanging down, bind the head of the tassel tightly, wrapping the thread around half a dozen times. Knot free ends of yarn firmly and trim.

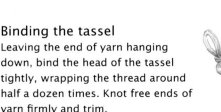

4 Shapes and fillings

All cushions need a good cushion pad. You can buy ready-made pads or make your own. Many fillings and fabrics are available to use, and you can make your own pads so that they can fit unusual spaces or oddly-sized cushion covers.

Cushion pads come in many shapes and sizes. For soft scatter cushions, choose between feather/down and firmer polyester fillings. Traditional kapok (cotton wadding), is less practical, but helps to give a firmly stuffed cushion. Firm seat cushions are normally made from fire-retardant foam which can be covered with cotton or polyester wadding to soften the lines. If you like a firm seat but prefer a softer look, try making a mini feather quilt to wrap around the foam.

If you cannot find scatter cushions of a suitable shape or size, you can buy heavy-duty feather-proof cambric to make your own. Buy loose feathers and down, or use polyester fibre filling.

Feather-filled cushion pad

If you have a special seat or cushion that is an irregular shape, or if you buy an unusual size cushion cover, you can make your own cushion pad to fit.

Measurements
Size of pad 20in (50cm) square pad

Suggested fabrics
Cotton, sheeting, calico, ticking

Materials
¾yd (70cm) of 48in- (120cm)-wide fabric • Feather or feather and down filling • Scissors and sewing equipment (see The workshop, pages 200–201) • White or matching sewing thread

Making the pad cover
Cut two panels of fabric, 20in (50cm) square. Place right sides together and raw edges matching. Taking a ½in (12mm) seam, stitch around three sides of the cover, and continue the seam for 2in (5cm) at each end of the longer open edge. Make a double line of stitching to prevent the feather filling coming out at the seams. Trim corners, turn right side out and press, turning under seam allowance along open edge and pressing.

Filling and finishing
Carefully fill with feathers, pushing it well into the corners. Use plenty of filling for a plump cushion. Pin folded seam allowances together. Slipstitch or topstitch the opening to secure the filling in place firmly. Now make a cushion cover following one of the techniques on the following pages.

Left *Cushions that are used for display or decoration need to be over-filled and plump, but conversely, for comfort, a cushion needs to be slightly under-filled. Feather and down cushions mould readily to shape and also plump up again easily.*

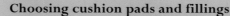

Gussetted cushion cover

If you want to cover a foam block; for a chair or window seat, for example, make a permanent covering of lining or calico before making the top cover. A layer of wadding softens the shape.

Materials

Block of foam, about 2in (5cm) thick, cut to seat size • Scissors and sewing equipment (see The workshop, pages 200–201) • Cotton lining fabric • Mediumweight polyester wadding • White or matching sewing thread

Measuring up

Measure each face of foam block. Cut panels of lining fabric, one for each face, adding 1in (2.5cm) seam allowance around each panel. Cut a piece of wadding: the measurement in one direction should be twice the foam's width, plus the depth, plus 1in (2.5cm) for overlap; the measurement in the other direction should be the foam's length, plus the depth, plus 2in (5cm) for two overlaps.

Wrapping the foam

Wrap wadding around the foam, positioning the overlap at one side. Make large basting stitches to hold wadding in place. Fold over ends, tucking in excess wadding at the corners, and stitch down edge of wadding to hold in place at front and back.

Making the gusset

Position the four lining gusset pieces, wrong side out, along each side face of the foam block. Pin seam allowances at corners. Remove from foam and stitch corner seams. The seam length should match the foam depth and not extend into the seam allowance. Trim seam allowances and clip off corners. Press seams open.

Choosing cushion pads and fillings

- Curled poultry feathers or duck feathers are the least expensive feather filling.
- A mix of either 85/15 or 51/49 feather and down gives a softer, more comfortable cushion especially for chair back cushions and pillows.
- Acrylic fibre fillings do not give a lasting shape, but are useful for people who are allergic to feathers.
- Sofa seat and back cushions need high-quality fillings and should be channelled to keep the filling evenly distributed: the cushion has several pockets.
- Feathers do not last for ever – they will uncurl and flatten so they will not plump up at all. Replace the pad rather than trying to revive it.
- Use feather-proof cambric or ticking to make up your own cushion pads with feather/down fillings. Cushion pads with cotton, polyester and foam fillings can be made up in lining material or sheeting.
- Make sure all foam is fire retardant.
- Wrap foam cushions in wadding and make a cover of curtain lining or calico to prevent the cushion fabric rubbing.
- Polystyrene beads are a firm filling for floor cushions. Once enclosed in a cover, the beads hold their shape well.

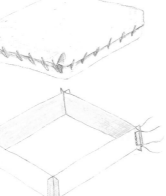

Fitting the top and bottom panels

Re-position the gusset, wrong side out, and lay top panel over foam block. Pin panel to gusset all around the edges. Turn over and repeat for back panel, leaving one edge open. Remove cover and stitch all the pinned seams.

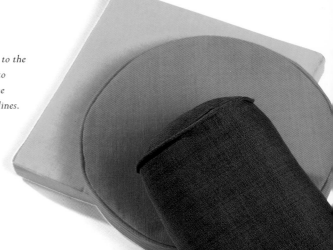

Trim seam allowances and clip excess fabric from corners. Press, turning under and pressing seam allowances along open edge. Turn right side out and insert foam through opening (unpick gusset seams at opening if foam is thick or firm). Stitch up opening by hand, or topstitch by machine, if you can slip the folded seam allowances under the foot of the machine.

Right *A permanent cover, fitted to the foam block makes the filling easy to handle. Emphasize the shape of the cover with piping along the seam lines.*

4 Closures and fastenings

Although zips are convenient for finishing a cover, there are many other alternatives. Buttons and ties can add a decorative touch, or ready-made tapes (with press studs or hooks-and-eyes) can be a discreet alternative to a zip.

The simplest cushion covers have no closure at all – the opening is just slipstitched together after inserting the pad. For a more professional finish there are many options. The fastening you choose depends on whether you want to make a feature of it, or keep it as unobtrusive as possible.

Type of closures

Zips and ready-made tapes are the most usual choice. These can be inserted along a seam line, but it is much simpler to set them into a panel of fabric for the back of the cover. The opening should be the same width as the cushion, to make it easy to insert the pad. For economy with rectangular cushions, make the opening across the width rather than down the length. This also makes the opening less obtrusive. The seam allowance and/or overlap between the back panels along the opening depends on the type of closure (see opposite).

Buttons are enjoying a revival as a decoration and closure in one. Old-fashioned pillow slips were often just rectangular bags, with buttons and buttonholes along matching hemmed edges at the opening. For a more decorative buttoned opening, the cover can be stitched on three sides, with a lined flap along the opening edge. Work bound or machine-stitched buttonholes in the flap, or stitch button loops along the edge. The flap may be rectangular or pointed, or be held with a set of buttons or a single button.

Other fastenings

Ties are easy to make and more decorative than zips. Fine tubes of fabric, known as rouleau (folded fabric ties) are also simple. You can make long thin lengths for trailing floppy bows or short wide ties for proud bows. Gingham checks in varying size and scale make attractive homemade pillow cases; floppy bows would be impractical and irritating, but short lengths quickly knotted would be functional, practical and stylish.

Instead of fabric ties, ribbons, binding tapes, cotton webbing and decorative braids could be substituted. As these are ready-made they just need cutting and hemming to contain any fraying.

Wrapping a cover over a seat cushion to tie at the front is the most stylish solution to keeping chair and sofa seat cushions clean, especially in family rooms. Truly washable upholstery fabrics are limited, and any plain colour will show stains. So an over cover – just a rectangle of washable fabric such as cotton piqué, with ties stitched to two sides, may be laundered and easily replaced. You can also quilt the cover yourself, backing the top fabric with ticking to make the cover reversible.

Envelope-style cushion

This attractive simple slip-over cover has just one opening edge, secured with ties, with a tuck-in flap, made in a similar way to a pillowcase.

Materials

Fabric to fit cover and make ties • Scissors and sewing equipment (see The workshop, pages 200–201) • Cushion pad • Matching sewing thread

Cutting out

Cut front and back pieces from fabric to match cushion pad, adding ⅝in (1.5cm) seam allowances. Cut two pieces of fabric to act as facings, 1¼in (3cm) longer than opening side by 5in (12.5cm) wide. Place any pattern to its best advantage. Cut two or three pairs of ties, 10 x 2in (25 x 5cm) for knotted ties or 18 x ¾in (46 x 2cm) for floppy bows. Use more ties for larger cushions.

Fitting ties and facings

Make up ties (see The workshop, page 217). Position ties on the right side of the front panel of fabric, along the opening side. The raw end of the tie should match the raw edge of the front panel. Pin in place. Place one of the facings on top, right sides together, sandwiching the ends of the ties. Pin to secure, and stitch along the seam line. Double stitch over each tie. Repeat for back panel.

Above *Simple knotted ties are a stylish and practical way of closing the outer cover over a inner pad which has been covered in an attractive fabric.*

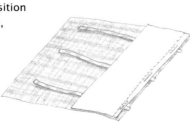

Above *Ties can really become a feature of a cushion closure, especially when they are made in a contrasting colour to the main fabric.*

Ready-made closures

	Type of closure	Details	When to use	Seam/turning allowances
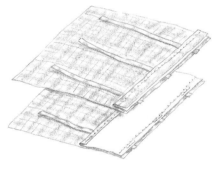	Zips	Available in a wide range of colours and lengths, and three or four different weights in plastic or metal.	Forms an unobtrusive closure on any type of cushion. Use chunky metal zips on large floor cushions, or lightweight dressmaking zips around the seam of a circular cushion.	Allow a ¾in (2cm) seam allowance down either side of opening where zip is to be inserted
	Hook-and-eye tape	Available by the yard or metre in two or three widths and weights. The eyes may be in the form of bars of metal or a series of eyelets down the length of the tape.	Particularly suitable for tailored covers – on foam seat cushions or boxed sofa cushions, for example.	On the underlapping edge, allow the width of the tape plus a turning half the width of the tape. On the overlapping edge, allow a turning half the width of the tape. Topstitch the tape in place on the right side of the underlap and the wrong side of the overlap, enclosing turnings. As for hook-and-eye tape.
	Press-stud tape	As for hook-and-eye tape. Studs may be plastic or metal.	Use on tailored covers. Use lightweight tapes with plastic studs on bed pillows.	

Finishing facings

Trim the front panel facing to 2½in (6cm). Fold under in half and then stitch the fabric close to fold. To neaten the raw back edge of the back facing, turn under ½in (1cm) to the wrong side and then stitch in place. Turn the facings to the wrong side of the panels and then press them in place.

Joining front and back panels

With the right sides together, pin the back panel onto the front panel, but open out the front panel facing, then fold and pin it over the back panel. Stitch the side and end seams. Trim all the corners and then turn the right sides out. Push the corners out using a point turner and then press each seam well.

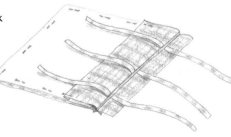

Right *This pile of cushions in blue and white country checks are mostly self-piped, but the casual ties of just one cushion provide welcome contrast and are the main point of interest.*

4 Scatter cushions

These are small accessories that can really make a big impact. Imagine a neutral room that is furnished with textures and tones of creams and stone and the impression just a single lime green satin cushion on one chair will make; or think about the same room with a row of stunning hyacinth-blue silk cushions standing up along the back of the sofa.

A basic scatter cushion can become a focal point on furniture and needs no adornment. It does not need braids and trimmings, frills and furbelows, piping or even a closure. If a cushion is to make an impact, then the fabric must be carefully chosen to be beautiful in its own right without the need of any further embellishment. So, for example, a beige fabric with white spots perhaps with a little sheen from a satin weave might be chosen to complement an old, weather-worn chair, or a subdued plaid or silky stripe might blend extremely well with a traditional floral chintz fabric.

Scatter cushion with zip

A zip closure makes a neat way of finishing a simple scatter cushion cover

Measurements

Size of finished cover 15in (38cm) square
Size of cushion pad 16in (40cm) square

Suggested fabrics

Glazed cotton is used here, but almost any fabric is fine.

Materials

Fabric for cover – ½yd (50cm) of 48in-(120cm)-wide fabric • Scissors and sewing equipment (see The workshop, pages 200–201) • 15in (37.5cm) long zip • Matching sewing thread

Measuring up and cutting out

Measure the pad from seam to seam. The cover should be 1in (2cm) smaller in each direction for a snug fit. Allow ⅝in (1.5cm) seam allowance on three sides and 1in (2.5cm) on the opening edge. Cut out two pieces, placing any pattern to its best advantage.

Inserting the zipper

Press 1in (2.5cm) to the wrong side of fabric along the lower edge of both pieces. Pin fabrics together along pressed line and stitch for just 1½in (4cm) at each end. Insert the zip (see The workshop, page 216).

Join the panels

Pin pieces together, right sides inward, taking care to match the corners. Open up the zip halfway and stitch around the remaining three sides, ⅝in (1.5cm) in from raw edges. Snip across each corner to within ¼in (5mm) of stitching line. Neaten raw edges and turn right sides out. Push the corners out with a point turner if necessary. Press each seam carefully from front and insert pad.

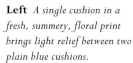

Left *A single cushion in a fresh, summery, floral print brings light relief between two plain blue cushions.*

Above *Rouleau and button closures are sophisticated at the back of a cushion or as features in their own right at the front. Make fabric rouleaux or purchase ribbon or tapes for ease.*

To make a quartered cushion

Cut some spare fabric to finished cushion size. Fold along the diagonals and cut to make four triangles. Place these onto your chosen fabric or fabrics, keeping the grain straight and cut out adding ⅝in (1.5cm) seam allowance all around.

Join in pairs, keeping stitching along the seam allowance absolutely straight. Press seams flat. Match at the centre pushing a pin through both joins to hold securely.

Pin fabrics together toward each corner. Stitch from centre to each corner in turn. As you return to the centre for the second seam insert the needle exactly where the last stitch finished. Do not try to back stitch, but leave long threads in the centre. Pull threads through, knot and stitch through one seam to secure. Press seam flat and continue to make up as for basic or piped cushion (see pages 104 and 110).

Rouleau and button closure

A rouleau and button closure can be added to a basic scatter cushion, if preferred.

Materials

Fabric for cushion • Cushion pad • Soft pencil • A strip of rouleau three times the length of the cushion (see The workshop, page 217) • Matching sewing thread • Fabric-covered or rounded buttons either one per ¾in (2cm) or one per 2¼in (6cm)

Cutting out

Cut a fabric panel for the cushion front, 1¼in (3cm) larger than the cushion pad; a panel for the cushion back 1¼in (3cm) larger than pad plus 3in (7.5cm) wider along the opening side; a strip to form a facing the length of the cushion 3in (7.5cm).

Fitting the rouleau

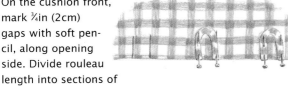

On the cushion front, mark ¾in (2cm) gaps with soft pencil, along opening side. Divide rouleau length into sections of 2½in (6.5cm), or more for larger buttons. Pin each section between the pencil marks, lining up raw edges. Stitch along seam line to hold rouleau in place.

Positioning facing

Pin fabric facing strip over, matching seam allowances and stitch just inside the last stitching line, so that no stitching shows from the front and the rouleau is sandwiched in place. Fold raw edge under ¼in (6mm) to the wrong side and stitch to neaten.

Joining front and back panels

Pin front and back pieces together, right sides together. Neaten raw edges of opening edge of the back panel by pressing ¼in (6mm) to wrong side and stitching close to fold line. Fold over to opposite side and pin securely. Stitch three sides along the seam allowance.

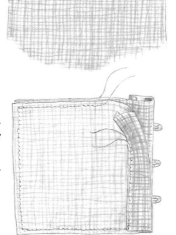

Adding closures

Cut across each corner, neaten the seams and turn right side out. Mark button positions with pins and stitch buttons securely in place. If the fabric is fine or might tear easily, stitch an interfacing along the length or stitch each button into a reinforcing square of fabric. Insert pad and button up.

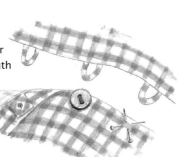

4 Piping and frills

Piping the outer edge of a cushion can make it much more stylish and interesting. Striped fabrics cut on the cross give a striking finish, as do checked fabrics which are cut on the diagonal. On a single cushion the exact colour and size of a piped, defined edge can be crucial; for example, the piping on cushions in an informal pile should be subtle and not too distinctive.

Frills are added to cushions for a softer touch. They work well with floral fabric and in bedroom furnishings. In the same fabric, a frill can be piped and bound with a contrasting colour, a striped edge can be combined with a floral print, or double frills can go with large and small prints or checks and stripes. In the sitting room a frilled cushion can sit behind a smaller plain, piped or corded cushion to fill the back of an armchair.

Piped cushion

Adding plain piping to a patterned cover gives it distinction and helps to define its shape and size.

Materials

Fabric for cover to fit pad • Cushion pad • Scissors and sewing equipment (see The workshop, pages 200–201) • Fabric and cord for piping to go all around cover, plus overlap • Matching sewing thread • Zip to match width of the pad

Cutting out

Cut two pieces of main fabric 1¼in (3cm) wider and 2in (5cm) longer than required cover, placing any pattern centrally. Make up enough piping to go around the cushion circumference (see The workshop, pages 210–211).

Positioning piping

Press 1⅜in (3.5cm) to the wrong side on both lower edges. Pin piping to cushion front, starting at the centre bottom, lining up piping stitching line with fold line along the opening and aligning raw edges on the other three sides. Clip into piping fabric at the corners to keep them square and overlap fabric at the join neatly.

Inserting the zip

Stitch as close to piping as possible. Join the front to the back along the lower edge, for just 1½in (4cm) at each end. Insert the zip. (see basic scatter cushion, page 108).

Making up the cover

Join the other three sides. Stitch as close to piping as possible. Turn to front to see that none of the piping stitching still shows. If it does, re-stitch even closer. Trim across corners and neaten raw edges. Turn right side out and press. Insert pad.

Above *Using the fabrics from one cushion to pipe another is a useful way of coordinating furnishings, and offers many interesting possibilities. Here, the fabric from the ticking pillows provides a smart striped piping for the white ones.*

Left *Selecting a single colour for the piping can be a difficult choice — if there are no restrictions just pick your favourite, or use this detail to coordinate with another colour in the room.*

Frilled edges

If you have made a cushion which is a little small, add a frill for more prominence. Frilled edges may be short and crisp or long and floppy, but should always be at least double fullness.

Measurements

Size of finished frill 2¼in (6cm) for a 16in (40cm) cushion, 3in (7.5cm) for a 18in (45cm) cushion, and 3½in (9cm) for a 20in (50cm) cushion.

Materials

Fabric for cushion and piping (see Piped cushion opposite) • Cushion pad • Fabric for frill • Scissors and sewing equipment (see The workshop, pages 200–201) • Matching sewing thread • Zip to match width of pad

Above *Overlong frills are overtly feminine and contrast beautifully with the polished wooden day bed.*

Cutting out and preparing frill

Cut out front, back and piping from main fabric as before. For the frill, cut out and join together fabric strips twice the circumference of the cushion by twice the finished width, allowing 1½in (4cm) for seam allowances on frill.

Preparing frill and piping

Make a continuous loop at least twice the cushion circumference and press all seams flat. Fold frill strip in half lengthwise, right side out. Stitch two gathering threads ⅝in (1.5cm) and ¾in (2cm) from the raw edge. Cut and notch front and back pieces to mark edges to be joined.

Positioning piping

Stitch piping to the front piece as for the piped cushion.

Gathering frill

Fold frill into four and mark with a pin to indicate position of each corner of the cushion front. Pull up gathers and distribute frill evenly, pinning with crosswise pins along the seam line. Align pins with corners. Stitch along seam line, as close to piping as possible. Check from front and stitch around again, even closer in, if necessary. Insert zip, stitch cover back to front and finish as above, inserting pad.

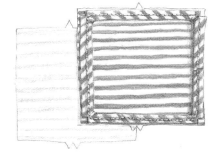

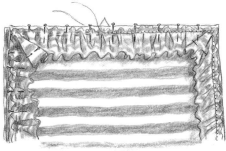

Optional finishes

Single frill For a single frill, use a fabric strip the width of the frill, plus 1⅛in (2.7cm) for turnings and seams. Allowing twice the circumference of the cushion for fullness, cut the length, joining and pressing seams as necessary. Make a ¼in (6mm) double hem along one long edge and stitch gathering lines along the other.

Double frill Make up two frills as for the single frill, with the outer frill ⅝in (1.5cm) wider than the inner one. Pin together along raw edges, stitch gathering threads through both frills and make up as one.

Bound frills Cut two lengths of main fabric for the frill, each the finished width plus ¾in (2cm). Cut and join a strip of contrasting fabric 1¾in (4.5cm) wide. Stitch a frill length to each side of this strip, right sides together, ⅜in (1cm) in from raw edges. Press seams to centre and then press the frill in half along centre line, so that the binding shows ⅜in (1cm) to each side. Stitch gathering threads and make up cushion as before.

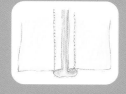

4 Buttons and beads

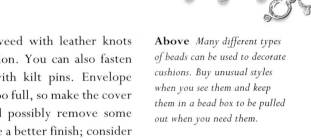

*E*laborate beading and decorative buttoning has been used extensively in the world of haute couture to enhance clothing and has long been the hallmark of individual couturiers. With thoughtful consideration, imagination and research, a few carefully placed decorative beads can really make a simple wool scatter cushion into something special. Look through photographs of couture collections, magazine features and advertising brochures, making a file of tear sheets and notes to bring colours, textures and shapes together ready for adaptation to cushion fronts. Historical pattern and ornament reference books plus transfer books from craft and art shops are invaluable for information on classical shapes.

Buttoned lined cushion

Buttons have long been the secret weapon of the fashion world. Every woman knows the trick of searching out a medium-priced, well cut jacket and simply changing the buttons to raise the profile. Paper-like taffeta and crunchy silks buttoned with mother of pearl, cashmere with gold drops and silk brocade with ribbon balls express sheer luxury. Try using white cotton with blue glass, navy blue wool with plaid buttons, plaids with blazer buttons and suiting tweed with leather knots to adorn your envelope cushion. You can also fasten traditional highland tartan with kilt pins. Envelope cushions are best not stuffed too full, so make the cover the same size as the pad and possibly remove some filling. Lining can also produce a better finish; consider featuring a narrow shirt stripe or small geometric print which you might just see as the corners turn up.

Materials

Fabric and lining fabric • Cushion pad • Scissors and sewing equipment (see The workshop, pages 200–201) • Matching sewing thread • Buttons • Buttonhole thread

Cutting out

Cut one front panel 1¼in (3cm) wider than the pad and twice the length plus 6⅝in (16cm). Cut lining to the same dimensions.

Lining the fabric

Place lining and fabric together with right sides together. Stitch along one short side. Stitch around the opposite end from 6in (15cm) along each side, taking a ⅝in (1.5cm) seam allowance. Snip into the seam allowance, at right angles to the raw edge, right to the seam, at the end of each stitching line. Snip across corners and turn right side out. Press.

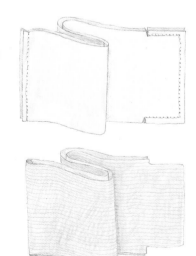

Above *Many different types of beads can be used to decorate cushions. Buy unusual styles when you see them and keep them in a bead box to be pulled out when you need them.*

Left *Choose your cushions' buttons to suit the situation. Self fabric-covered buttons are sophisticated and understated, but you might prefer to reverse the colours, use the buttons as accent points, or stitch a row of bunnies for cushions to go into a children's bedroom.*

Joining side seams

Pin the raw edges together, with enough pins to prevent any slippage – especially if using silks or velvets. Fold over, with right sides inside and lining up the short side with the 5⅜in (14cm) stitching notches. Stitch these two long sides together.

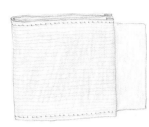

Finishing the cover

Snip across corners and neaten seams. Turn right side out. Topstitch around the flaps and across the opposite short end, about ¾in (2cm) from the edge. Make buttonholes in the flap and fold it over so you can mark button positions (see The workshop, page 217) Stitch buttons in place through fabric layers to secure.

Beaded cushion

Liven up a plain cushion with a beaded design to suit your room scheme. Silks, or textured fabrics, go beautifully with beads to make an unusual decorative cushion.

Select a design that you feel comfortable with and then translate the idea into something which is workable. Magazines, books and photographs are good sources for inspiration. An abstract design might catch your eye, a pastoral scene or a specific geometric pattern. Embroidery books will also be useful to help you to put your ideas onto paper. Choose your material and cut out front and back cushion panels. Draw your design freehand on the panel of the fabric (with a soft drawing pencil or tailor's chalk). Mark the design's pattern with glass-headed dressmaker's pins to represent each bead. Stitch one bead at a time replacing each pin in turn. Hold each bead in place with a backstitch using thread the same colour as the bead. Make up the cushion following the envelope or zipped scatter cushion style.

Left *Brightly coloured ethnic printed material used on cushions offers scope for unusual and novel decoration. Here small sea shore shells decorate the cushion's border.*

4 Tied corner cushion

A very smart way of introducing bows or knots to cushions, this cover has topstitched borders that tie at the corners. The cover is best made up in mediumweight cotton fabrics, selected to suit your scheme – understated when made with simple striped fabrics such as fine ticking, or elaborate with full-blown roses and complementary checks. Use the cushion on its own in the back of a side chair, as the centrepiece on a sofa, or as a focal point on a bed.

Measurements
Size of finished cover and cushion 20in (50cm) square cushion pad.

Suggested fabric
Glazed cotton, natural ticking, colour-woven stripes and checks.

Materials
¾yd (70cm) of 48in-(120cm)-wide main fabric • ½yd (0.50m) contrast fabric for borders/ties • Scissors and sewing equipment (see The workshop, pages 200–201) • Matching sewing thread • 20cm (50in) zip to match main fabric

Right *Striped ticking has been used for both the cushion cover and the topstitched border ties. By cutting the panels with the fabric grain running in different directions, a contrast is achieved without having to introduce another fabric.*

Rouleau corners
For a more delicate finish, you could make lengths of rouleau (see The workshop, page 217) and insert the unstitched middle section between the front and back pieces to look like piping. If using striped fabrics, cut the border stripes in the opposite way to the cushion front so that at each side the border stripes sit at right angles to the cushion; or alternatively cut checks on the cross for the border strips to contrast with the front. Longer, narrower strips can be tied into double bows or loops.

Cutting out
Cut a panel of main fabric for the front and back, 21¼in (53cm) by 22in (55cm). Cut four strips 5in (12.5cm) wide and 40in (100cm) long from contrasting fabric. Cut the pieces putting any pattern to its best advantage.

Making up borders/ties
Fold one strip in half lengthwise, right side inside, and stitch along raw edges, taking a ½in (12mm) seam, 10⅜in (26.5cm) from each end. Press seams open and fold each end so that the seams are in the centre. Stitch across each end securely. Trim across the corners and turn right side out. Pull the corners square and press. Repeat with other three strips.

Positioning strips
Place one length along each edge of right side of top panel, ¾in (2cm) from the top and two sides, 1⅛in (2.8cm) from the bottom edge, and pin with cross pins. Align centre of strip with the mid-point of each side of the panels, leaving tails at each end. Topstitch each in place ⅛in (3mm) from each side and between the ties which run across the cushion.

Bunched Corners

This method is a simple way to make fun floor cushions. Almost any fabric can be used, from fine cotton to heavy chenille. Each corner will need to be finished with tassels or knotted cords or rouleau loops. Just choose the detail to suit the situation and fabric. For instance, chenille cords and key tassels would be perfect for heavy damasks and chunky weaves, whereas rouleau loops and fine cut fringe tassels would complement fine linen or upholstery-weight silks.

Use cushion pads that are at least 24in (60cm) square and preferably 30in (75cm) square. A pile of two or three cushions will make a comfortable stool. Make unpiped covers to the same size as the cushion pads. Take each corner in turn and pinch up the excess fabric to make rounded corners and a fat cushion. Tie in place with some narrow tape or spare fabric strips. Repeat with the other three corners until you have a plump cushion with four 'ears'. Tie these corners very tightly and knot the tape or fabric. An elastic band can be used if you find it hard to tie the corners tightly enough. Knot cord and tassels around each, either crunching the ears into squashy rosettes or leaving them to stand out.

Right *Ties which are short and wide can make good chunky knots at the corners, on the sides or around cushion covers themselves.*

Inserting the zip

Press 1in (2.5cm) toward the wrong side along the lower edge of the front and the back pieces. Stitch them together for 1½in (4cm) at either end. Insert the zip (see The workshop, page 216), then open up the cover halfway.

Joining front and back panels

Pin the other three sides together, with right sides together, folding the ends of the ties inside so they do not get caught in the seam. Stitch around keeping exactly ⅝in (1.5cm) from the edges to avoid catching the border strips. Trim across the corners and then neaten seams. Turn the right side out. Press. Fill with the cushion pad and then tie each corner in double knots or make them into tight bows.

4 Bolsters

The bolster that was used as a cushion to support the head along the top of the bed was the forerunner of today's softer and more comfortable pillow. Bolsters were also more formally used as decorative side cushions on early wood-frame sofas, and they are the forerunners of today's scatter cushion. In the bedroom a firm bolster running down the width of the bed, with soft down cushions on top, is comfortable to sleep with and gives good support for reading in bed. But generally bolsters are made to look decorative. They can be feminine, frilled affairs for the bedroom but can also be made in a more formal style with piped, fringed and tasselled finishes for wood-frame sofas. Feather/down mix is the best filling for the bolster pad, as they need to be firm enough to hold their shape.

Tailored bolster cover

Smart piping detail emphasizes the shape of a tailored bolster at the end of a sofa. Dimensions given here are for a standard sofa bolster; adjust measurements if you are making the bolster to fit a specific piece of furniture.

Measurements

Size of finished cover and bolster 18in (45cm) long × 7in (17cm) diameter. The circumference will be 22in (55cm).

Suggested fabrics

Upholstery weight fabrics: heavy cotton, linen union, velvet or brocade are all ideal.

Materials

¾yd (70cm) of 36in-(90cm)-wide fabric • Scissors and sewing equipment (see The workshop, pages 200–201) • ¾yd (70cm) handmade piping or ready-made flanged insertion cording • Matching sewing thread • 16in (40cm) zip

Cutting out

Cut a piece of fabric 25 x 19¼in (62.5 x 48cm) (i.e. circumference of bolster plus 1½in (4cm) by the length of the bolster plus 1¼in (3cm). Cut two circles 8¼in (20.5cm) in diameter for bolster ends (⅝in (1.5cm) seam allowance included).

Above *Bolsters are almost always used for decoration before comfort, so they need to be filled and stuffed firmly. Make the inner pad about 10 percent larger than the cover. Use a soft filling such as down or fibre for a squashy bed bolster.*

Setting in the zip

Join the long sides of bolster tube, taking ¾in (2cm) seams and setting a zip into the seam (see page 216). Press seam and open zip. Turn right side out.

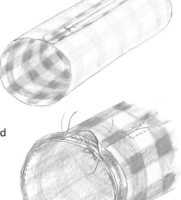

Adding the piping

Pin piping or flanged insertion cord all around each end of the tube. Position the raw edges of the piping level with the raw edge of the fabric, on the right side. Where the piping meets, unravel ends, twist together and neaten fabric covering. Stitch piping in place.

Joining the ends

Make ⅝in (2.5cm) snips at about 1in (3cm) intervals in the seam allowances around both tube ends, including the seam allowance of the piping. Pin around flat ends, right sides together, making more snips as needed to keep the fabric flat. Baste in place Stitch as close to piping cord as possible. Check from right side that the stitching is as tight to the cord as you thought and stitch around again, if necessary.

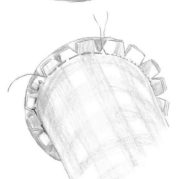

Finishing the pad

Neaten seams, turn right side out and press. Insert pad, plumping it to make neat ends.

Knotted bolster cover

This delightful cover adds a casual, stylish touch to a bed head bolster.

Measurements

Size of bolster and cover 18in (45cm) long × 7in (17cm) diameter. The circumference will be 22in (55cm).

Suggested fabrics

Cotton sheeting, broderie anglaise

Materials

⅛yd (1.3m) of 36in (90cm) wide fabric (any pattern will run along the length of the bolster) • Scissors and sewing equipment (see The workshop, pages 200–201) • Matching sewing thread • 2yd (1.80m) ribbon, braid or lace to trim ends (optional)

Cutting out

Cut out one piece of fabric, 37 x 23 ½in (120 x 59cm) (i.e. 30in (75cm) longer than the bolster by the circumference of the bolster plus 1 ½in (4cm).

Joining the sides

Fold fabric in half lengthwise, right sides together, and stitch the length of the bolster cover ¼in (6mm) from the raw edges. Turn out, press, and continue to make a French seam (see The Workshop, page 205).

Finishing the ends

Press under ⅝in (1.5cm) double hems around each end. Stitch with a plain stitch or use a decorative stitch. Alternatively, attach lace, ribbon or braid all around. Press.

Finishing the cover

Insert the bolster pad and tie each end in a chunky, loose knot. Alternatively, make up long, fine ties in plain cotton to bind the ends in place.

Above *Crisp white cotton is so rewarding – it is easy to launder, and is fresh in summer and winter. Add any topstitched lace decoration before making up the cover.*

Drawstring bolster cover

For a simple bolster cover, cut out a piece of fabric 16in (40cm) longer than the bolster by the circumference of the bolster plus 1¼in (3cm). Fold fabric in half lengthwise, right sides together and stitch along length, taking ⅝in (1.5cm) seams. Neaten seam, turn out and press. Press under a ⅝in (1.5cm) double hem at each end to form a casing. Stitch close to fold line, leaving a ¾in (2cm) gap at each seam. Thread narrow ribbon or cord through each channel. Insert bolster pad, pull up ends. Tuck knots inside. Cover two buttons with fabric and stitch in place, or stitch rosettes or ready-made heavy tassels over the hole.

4 Boxed cushions

Boxed cushions are very useful soft furnishings to make. They are suitable as chair and sofa seats and backs, as loose cushions in occasional chair seats, or they can be floor cushions, window seats and head rests. Any seat cushion which is to provide long-term comfort needs depth, so the cover will need to be gusseted, turning the cushion into a 'box'. Most fabrics are suitable, but washable fabrics are best for outdoor or heavily-used chairs. Metal framed chairs are structurally strong and look good with a brightly coloured or patterned cushion. Wicker chairs can look stunning in strong fabrics but as they have a lighter feel, they can also suit a softer stripe, floral chintz or country check. Sofa cushions usually have piping, often of a different fabric, to emphasize the shape. Avoid too strong a contrast, just choose a very hard-wearing fabric one or two tones deeper than the main fabric. Buttoning any box cushion stops the cover moving, adds interest and a natural formality. Choose from fabric-covered buttons to match or contrast, carved shell or bone, or wool or cotton tufts.

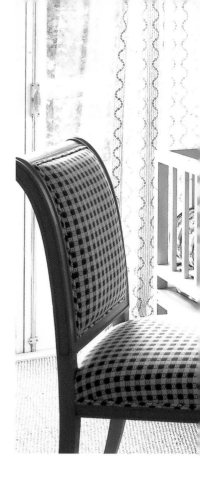

Right A boxed cushion can transform a table into a comfortable stool. Here deep buttoning keeps the cover in place and cotton tufts pick up the small geometric design in the weave. Buttoning also makes the cushion firm to act as an occasional table as well.

Measurements

Size of cushion and finished cover Use a cushion pad to fit snugly in the chair, or one the size of the seat it has to go on. It may have one or more curved edges.

Materials

Fabric for cover • Scissors and sewing equipment (see The workshop, pages 200–201) • Fabric and cord for piping • Zip (the length should match the width of the cushion) • Matching thread

Cutting out

Cut top and bottom pieces of fabric 1¼in (3cm) larger all around than finished cushion size, a gusset to fit three sides and 1¼in (3cm) wider than the finished cushion depth, and one piece for the zip gusset 12in (30cm) longer than the opening end and 3¼in (8cm) wider than the depth. Cut out the pieces, matching the pattern and making allowance for the checks and stripes. You will need enough to allow piping cord to go twice around the cushion.

Left *Foam blocks covered in soft polyester wadding are substantial enough to make comfortable seats over a metal chair frame. Washable colourfast fabrics are most suitable for outdoor use where constant laundering is necessary to maintain a fresh appearance.*

Inserting the zip

To set the zip into the gusset, cut the zip strip in half lengthwise and press 1in (2.5cm) to the wrong side along centre edges. Open up zip and pin one side very close to teeth. Stitch. Close zip and place the other fold over the teeth so that the first stitching line is not visible. Pin and stitch. Join one short end of the long gusset piece to the closed zip end.

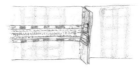

Setting in the gusset

Placing the open end of the gusset 4in (10cm) from one back corner, pin the gusset to the front piece ⅝in (1.5cm) from raw edge. At each corner stop ⅝in (1.5cm) from the end and snip ⅝in (1.5cm) into the seam allowance of the gusset. Fold fabric to make a right angle and continue pinning.

Finishing the corner

Unpin approx 4in (10cm) and stitch two gusset ends together. Re-pin and stitch all around.

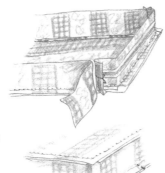

Joining back piece

Open up zip about 4in (10cm) and pin the gusset to the back piece in the same way. Take care to match all notches and check that the corners are straight. Stitch. Turn right side out and press. Insert cushion.

Buttoning a cushion

Plan the button positions straight onto the cover once the pad has been inserted. Use crossed pins to mark the button positions and a small ruler to keep each row parallel to both sides and to the next row. Ideally, the distance between buttons should form a perfect 'square' or diamond. Mark both top and bottom of the pad. If necessary, make a plan of the top side on graph paper and transfer this to the under side. You must have these marks on both sides to enable you to guide the needle through vertically. Bring the thread (use button thread) from the bottom to the top with an upholsterer's needle, thread the button on and knot. Push needle back down and thread another button on. Tie the two cords together and pull tightly, so that both buttons are well indented. Secure knot at least twice and tuck in the loose ends.

Above *Simple calico covers are not only inexpensive to buy, but authentic in texture. They also allow the beauty of the natural wood to remain predominant.*

119

4 Bed pillows

Pillow covers are divided into two types: the pillow-case, a functional cover for the pillow used for head support while sleeping and pillow 'shams', the covers for any extra pillows used for decoration or back support. Housewife style describes the cover with a flap at the back which allows you to insert the pillow. The edges might be plain, flat bordered, scalloped or frilled and pillows are made in the same way as scatter cushions, but without zips. Pillow shams are usually open at one end with the decorated edge, whether frilled or embroidered, hanging beyond the pillow. Large pillow covers often have only three bordered sides, with the fourth side containing the closure. A decorative pillow opening can be made with ties, buttons and rouleaux or laces following the ideas given for scatter cushions (see pages 108–109).

Housewife pillow

This simple style of pillow is very straightforward to make and can look good on any style of bed.

Measurements

Size of pillow and finished cover 19 × 29in (48 × 74cm) – standard pillow

Suggested fabrics

Fine cotton, polyester cotton mix or linen. Fabric must be fully washable.

Materials

1¼yd (1.10m) of 44/45in (120cm)-wide fabric • Scissors and sewing equipment (see The workshop, pages 200–201) • Matching sewing thread

Measurements and cutting out

Cut out one back piece of fabric 1¼in (3cm) larger all around than the pillow and one front piece 1¼in (3cm) wider and 9¼in (23cm) longer than the pillow, placing any pattern to its best advantage.

Hemming the panels

Make ⅝in (1.5cm) double hems on the right-hand side of the front piece and the left-hand side of the back piece.

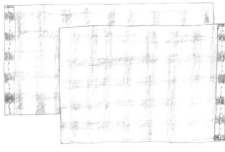

Joining panels

Pin the back and front pieces together, matching three raw edges and folding the flap onto the back. Stitch along the three sides. Trim corners, neaten seams, turn out, then press. Insert pillow.

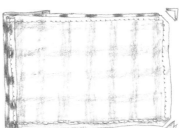

Left *A bold line of broad satin stitch helps create a crisp border, and picks up the colours in these cheerful plaid pillowslips.*

Above *The simple housewife pillow still remains the first choice of many. You can make your own to coordinate with your curtains and cushions.*

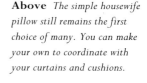

Flat border cushions

A crisp border turns an ordinary housewife pillow into an Oxford pillow. The cover can be made in the same way as the housewife pillow, just adding extra fabric to form the border.

Measurements

Size of pillow 19 × 29in (48 × 74cm)
Finished cover 25 ½ × 35 ½in (64 × 89cm)

Materials

1¼yd (1.10m) of 44/45in (115cm) wide fabric ● Scissors and sewing equipment (see The workshop, pages 120–121) ● Matching sewing thread

Measurements and cutting out

Cut out one back piece of fabric, 7½in (19cm) wider than the pillow and 5⅛in (12.8cm) longer. Cut one front piece 7½in (19cm) wider than the pillow and 20½in (51.5cm) longer.

Hemming the panels

Make ⅝in (1.5cm) double hems on the right-hand side of the front piece and the left-hand side of the back piece.

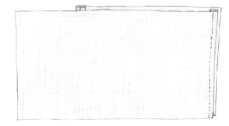

Joining front and back panels

Pin the back and front pieces together, right sides facing and raw edges matching around three sides. Fold a 12⅛in-(31cm) wide flap at the end of the front piece back, leaving a 3¼in (8cm) border at the end. Stitch around the three sides, including the border of the front panel. Clip corners, neaten seams, press and turn right side out. Poke out the corners neatly with the tip of a pair of scissors. Press again.

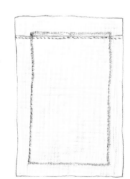

Stitching the border

Baste all around the cover, 3 ¼in (8cm) from edge, taking care not to catch in the hemmed edge of the back panel. Stitch a decorative, plain or satin stitch along the baste lines.

4 Bordered cushions

*C*ushions with additional borders or embellishments fit easily together and blend well on a garden bench, piled into a squashy sofa, or displayed on a bed. Frilled edges, cords and pipings, fringes and tassels are pretty decoration and encourage a romantic and period atmosphere. Padded and double borders are more contemporary in style and can be used on their own or with other decorative edgings. These covers can be made with an Oxford-style opening (a tuck-in flap), or you can set a zip across the back of the cushion, close to the stitched edge of the border. For the double-border cushion, make the front panel out of two overlapping panels so that you can add a buttoned finish, if preferred.

Double border cushion

This style of cushion looks very effective when finished with a decorative trim.

Materials

Fabric (as dimensions of cushion pad) • Cushion pad • Scissors and sewing equipment (see The workshop, pages 200–201) • Matching sewing thread • Zip the width of the pad • Contrasting thread or braid to trim (optional)

Right *A cushion cover with a double border, also known as an Oxford cushion, is extravagant with fabric, but the elegant result is well worth it.*

Measuring and cutting out

Measure cushion pad from seam to seam and cut front piece 6¾in (17cm) wider and longer than the finished cover, and the back piece 6¾in (17cm) wider and 8in (21cm) longer. Place any pattern to its best advantage. Cut a 8¼in (21.5cm) strip from bottom of back piece.

Inserting zip

Pin two back pieces together again. Stitch ¾in (2cm) from raw edges for 7½in (19cm) from either side. Insert the zip (see The workshop, page 216) and open up halfway.

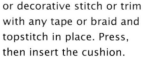

Folding the borders

Place the front piece on the table, right side down, and press 3⅜in (8.5cm) of each side to the wrong side. Fold each corner under in a clockwise direction to make a false mitre. Repeat with the back piece, also folding each corner in a clockwise direction.

Joining front and back

Place back and front pieces together, with wrong sides facing inward, so that at the corner the adjacent folds go in opposite directions. Pin and baste 2¾in (7cm) from outside. Stitch all around with plain or decorative stitch or trim with any tape or braid and topstitch in place. Press, then insert the cushion.

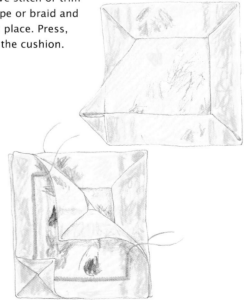

Padded border cushions

A layer of wadding or iron-on fleece adds softness to the front of the cushion and emphasizes the bordered edge.

Suggested fabrics

Glazed cotton or sateen, to show off the texture.

Materials

Fabric (see cutting out instructions) • Mediumweight wadding or iron-on fleece • Cushion pad • Scissors and sewing equipment (see The workshop, pages 200-201) • Zip the width of the pad • Matching sewing thread • Contrasting thread for border (optional)

Cutting out

Measure the cushion pad from seam to seam. To make a 2in (5cm) wide border, cut out one fabric front piece 2⅝ in (6.7cm) larger all round than the cushion. Cut two back pieces: one should be a total of 5½in (14cm) wider than the cushion and 1⅝in (4.5cm) longer; the other should be the same width as the first, and a total of 5⅝in (14.5cm) in the other direction.

Setting in the zip

Join the two back panels with a line of basting stitches, taking 1in (2.5cm) seams, to make up a panel the same size as the front panel. Stitch the seam at each end for 2⅝in (6.7cm), press and press seam open. Position the zip along the seamline on wrong side of fabric and stitch in place. Remove basting and open zip slightly.

Padding the front panel

Cut a piece of wadding or iron-on fleece adding 2in (5cm) to the measurements of the cushion pad all round the edge. Position padding centrally on wrong side of front panel. Baste wadding in place around edge, or fuse to fabric with an iron.

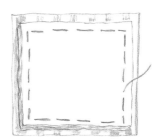

Joining front and back panels

With right sides of cushion facing, and raw edges matching, stitch front and back panels together all around edge, taking care not to catch the wadding into the seam. Press, clip corners, turn right side out, poke out corners neatly and press again.

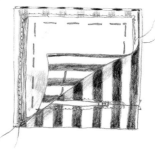

Finishing the borders

Baste all around edge of cushion, positioning stitches 2in (5cm) from the seamed edge. Topstitch with a double row of stitching or a narrow satin stitch.

Left *To transform a single bed into an inviting sofa, pile soft squashy cushions along the back and sides, supported by chunky bolsters at the ends. To make the padded borders, follow the instructions for a flat border, but before stitching around from the front, insert folds of polyester wadding along each side, cut just a fraction narrower than the finished border width.*

4 No-sew cushions

For those people who do not like the thought of doing any sewing, or really do not have the time, there are always different ways to improvise and create interesting soft furnishings, such as cushions, without a stitch needing to be sewn. Long scarves in luxury fabrics such as silk and chenille, brilliantly painted squares, woven plaids, linen tablecloths, napkins and glass cloths can all be used imaginatively to make cushion covers. The chosen material can then be knotted over a cushion pad, can be fixed with some laces, toggles and buttons or possibly tied with ribbons in blending colours.

Above *Striped tea towels are laced together with sash cord through eyelet holes. Eyelet hole kits are available from most craft stores and take very little time to fit.*

Left *Take advantage of pre-embroidered motifs. The sides of this towel were simply stitched together to make a luxurious garden cushion.*

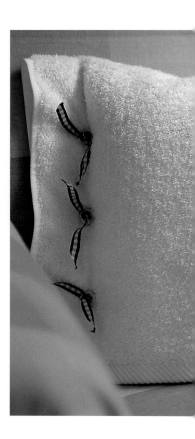

No-sew cushions do not need to be boring – in fact many new opportunities to incorporate imaginative designs and ideas present themselves only once the no-sew boundary is applied. People who love sewing will automatically start looking at the fabric sections of department stores and study special collections and books. They will rummage through material remnants, choose from fabric rolls and match samples with sofa and chair covers, or other cushions and curtains. The person who does not sew will need to be on the look-out for finished items, however, with an eye to adaptation. Of course, colours still need to match or tone, but in objects already made there is sometimes more room for unexpected combinations. For instance, a paisley shawl or a chenille wrap might generally be described as terracotta but might contain colours as diverse as bright pink and bottle green within the mix.

Tablecloths and napkins can be buttoned together or folded and buttoned over to accommodate a cushion pad or a pillow – as can a towel or cot sheet. A quilt can be folded over a mattress to make a squashy, comfortable cushion, and transforming a bed into a useful daytime sofa. Large squares of fabric – from scarves to Indian bed covers – can be used to parcel up cushion pads, and be knotted at the front or side to become part of the overall design. Fastenings such as toggles, ribbons, laces and eyelets are all practical and can be most attractive on cushions. They may need a needle and thread to put them in place but no sewing machine is necessary – or any great sewing skill, either.

Ribbons can be as narrow as 1⁄16in (2mm) or as wide as 4in (10cm) in organdie with wired edges, tartan check or calico. They can also be as shiny as double satin or matt as unbleached linen. Buttons to suit any fabric and any situation can also be easily purchased. You can choose from two-hole oyster pearl buttons, coloured glass buttons or use bejewelled ornaments or numbers and alphabet letters.

Below *Lace panels are wrapped around a fat bolster cushion and just held at either end with scrunchy knots. A small cushion pad is covered in a tray cloth that is then fixed firmly in place with tiny French knots along the edges.*

Left *A small hand towel can easily be made into a baby's cushion with a decorative botton and ribbon fastening, and an attractive teddy bear motif.*

125

4 Children's cushions

All children love sitting on the floor and will enjoy bouncing around on these dice blocks or just lounging on the squashy bean bags. As the seating will get very dirty, choose easily washed fabrics in bright, strong colours to liven up a play room. With the dice blocks, each square must be the same size. Make the first square from cardboard and use this as a template for all six sides. It is unlikely that you would make just one dice, so buy three or four different fabrics to mix and match. Order foam blocks beforehand, if possible already wrapped in polyester wadding, which gives a much softer finish.

Dice blocks

Children will love these bright blocks. They are not difficult to make as long as you cut them out carefully, and they are hard wearing.

Measurements

Size of finished dice About 20in (55cm) square

Suggested fabrics

Heavy cottons, preferably washable.

Materials

⅝yd (60cm) of fabric, 48in-(120cm)-wide in each of the colours • 20in (55cm) cube of foam • Scissors and sewing equipment (see The workshop, pages 200–201) • Matching sewing thread • 60in (160cm) lightweight zip closure (optional)

Cutting out

Cut out two squares of fabric in each of the three fabrics, each 1¼in (3cm) larger all around than the dice. Plan which squares are going around the side and which will be top and bottom pieces.

Joining the sides

Stitch four sides together, taking ⅝in (1.5cm) seam allowance and stopping ⅝in (1.5cm) exactly from each end. Secure stitches. The tops and bottoms of each adjacent piece must line up exactly, so if any have slipped, re-stitch them.

Adding the top square

Pin one side piece to top square. Position each corner so that the top of the stitching line is exactly ⅝in (1.5cm) from each side. Pin to hold. Pin between corners, keeping fabrics flat. Stitch, securing the stitching at each end. Repeat with the other three sides, positioning the corners first.

Finishing the bottom

Stitch one side of the bottom square to one side piece. Press the other six raw edges ⅝in (1.5cm) to wrong side. Turn right side out. At this point insert the zip around three sides if you will be using a closure. If not, insert the foam block and slipstitch the folded edges together, using buttonhole or doubled thread.

Left *Dice cushions can be made from printed fabric, but if you feel more adventurous you can appliqué dots to plain fabric to make them look like real dice.*

Above *These cushions can make brilliant gifts. Just use those small fabric remnants and left-over fabrics. Alter the number and appliqué the design to suit the chosen recipient.*

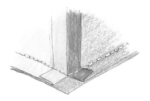

Bean bag

This is the simplest bean bag to make; it is easy to take off and wash, and even a child could put it together!

Measurements

Size of finished bean bag 28in (70cm) across and 24in (60cm) high

Materials

2½yd (2.20m) lining fabric, at least 48in-(120cm)-wide • 3yd (2.80m) main fabric • Scissors and sewing equipment (see The workshop, pages 200–201) • 1 bag of polystyrene beans weighing 10lb(4½kg) • Matching sewing thread • 2yd (2m) ribbon, cord or tape for drawstring

Cutting out

From the lining fabric, cut two circles 29¼in (73cm) in diameter and cut and join the remaining fabric to make one strip 25¼ x 87in (63 x 215cm). Cut and join the main fabric to make one strip 58 x 87in (140 x 215cm).

Making up the inner bag

For the inner bag, stitch the short ends of the lining to make a tube, leaving an 8in (20cm) gap in the middle. Pin each edge around one of the circles, snipping fabric as necessary to keep it lying flat. Stitch around twice and neaten seams. Press. (If the side and circles do not quite match, just make a tuck in the side piece.) Fill with the beans and machine stitch the side gap closed. The bag should be quite loosely filled, so that it flops around on the floor and is comfortable to sit in.

Making the outer cover

Join short ends of main fabric to make a tube. Neaten seam. Pin ¾in (2cm) double hems at either end. Stitch around twice, once close to the outside edge, and again close to the hem line, this time leaving a 2in (5cm) gap at each seam. Thread ribbon or tape through. Pull up one end and tie in a knot. Insert bag and pull up other end.

Optional trim

You can make large fabric-covered buttons to go over the gathering channels at each end, or cut a circle of fabric and turn under the ends before slipstitching in place.

Above *This is the second most popular idea that has come from America! Bean bags are ideal for children, pets and students as they provide comfortable and versatile seating. They are easy and inexpensive to make, and light enough to move around.*

Alternative bean bag

Make up inner lining and fill with beads as before. Pin the opening sides together.

Cut six sections of fabric which are 54⅜in (136cm) long and 16in (40cm) wide. Fold one in half lengthwise and then in half widths. Pencil a rounded curve starting from outside edge of folded centre and stopping ⅝in (1.5 cm) from ends. Cut through all layers and use this as a template for the other five sections.

Stitch all pieces together along long sides, taking care to stitch to the centre of each piece at either end, and the next piece starts at the centre. There should not be holes at the ends. Leave a 45in (115cm) gap along the last long side. Turn right side out, insert filled bag, slipstitch opening.

4 Appliqué cushions

Traditionally, appliqué was a hand-sewn technique. The motif was cut out, the edges turned under, and the shape stitched to the background fabric by hand. However, the process is much less laborious with a sewing machine. Appliqué is particularly effective when using a patterned fabric with bold motifs, so that you have a ready-made design. Otherwise, mark out the motif on fabric before beginning. If using fine fabric, use iron-on interfacing to prevent the motif from distorting (see The workshop, pages 208-209). Double-sided iron-on interfacing both stiffens the fabric and holds it in place while you stitch. It has a paper backing, so you can iron it onto the fabric, then remove backing paper and iron it onto the fabric you are stitching to.

Enlarge the motifs shown here using a photocopier or squared grid (see The workshop, page 215). The motifs here are about 50 percent of the actual size.

Cutting out
Cut out motif in fabric and interfacing, leaving a generous border around the edge, and fuse together.

Stitching and clipping
Transfer the design using dressmaker's carbon paper. Work a very fine line of running stitches, in matching thread, around the complete design outline. Trim seam allowances around design to $\frac{1}{8}$in (4mm) and snip in toward design outline on all curved lines.

Fixing into position
Place onto cushion cover and tack securely into place leaving sufficient room around edges to turn under edges. Turn under seam allowance so that the running stitch outline is just hidden and finely hem edge into place.

5 Soft seating and cover-ups

Soft seating and cover-ups

*A*ll furniture deteriorates in time, and all too often it is the fabric on your favourite sofa or set of dining chairs that starts to look faded, shabby or gets stained or torn. But you do not have to discard this type of furniture just because it is past its best. Drop-in dining seats, for example, can be easily revamped by just removing the seats and recovering them with a new fabric. Old, tired sofas can be revived with

loose covers, throws or rugs in traditional muted colours or more modern, lively patterns that can be chosen to match in with your existing decorating scheme. You can also disguise any mis-matched furniture or update old dining chairs by making contemporary floor length covers, which you cut out in panels. Always choose your furnishing fabrics carefully before you start your furnishing project. Closely woven heavy cotton, twill, wool and acrylic mixtures are suitable for fixed upholstery covers but for loose covers, mediumweight cottons or tougher cotton and polyester mixtures, and linen-union are more suitable materials. If you know you want a washable cover, check that the fabric is shrink resistant before you buy.

A wide range of chairs, both upholstered and timber framed, can be given a new lease of life with a decorative fabric cover. If you no longer admire your dining table and chairs, hide them with floor-length covers, as shown far left. Moving to a new home and different decorations can create problems with patterned textiles that no longer fit the bill or blend with their new surroundings, but new shaped loose covers, see above and left, can be the answer. Even easier to create are simple straight-sided slip-over covers, see lower left.

5 Drop-in chair seat cover

Drop-in chair seats are easy to re-cover at a very low cost. The seat slips out of the chair making it simple to work on, and the quantity of material needed is minimal. Use any hard-wearing furnishing fabric, but if you choose one with a large design, the pattern will need to be centred on each chair you cover. This is a good time to smarten up the chair frame too. You can clean and repolish it if it is in a good condition, or you can give it a decorative paint finish to coordinate with your room's colour scheme.

Right *Traditional shape balloon-back dining chairs are given a modern look with white paint and seats covered in a bold check fabric.*

Tools and materials

Upholstery-weight furnishing fabric • Calico or lining fabric for underside • Old chisel or screwdriver to lever up old tacks • Pincers to remove old tacks • Scissors • Iron • Soft pencil • Hammer • ½in (12mm) fine tacks

Measuring up

Measure the fabric-covered top of the seat from front to back and also from side to side. Add 4in (10cm) to each measurement for the size of the new fabric piece. If you choose a patterned fabric, remember to allow for the design to be centred on the seat. For the undercover, measure the underside and then add a further 2in (5cm) to each measurement.

Below left *A rich red seat cover highlights the warmth of natural wood on a traditional dining chair. Upholstered chair seats need to be covered in tough, close-woven fabric to withstand extensive wear.*

Removing old cover

Take out the seat by pushing it upward. These seats are usually made from a wooden frame, with a base of webbing or plywood to hold the wadding or other stuffing. The wadding should be covered with a calico lining and then the main fabric cover. To remove the old cover, turn the seat upside down and gently lever up the tacks with the screwdriver. Once you can get the pincers under each tack head remove it.

Positioning new fabric

Cut out cover piece, making sure that any design is centred. Press, then fold in half from back to front and mark the fold line in pencil. Repeat, folding in half widthwise. Mark corresponding centre points on the underside of the front and back frame pieces and the two side sections. Lay out the fabric, wrong side up, and position the frame on top, lining up the centre point marks on fabric and frame.

Tacking cover sides in place

Pull fabric fairly taut and partially hammer in one tack at each marked position to hold fabric in place. Turn seat over and check from top side that the cover is positioned accurately. Adjust if necessary, then add more temporary tacks at 1in (2.5cm) intervals along each edge.

Temporary tacking
To ensure a professional finish, temporary-tack the cover first. To do this, the tacks are only partially driven in, just far enough to hold the fabric in place, then at each stage the seat is turned the right side up to check that the design remains accurately centred. The fabric grain should also run straight in each direction, and the cover should be smoothly taut but not pulled so tight that the tack points show. Once you are completely satisfied with the finished effect, tack the cover firmly into position, using a small pin hammer.

Fixing corners
Stretch the fabric taut diagonally at each corner and put in a temporary tack through the fabric into the frame corner to hold it. Ensure that loose fabric is equal on each side and fold each piece into a pleat. Before fixing down, trim away any excess fabric beneath the pleat, leaving no more than a ⅜in (1cm) turn. Tack the pleats down. Check the fit from the top side, adjust tacks if necessary, then hammer them all home.

Covering the underside
Cut out the fabric for the underside, then turn under 1¼in (3cm) along all the sides and press. Place the fabric, right side up on the underside of the seat, positioning it centrally to cover all top fabric's raw edges. Tack firmly in position at about 1in (2.5cm) intervals on all four sides.

Finishing cut-out corners
Pull the fabric taut diagonally, as for ordinary covers, and then temporarily fix a tack in the centre of the cut out on the back of the seat. Pleat the fabric carefully at each outer corner and then tack down.

Above *Bold plaid fabric creates a crisp look for this old carver chair. You can match up a group of differently designed chairs by painting them to match and using the same fabric for the new seat covers throughout.*

5 Over-stuffed chair seat cover

An over-stuffed seat is an upholstered seat which is fixed permanently to the frame and wraps over the edge of it. On a over-stuffed seat, unlike a drop-in seat, you need to work from the top side of the chair, so it is easy to check that any design remains centred and that the grain of the fabric runs straight from front to back and across the chair. Use any upholstery weight furnishing fabric but ensure that you buy enough material if you have chosen a bold design so that the pattern can be easily centred on each chair that you cover.

Below *A stylish period feel is created with this traditional frame and over-stuffed chair seat cover in green and gold fabric with a coordinating trim.*

Tools and materials

Upholstery-weight furnishing fabric • Calico or lining fabric for lining • Cotton wadding to go between under and top covers • Braid to edge seat cover • Old chisel or screwdriver • Pincers to remove old tacks • Scissors • Craft knife • Hammer • ½in (12mm) fine tacks • Fabric adhesive

Measuring up

Measure the fabric-covered top of the seat from front to back and from side to side. Add 4in (10cm) to each measurement for the size of the new fabric piece to allow for a 2in (5cm) deep seat, or more for a bigger chair. If you choose a patterned fabric allow for the design to be centred on the seat.
• For the lining, use the same measurements, adding 2in (5cm) to each length.
• For the wadding, use the same measurements, adding 1in (2cm) to each length.
• For the braid, measure all four sides of the chair seat and add 2in (5cm) for turnings.

Removing old cover and lining

Pull away the braid. Gently lever up the tacks with the chisel or screwdriver holding the braid end and old cover to the frame, then get the pincers under each tack head to remove it. Discard the old wadding between the lining and top cover, then remove lining in the same way as the top cover.

Replacing lining and wadding

Cut the lining piece 2in (5cm) larger than the seat on all sides and fit, following the next two steps for positioning and fixing the top cover. Make small, evenly spaced pleats at the front corners. Trim away excess lining with the craft knife. Cut the wadding slightly larger than the seat top and place over lining.

Positioning top cover

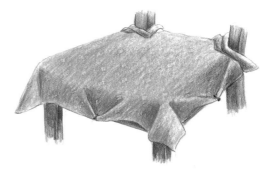

Press top fabric, cut to 2in (5cm) larger than the seat on all sides, and place over the seat centring any pattern. Partially hammer in one tack in the centre of each chair side edge and the front to temporarily hold the cover in position.

Left *Here a back view of one chair is shown lined and ready for covering. Instead of a fixed cover this could be given a slip-on style with a gathered skirt as shown on the other chair (right).*

Below *Re-fitting webbing and springs in upholstered furniture is a specialist task. You can learn the skills at an upholstery class.*

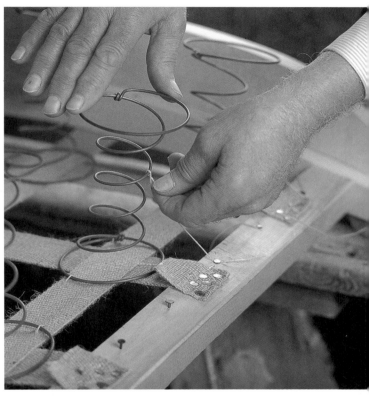

Fixing back corners

Fold cover fabric forward to line up with the chair back struts and make one cut from each fabric back corner to within ⅜in (lcm) of each upright strut. Turn under the raw edges, trim excess fabric, fold under again and fit neatly around each strut. Tack down. Put in tacks all along the sides and back of the seat, so that they are spaced at about 1in (2.5cm) intervals.

Fixing front corners

You can use a double pleat on the front corners, (see Fixing corners, page 133) or for a squarer corner, use a single pleat. Fix a temporary tack to hold the fabric near the corner on the side edge, then fold fabric round toward the front edge and tack here after cutting away any surplus fabric along the edge. Fold extra fabric under to form a neat single pleat on the corner. Cut away any surplus fabric below the pleat and fix in place with two tacks. Tack front edge down. Make sure that all the tacks are knocked in and then trim fabric close to tacks.

Adding edging braid

Turn under ⅜in (1cm) at end of braid and tack to line up with chair's back strut and to go over raw edge of cover. Add some adhesive to the wrong side of the braid and over tacked edge of cover, and press braid down along cover edge. At the opposite back strut, turn under the raw edge and glue in place. Cover the back edge similarly.

Tips

• If, on removing the old cover, you find that the upholstery beneath is in poor condition, it is wise to replace this before fitting the new cover. In most areas local upholstery classes are available and are led by an expert upholsterer who will oversee you through all the stages of replacing the webbing and springs, and also fixing the stuffing.

• Temporary tacking, (see Temporary tacking, page 133), allows you to make any adjustments so that you can be sure the cover is positioned accurately and fits smoothly before all the tacks are finally driven home.

5 Classic loose covers

Loose covers provide an instant new look for old and worn, but still comfortable, sofas and chairs and they are not difficult to make. These traditional loose covers form a second skin to upholstered furniture, following the shape and contours closely. You can also use covers to protect a special upholstered finish from dust, general wear and damage from enthusiastic children and pets. However, no cover can be made to sit neatly over shiny finishes like leather and plastic.

Types of fabric

Use only loose-cover or upholstery-weight fabric which is crease-resistant, firmly woven and tough so that it is able to withstand the wear demanded of it. Thick or heavy fabric is unsuitable to use as it is difficult to sew, particularly where piping is included, and where a number of layers of fabric must be stitched together. If the covers are to be washed, check that the fabric is colour-fast and non-shrink. Piping shows off the shape and can be finished in matching fabric or used as a feature. For contrast piping, choose a similar weight fabric to that picked for the main part of the covers.

Choosing a design

Plain fabrics look smart, especially if the seams are out-lined with contrasting coloured piping; they are also economic. Small, random designs which do not need careful matching are also economic and easy to work with. Bold motifs, checks and stripes look effective but require more care and extra fabric as designs need to be matched both up and down and across the furniture.

Below *A country look is created for this traditional armchair with an attractive fabric of fruit, flowers and leaves, which is offset by the ebullient gathered skirt.*

Left *A comfortable sofa gets a new look with a subtle modern fabric cover. Piping accentuates the curves and a simple skirt with corner pleats provides an uncluttered finish.*

Style of openings

Traditionally, openings are held closed with a long, tough zip but alternative choices are touch-and-close fastening, press stud fastening tape or hook and eye tape. If you want to make a feature of the opening, use bow ties, which can then be repeated on the opposite back and the front corners for decorative effect, or use colourful buttons and fabric or cord tabs.

Skirt design choices

The simplest loose covers are held beneath the furniture with a casing and cord ties, and this design suits modern straight-sided sofas with long legs and traditional chairs with ornate legs. A tailored skirt with corner pleats gives a classic look, while box pleats or a gathered skirt blend well with country-look fabrics and furniture styles. For a more unusual skirt, consider the two-tier effect of a double frill or a straight, tailored design with a scalloped over skirt.

Right *Comfort and warmth are added to a cool bathroom with a Victorian chair covered in classic red and white fabric. Note the short frilled skirt which allows the shapely legs to be on display.*

Below *The simple shape of a sofa and footstool are highlighted by both the fabric and a plain floor-length skirt. Colour is cleverly added to the muted scheme in the cushion covers and striped fabric of the slip-on chair cover displayed in the background.*

Fitting loose covers

Loose covers are not difficult to make but for a successful result they require careful fitting before the sections are sewn together.

- First measure each section of the furniture. Follow original seam lines and measure at the widest point.
- Add 4in (10cm) to all measurements for seams for adjustments. Also allow extra fabric for a tuck-in to hold cover in place. Add an extra 6in (15cm) to inside back, back and sides of seat and inside arm sections for this.
- Cut out squares and rectangles from fabric to correspond to these measurements. Then pin them, wrong side out, onto the chair and to each other for an accurate fit.
- Chalk in the seam line positions, remove the cover pieces, trim to 1in (2.5cm) seam allowance.
- Stitch sections together including piping in the seams, if required. Leave an opening along one back corner seam for taking the cover on and off.
- Finish the opening and the lower edge.

5 Dressed-up dining chair

A surface worn or unattractive looking upright chair can be transformed with a slip-over floor-length cover made from a series of squares and rectangles. The cover shown here fits back and seat, and has a smart straight-sided skirt with a false pleat at each corner. The skirt sections are lined with a contrasting fabric that is echoed in the false pleats which peep out between the skirt sections. Instructions are for a straightforward cover which can easily be dressed up using one or more of the ideas featured here.

Tools and materials

Closely woven furnishing fabric for top cover • Contrasting fabric for lining skirt and false corner pleats • Tape measure • Pencil and paper to make pattern pieces • Scissors and sewing equipment (see The workshop, pages 200–201) • Matching sewing thread

Measuring up

Do a rough sketch of the chair to be covered and mark on it the following measurements (always measure each section at the widest or longest point). Add 2in (5cm) to back and seat measurements to allow for adjustment when fitting and 1in (2.5cm) for seam allowances. Remember that if you choose a design with a large motif this will need to be centred and matched up on each of the six main sections of the cover, so allow extra material for this (not necessary on the skirt lining pieces).

• *outside back* cover (A) Measure the chair back width and the length from top edge to floor. Also measure from seat to floor for back panel lining.
• *inside back cover* (B) Measure width including frame sides, and length from top back edge to seat.
• *seat* (C) Measure from side to side and back to front to frame edge.
• *side panels* (D) Measure from top of seat frame to floor and from outer edge of back to outer edge of front leg.
• *front panel* (E) Measure from top of seat frame to floor and from outer edge to outer edge of each front leg.
• *false corner pleats* (F) Measure from seat frame top to floor and cut each 9in (22.5cm) wide.

Cutting out the cover

Make pattern pieces of each section from paper, label them with section name and arrange on the fabric. Check that each section follows the straight grain of the fabric and that the motifs are centred. When you are happy with the arrangement and have ensured that the design matches on all sections, pin each pattern piece in place and cut out. From lining, cut two side panels, one front panel, one short outer back panel and eight false pleat pieces.

Lining the skirt pieces

Right sides together, pin and baste one skirt side panel lining piece to top fabric section, ½in (1.25cm) from raw edges along sides and bottom. Stitch, then repeat on second side panel and front panel. Attach back skirt lining to lower back panel section in same way, stitching to 1in (2.5cm) of lining's top raw edge. Turn under a ½in (1.25cm) hem along lining's top edge and slipstitch in place to outer back panel. On skirt pieces, trim diagonally across raw edges on bottom corners, turn right side out; press.

Left *A plain dining chair is transformed into a stunning focal point with a beautiful floor-length cover. Comfort has been added with cushions tied to the chair below the cover.*

Lining the false corner pleats

Right sides together, pin, baste and stitch two false corner pleat pieces together along the sides and lower edges as for the skirt sections. Repeat with the remaining six pleat pieces to make the other three corner pleats. Finish, trim, press and turn right side out as for skirt sections.

Fitting the back sections on the chair

With wrong sides outside, place the chair back and inside back sections together on the chair. Pin in place to fit, ensuring that the seam runs along the outer back edge of the frame. Make a small dart in the inside back piece at each of the top back corners to fit the frame shape. Remove and stitch darts. Trim raw edges outside seam line to ½in (1.25cm) then stitch the two back sections to each other along the top and sides. Neaten raw edges.

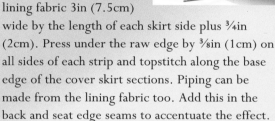

Adding the seat piece and skirt

Replace the back sections on the chair, inside out and pin the chair seat section, wrong side uppermost, to the inside chair back along the back edge. Add the side and front skirt pieces, lining side outward and pin to the seat section so that the seam runs along the outer frame edge and skirt edges meet at the back and front leg corners. Remove, trim seat seams, if necessary and tack all pinned seams.

Positioning the false pleats

Centrally position one pleat section over each skirt corner. Pin and baste in place along seam line through all the layers. Stitch seams. Neaten raw edges. Press seams, turn cover right side out and fit.

Adding a border and piping

To add a border, as shown in picture (left), cut four strips of lining fabric 3in (7.5cm) wide by length of each skirt side plus ¾in (2cm). Press under raw edge by ⅜in (1cm) on all sides of strips and topstitch along base edge of cover skirt sections. Piping (from lining fabric) can be added to back and seat edge seams for effect.

Right *Button-through covers liven up the appearance of matching chairs with upholstered seats and backs; in this case the covers finish with a short gathered frill.*

Optional extras

- Use some ribbon or make matching fabric ties to highlight corner pleats.
- On a chair with a shaped back include side openings and use bow ties or touch-and-close fastening to hold closed.
- Add a seat cushion made to match the chair cover.
- To add a border, as shown in the picture (left), cut four strips of lining fabric 3in (7.5cm) wide by the length of each skirt side plus ¾in (2cm). Press under the raw edge by ⅜in (1cm) on all sides of each strip and topstitch along the base edge of the cover skirt sections. Piping can be made from the lining fabric too. Add this in the back and seat edge seams to accentuate the effect.

5 Slip-on chair cover

This semi-fitted chair cover simply slips over the chair like an egg cosy. The inverted pleats on each back corner allow for this and bow ties along the pleat lines hold the cover neatly in place and help to provide some extra decoration. The upholstered cover drops to just above floor level and is finished with a plain hemmed edge.

Tools and materials

Loose cover furnishing fabric • Soft tape measure • Marking pen • Wallpaper lining or brown paper to make a pattern • Scissors and sewing equipment (see The workshop, pages 200–201) • Soft pencil • Tailor's chalk

Measuring up

Using some wallpaper lining paper or brown paper, do a rough sketch of the chair to be covered and mark on it with the marking pen the following measurements using the soft tape measure. Always remember to measure each section of the chair carefully at their widest or longest point as accuracy is essential. You will then need to add an extra 2in (5cm) to all the measurements to allow for any necessary adjustment when fitting the cover. Also remember to leave an extra 1in (2.5cm) for the seam allowances.

Right *A close up of the opening shows the gusset and the decorative bow ties which hold this decorative cover in place.*

Below *Full length curtains and matching chair cover fabric both echo the pattern of the wallpaper in this relaxing bedroom. The chair cover simply slips over the upholstery and ties in place easily.*

Making a pattern

When you start to make your pattern, take your time to take the following measurements so that you will get a good fit for your cover.

• *outside back cover* Measure the chair back width and the length from top edge to floor.
• *inside back cover* Measure width and length from top back edge to seat. Allow an extra 6in (15cm) to length for the seat tuck-in.
• *seat* Measure from side to side and back to front. Allow an extra 12in (30cm) to both measurements for seat tuck-in.
• *lower front section* Measure chair width and drop from seat front edge to floor.
• *inside arm* Measure width and length at widest and longest points. Allow an extra 6in (15cm) to length for seat tuck-in. If your chair has arms with gussets along the top and side edges, you will need to measure, fit and stitch these as separate sections.
• *outside arm* Measure width and length at widest and longest points.
• *inverted back corner pleats* Use outside back cover length measurement and make two gusset strips to this length and 10in (25cm) wide.
• *bow ties* Make each strip 3in (7.5cm) wide by 13in (32.5cm) long and make enough pairs to space them evenly about every 5–6in (12.5–15cm) down each pleat edge.
• *seat cushion* (Follow cutting out and making instructions on pages104–105).

Note: some chairs, such as the one shown here, also require a tuck-in between back and inside arm edge.

Cutting out the cover

Using your measurements (left), cut out pattern pieces of each main section from lining or brown paper and label them with section name. Place on chair and pin together, starting with inner and outer back and arms, then add other sections. Make folds in the paper around curves and slip tuck-ins in place. Pencil in fitting lines. Remove pieces and cut paper pattern to follow curves, allowing 3in (7.5cm) outside line for accurate fitting and seam allowance. Arrange pattern pieces on fabric ensuring any fabric design lines up. Pin in place and cut out. Also include pleat, cushion and bow tie pieces in layout.

Fitting the cover pieces

Wrong side out, pin all the main fabric sections to each other on the chair, making any minor adjustments where you think they are necessary so that they fit very well. Then mark in all the seam lines using the tailor's chalk. Remove all the fabric sections from the chair and trim the seam allowance to 1in (2.5cm). Neaten all the raw edges with scissors.

Attaching corner pleat pieces

Right sides together, pin, baste and stitch one gusset strip down one outer back edge. Pin opposite edge of gusset piece to outer back edge of side panel and stitch. Temporarily remove adjoining pinned pieces to make stitching easier. Repeat to stitch second gusset strip to opposite back corner. With right sides together, fold gusset in half along its length, and pin in place through seam lines. Stitch along seam line for 2in (5cm) down from top raw edge. Open out and centre pleat at back of this seam. Pin, then stitch across top edge to hold. Press pleat.

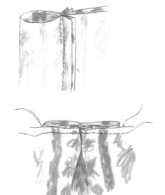

Stitching the cover

Repin pieces together where necessary and stitch to join all cover sections along marked lines. Press seams open and replace cover on chair, right side out.

Hemming the cover

Turn the fabric under and pin a double hem along the lower edge of the cover, making sure that the hem edge hangs just above floor level. When the length is correct, remove the cover and stitch the hem.

Making and fitting the ties

With wrong side uppermost, fold one long edge of one strip to its centre and press. Repeat along opposite side so that raw edges meet. Press in ½in (1.25cm) to the wrong side across one short end. With right side outside, fold the strip in half along its length. Press well.

Stitch close to all edges. Repeat to make all ties. Mark tie positions along back corner seams, spacing these equally 5–6in (12.5–15cm) apart. Undo the seam at each point and insert 1in (2.5cm) of tie raw end. Stitch the seam again to hold the tie ends in place. Replace the cover and tie bows.

Cushion cover

Follow the instructions detailed on pages 104–105 to make up the cushion cover. Remember to make sure that the pattern matches the one that appears on the chair cover.

Ties

Ribbon, braid, fabric strips and cord can all be used to hold chair covers in place in a number of decorative ways or can appear simply to define a design point. The two pictures shown here provide some suggestions.

• Use long strips of narrow ribbon or cord to lace up an opening.

• Use cord or ribbon to make loops that fix buttons in position.

• Create broad, bold and bountiful bows, or slim bootlace fixings.

5 Instant cover-ups

*I*f you are short of time, tight for cash, or like a casual furnishing effect, then a no-sew throw-over cover is a simple way to give a sofa or upholstered chair a new lease of life. Where over-exuberant children and pets cause problems for favourite furniture, throws also provide a quick method of protection and can be cleverly used to hide the damage from a cat's sharp claws. They can also add zest to a too-bland colour scheme in a room or help to create a change of look between summer and winter.*

Throws and rugs

Throws are now widely available in a huge range of designs. However, there are many other equally successful alternatives. Exotic rugs that are too precious to cover the floor or cotton rag rugs stay in place well on furniture. Throws can also be a perfect way to show off a beautiful bedspread, antique shawl or embroidered tablecloth. Lengths of fabric can be joined together to make an all-embracing cover or you can use a decorative flat sheet that falls in graceful folds around a chair base. More texture can be added by outlining the chosen textiles with braid or a fringe or by adding decorative corner tassels.

Alternative effects

Quick cover-ups provide a chance to create a very individual look. Here are some ideas that can start you experimenting:

Simply draped

A quick, stylish effect is gained by literally throwing soft draping fabric over a sofa or chair. Adding scatter cushions or placing a seat cushion on top of the throw helps to keep it in position.

Sculptured finish

A number of small-size rugs can be used to follow a sofa's shape. Use one over the sofa back, another over the seat, tucking the rug sides into the space behind the seat cushions to help pin them in place. You could add a further couple, draping one over each arm. Choose rug shades that blend for a subtle effect, or pick strongly

Above *A large size bedspread acts as an all-enveloping throw on a sofa to hide wear, damage or stains from view.*

Left *Here a neat look is created by matching the colour of the throw to the upholstery beneath. The only disadvantage of this type of cover-up is that regular smoothing is required to maintain a neat finish.*

contrasting colours to create a focal point. Before you buy any rugs, check that light-coloured textiles can be washed or easily cleaned.

The layered look

This is a much more casual effect which is created with rugs or a range of textiles draped, angled and folded over back, arms and seat to give a patchwork of wonderful shapes and colours.

Using ties

Fabric can be draped on furniture and then the corners can be tied in place on either side, or the fabric can be swathed around a chair and tied in the lower centre front or at the back. Alternatively, use contrasting-coloured cords to encircle the back and base of a fabric-covered sofa or chair.

Taking a tuck

A large sheet or bedspread can be tucked in to give a neat, structured look to furniture. Lay your chosen material over a sofa from back to front, tucking it in both behind and in front of the seat cushions as well as along the sides. Extend the tucks as pleats over the back and then secure in place with a few stitches where necessary. Slim strips of foam that are pushed into the tuck-in spaces around the cushions help to keep the cover in place.

Taking measurements

To work out the size of an all-enveloping throw-over cover, measure the chair or sofa from the floor at the back to the floor at the front, following the curves of the furniture. Then add about 12in (30cm) extra for every tuck-in that you want. Do the same from side to side, adding 24in (60cm) for two tuck-ins, one on either side of the seat.

Above right *An ethnic throw and tapestry cushions add an colourful look to a room. Mix and match texture and patterns for an exotic effect, echoed here in the cushion covers.*

Right *To coordinate furniture with a new decorative room scheme, temporarily hide their colours with a plain sheet or fabric length until you have time to make a matching cover.*

5 Buying old chairs

Finding suitable furniture to cover

Second-hand dining chairs and upholstered furniture that are in good condition can still be bought at bargain prices. If you want a genuine antique, go to a reputable antique shop, unless you are an expert on the subject yourself. If you have the time, visit house sales and auctions. Most have a day's viewing before the auction and you can leave a bid with the sales staff if you are unable to return on the day of the sale itself. This also ensures that sale fever does not tempt you to pay too high a price for your chosen piece! Market stalls and junk shops often turn up some interesting individual pieces. You can also look through the advertisements in local papers for second-hand furniture as these can produce some great bargains.

What to look for when buying

Always make the following checks before buying furniture second-hand:

- Sit on a chair or sofa to check how comfortable it is.
- Check from the top that the upholstery is still firm. Press down on it; it should spring back into place again. Look at the arms and make sure that they are still secure.
- Look at the underside of upholstered furniture to see if the seat sags and feel to make sure that the springs are still in place and attached to the webbing.
- On a dining chair, place one hand on the back and the other on the seat. Then rock it to test for any loose joints or unsteady legs. Creaking may indicate that it has woodworm. Look for woodworm holes and a sawdust-like deposit. Many holes point to a weakened frame, so avoid buying this type of chair.

Above and Below *Clean up wooden and painted frames before recovering old chairs with new upholstery fabric and trimming. The best bargains are often found outside antique shops and second-hand stores.*

Safety point

Try to obtain a guarantee that foam has not been included in the making of the furniture as if this becomes ignited it can be a smoke and fire hazard. It is now illegal in most countries to sell upholstered furniture which has not been tested for fire resistance following upholstered furniture safety regulations.

6 **Merging the indoors and outdoors**

Merging the indoors and outdoors

Outdoor living offers great possibilities for soft furnishings: umbrellas, deck chairs or soft mattresses can be easily adapted to suit the smallest roof terrace or the largest garden. You can make a small patio or back yard into a summer dining room; a sunny terrace can add an instant extension to a living room, or a secret bower in a quiet corner of the garden can become an escape from the world. Conservatories and garden rooms can be decorated with

furnishings to create a further area for living and entertaining throughout the whole year.

Outdoor soft furnishings may be made to complement an existing interior decorating scheme or they can be used to introduce different colours, patterns and textures to the home. Choose schemes to blend with your furniture. Bright patterns can liven up moulded plastic furniture, while bold stripes can be ideal for deck chairs, for example. Awnings and blinds for patios, hammocks, garden parasols and dining tents can all be created in matching fabrics. As outdoor furniture is only used occasionally for entertaining, it also lends itself to more adventurous use of colour and pattern. Items such as windbreaks, linings for picnic hampers and matching accessories such as cutlery rolls, napkins and tablecloths can all be made in a range of attractive, colourful, hardwearing and washable fabrics.

You can continue the decorating theme from the inside of your home to a terrace as this checked blanket and accessories, above, shows. The iron bench, above left and below, subtly links inside to outside by being covered in a delicate floral print. A lounger cushion, far left, or a striped sofa and wicker furniture on a verandah, left, can tempt you to sit outside.

6 Setting the scene

Your garden or terrace may be used as an extension of your home for entertaining during the warm summer months. The fashion for al fresco dining has meant that these areas can be used as a delightful setting for Mediterranean-style meals as well as general relaxation. The choice of colours and fabrics for outdoor furnishings may be inspired by a number of factors. The amount of light and the direction of the sun on a patio or in a garden may dictate your choice of colour. A terrace or patio which benefits from a great deal of sunlight would suit cool Californian blues and greens, while a shadier aspect could be brightened up by using such stunning colours as brilliant oranges, reds and pinks.

Inspiration for colour and pattern in furnishings may be drawn from many sources – from the flowers and plants in pots on the terrace or growing in the garden, or from mementoes and photographs from foreign holidays where more tropical climates can be reflected in a bolder use of design and colour.

Using different patterns

Prints and pattern designs for fabrics may also reflect the outdoors in delicate botanical motifs, floral and topiary designs, while plain colours can be mixed and matched together with equally good effect. A simple tie-on seat cover for a foldaway bistro chair can be used to introduce interest, colour and decoration to a terrace or conservatory while a plain garden bench can be painted, and dressed with a fabric-covered seat and matching tasselled bolsters to create an elegant and inviting outdoor seat.

Choosing fabrics

Fabrics for outdoor furnishings are largely dictated by how they will be used. Washable fabrics are obviously most suitable since such covers when they are out in all weathers are more likely to need regular cleaning during the summer months. Check how light-resistant the fabric is as some weaves and prints are more suitable than others. Generally, curtain fabrics and deck chair canvases will wear well. Plasticized fabrics are useful out of doors, and are particularly suitable for tablecloths and mats. The PVC coating helps to prevent any colour fading, eliminates the need for hems, and makes for an easy-care, wipe-clean surface.

Quilted fabrics provide an instant soft touch for table accessories and cushions, but pre-quilted fabrics often have only a dress-weight top layer, which may not be as fade-resistant or durable as other heavier fabrics. Cushions and mattresses should always be chosen with washable polyester fillings, so that it does not matter if they are left out in the garden overnight and get caught in the rain by mistake.

Left *The light and airy feel of this sitting room, with its doors leading to the garden, is achieved with chic black and white striped cotton furnishings. The two wrought iron daybeds have loose box mattress covers made up in the cotton stripe. Slatted wood folding garden chairs make ideal dining chairs for this summery room.*

Right *A perfect setting for a summer lunch by the river has been created in this scheme, using a combination of bold painterly spots, checks and stripes in cobalt blue and lime on a crisp white background, as tie-on seat covers, plump cushions and matching tablelinen. The parasol and deck chair have also been covered to match the scheme.*

Above *Give old sofas and chairs a new lease of life in a garden room by draping them with fabric or readymade throws. Here, a simple printed design on white cotton has been used as covers, accentuated by brick red terracotta cushions.*

New covers and linings for outdoor furniture and accessories can be used for both old and new pieces. The wooden frames of deck chairs and director's chairs usually outlast their slings, so new covers can be very economical to make.

A quilted lining for an old picnic hamper, tied with simple bows, can give it a new lease of life, making it an attractive accessory, as well as providing good protection for all the hamper contents. The lining can also be coordinated with some matching cutlery rolls and napkins to make a complete picnic set that is ideal for a day out in the country.

6 Tie-on chair cushion

This tie-on cushion cover can be adapted to suit a wide variety of indoor and garden chairs, making a colourful and comfortable addition to any furnishing scheme. Make up the tie-on covers in matching fabrics or try using contrasting plain fabrics for each seat to add more style and interest. The cover can be filled with a conventional cushion pad. Alternatively, you can use sheet foam cut to size, which can be left outside during the summer months.

Suggested fabrics

Linen and cotton in plain, woven or printed designs. Avoid using very large repeat designs on fabric as they will result in fabric wastage if you are making a set of matching seat covers.

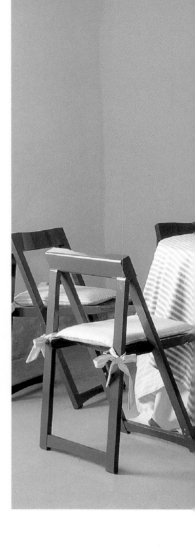

Materials

Approximately ⅝yd (60cm) of 48in-(120cm)-wide fabric for each chair seat cover • Paper and pencil for chair template • Scissors and sewing equipment (see The workshop, pages 120–121) • 1¼yd (1.10m) cotton ribbon or braid ⅝in (1.5cm) wide per chair for ties • Matching sewing thread • 4 plastic or metal stud fastenings for opening • Cushion pad to fit finished cover or ¾in (2cm) thick sheet foam cut to size

Making the chair seat template

Draw around the chair seat with the paper and pencil to make the template for the top panel of the cover. Add ⅝in (1.5cm) all round for seam allowances. Use the same pattern for the bottom panel, allowing a total of 2in (5cm) along back edge for a turning.

Above *A loose chair cover for this traditional bamboo chair has been made up in a pretty floral chintz design with long, beige ribbon ties.*

Left *Use simple braid or ribbon to give a decorative trim to a simple tie-on cushion made from plain fabric.*

Adding a frill

A frill is a particularly appropriate finish for covers made up in floral prints. Make up the frill from strips of fabric 6in (15cm) wide. Cut one strip 1½ times the length of the back of the seat. Cut a second strip 1½ times the total length of the remaining three sides (join lengths if needed to make the frill long enough).

Fold fabric for frills in half lengthwise, right sides together. Stitch across the ends, taking ⅜in (1cm) seams. Clip corners, turn right side out and press. Make lines of gathering stitches ⅜in (1cm) from the raw edges. Position the ties on the top panel, then add the frills.

Gather up the short strip to fit across the back edge of the cover, excluding the seam allowance. Pin to the right side of the top of the top panel, with raw edges matching, leaving the ⅝in (1.5cm) seam allowance free at each end. Gather up the second strip and pin around the remaining three sides of the panel in the same way, allowing extra fullness at the corners so the frill will hang neatly. Stitch in place ⅝in (1.5cm) from raw edges. Finish the facing and make up the cover as described below.

Cutting out

Cut out two panels of fabric using the pattern template. Position the pattern centrally over any pattern motif. Cut a facing strip to match the width of the pattern and 2in (5cm) wide.

Positioning the ties

Cut the ribbon or braid in half, then fold each piece in half. Position the folded edge of first ribbon 1in (2.5cm) in from the back corner of the right side of the top panel of the cover, so that the fold is toward the raw edge and ¼in (6mm) from it. Pin in place. Repeat for the second tie.

Above *The plainest tie-on seat covers transform these wooden folding chairs into a coordinated green and white dining room scheme with a sunny, relaxed outdoor style.*

Positioning the facing

Turn under and stitch a double, ½in (1.25cm) wide hem along one long edge of facing strip. Position strip across back edge of the top panel, with right side downward and long raw edge matching raw edge of top seat panel. Stitch in place taking a ⅝in (1.5cm) seam. Turn facing over to wrong side of fabric and press.

Finishing the bottom panel

Turn under a 1in (2.5cm) double hem along the back edge of bottom seat panel. Topstitch in place.

Making up the cover

With right sides together, pin, baste and stitch around three edges of the seat cover, catching in the ends of the facings but leaving the back of the cover open. Trim seam allowance and clip diagonally across the corners of the cover and turn to right side. Press.

Finishing the back opening

Sew stud part of fastenings to the double hem along the edge of bottom panel. Sew socket part of fastenings to the facing along the open edge of the top panel. Insert cushion pad or sheet foam cut to size using a paper template without seam allowances.

6 | Picnics outdoors

E *ating outdoors during the limited time that we have during the summer months can be great fun. If you like to go for trips to the country or seaside making your own lining for your picnic basket and then coordinating a cutlery roll can give you the ideal picnic set.*

Cutlery roll

Make up individual cutlery rolls to hold knives, forks and spoons to match the lining of a picnic hamper.

Measurements

Size of four-piece cutlery roll 12 × 10in (30 × 25cm)

Suggested fabrics

Mediumweight canvas or drill; heavyweight furnishing cotton. Use plain, printed or colour-woven checks or stripes. Avoid large patterns because of the cutlery roll's size.

Materials

½ yd (45cm) of 36in (90cm) wide fabric • Scissors and sewing equipment (see The workshop, pages 200–201) • 1 glass as a guide • Matching sewing thread • 1⅝yd (1.70m) bias binding, 1in (2.5cm) wide

Cutting out

Cut out a front panel measuring 12 x 10in (30 x 25cm). Cut out a matching inside panel measuring 12 x 10in (30 x 25cm). Round off the corners of the two main pieces using a glass as a guide to make an even curve. Cut out a cutlery insert panel measuring 12 x 5in (30 x 12.5cm) and round off two corners in the same way.

Sewing the cutlery insert panel

Make a turning of ⅝in (1.5cm) along one long edge of the insert panel and topstitch in place. Position insert panel on the right side of the inside panel, matching raw edges. Pin together, then trim insert panel to match curved corners of inside panel.

Sewing the cutlery inserts

Mark off three equally spaced lines vertically on the insert panel to form cutlery inserts and topstitch along these lines, reverse stitching at the neatened edge of the insert panel to strengthen the pockets.

Sewing the front panel

With wrong sides together, lay inside panel on top of front panel and pin together. Using ready-made bias binding, fold it in half lengthwise and baste in position, enclosing raw edges of cutlery roll. Turn raw ends of the bias binding under and topstitch binding in place.

Making the cutlery roll ties

Cut one tie piece from bias binding, 20in (50cm) long. Fold the binding in half along its length so that the raw edges are enclosed and press. Turn in ⅝in (1.5cm) at each end and press. Topstitch close to the folded edges along the length and across ends of tie.

Attaching the ties

Fold tie piece in half across width and stitch to centre of one side of cutlery roll. Insert cutlery, roll and tie in a bow to finish.

Left *Individual cutlery rolls for picnics and outdoor eating make a lovely finishing touch, and can be made to coordinate with a picnic hamper or to match your tablelinen.*

*Make your garden a place to relax.
Sling your seat from an overhanging
branch: this hammock is edged with
crochet and piled with cushions (above
and right).*

Trimmed and tailored cushions create an
unexpected seaside welcome even on the dullest
day (left). The cushions are easy to remove
and stow away. This traditional wooden
lounger (above) takes on a new lease of life
when re-covered in an Ikat-style print fabric.

Outdoor *living*

Mix and match boldly striped deck chair fabrics for a splash of sunny colour in a seaside setting (left) or select a single shade for a quiet corner of the garden (below). This brightly checked fabric is equally at home in a grand garden or a cool conservatory (right). Carry your colour scheme through into the garden to bring the great outdoors into your home (overleaf).

A boldly striped hammock brightens a quiet corner (above) but don't let prints and patterned weaves fight with pastel planting schemes.

Cutting out

Cut out one hamper base, 17 ¾ x 11 ¼in (44 x 28cm).
Cut out one hamper side lining 55 ¼ x 7 ⅜in (135 x 17 ⅜cm).

Sewing the hamper side lining

With right sides facing, stitch the side lining together at the shorter side. Then press the seam flat.

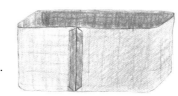

Finishing the top edge

Turn under a ⅜in (1cm) double hem all around top edge of side lining and press. Stitch in place by machine, close to fold of hem.

Above *An old or new picnic basket can be lined in fabric to coordinate with picnic rugs, tableware and napkins. Quilted fabric adds an interesting dimension to the lining as well as providing protection for the hamper's contents.*

Lining a picnic hamper

Line an old or new picnic hamper with some pretty fabric as a finishing touch for your outdoor eating. This design can be adapted to suit most hamper shapes and features ribbon ties so that it can be easily removed for washing. It can be made in plain cotton or plastic-coated cotton if you prefer a water-resistant lining that can be wiped clean after use.

Measurements

Size of picnic hamper (internal dimensions) 16½ x 10 x 6in (41 x 25 x 15cm) (If your hamper has different measurements, make two paper templates – one to fit the hamper's base and a long strip to fit around the inside. Add a ⅝in (1.5cm) seam allowance around the base and along one long edge, and the two short ends of the side strip. Add ¾in (2cm) hem allowance along top edge of long strip.

Below *Simple fabric ties are threaded through the basketwork so that the lining can be removed for laundering.*

Suggested fabrics

Heavy furnishing cotton, plastic-coated cotton, ready-quilted cotton. (If using ready-quilted cotton, omit hem allowance along top edge and bind the edge instead.)

Materials

⅝yd (0.50m) of 60in-(150cm)-wide fabric ● Scissors and sewing equipment (see The workshop, pages 200–201) ● Matching sewing thread

Sewing the lining to the base

With right sides together, sew lining to base, starting the sewing from one corner matching the side seam of the lining. Clip into seam allowance of side panel at each corner and clip across corners of base. Press.

Attaching the ties to the lining

Cut 10 pieces of fabric for ties, measuring approximately 8 x 2in (20 x 5cm). Make up 10 ties following the instructions in The workshop, page 217. Fold the ties in half and stitch to top edge of hem by hand, positioning one at each corner, one in the centre of each short edge and two, evenly spaced, down the longer sides of the basket.

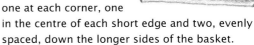

Attaching the ribbon ties to the hamper

Position lining in hamper. Thread one tail of each tie through the gaps in the woven wicker. Tie into bows to hold the lining firmly in place.

6 Soft mattresses

The soft mattress is a less structured version of the boxed seat and can be adapted to fit deck chairs, sun loungers and benches. The fat, softly stuffed piping gives a distinctive edge to the mattress. It is filled with wadding which can be multi-layered depending on the depth required. The buttoned effect can be created by using standard buttons or knotted ties.

Suggested fabric

Mediumweight furnishing fabric; cotton towelling.

Materials

Fabric (see measurements below) • Paper, pencil and plate to make mattress template • Scissors and sewing equipment (see The workshop, pages 200–201) • Heavyweight polyester wadding (two layers for a thin soft mattress, up to five layers for a firmer mattress), plus extra for making soft piping • Matching sewing thread • Covering buttons

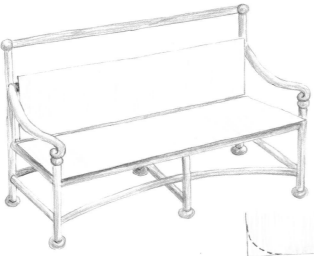

Making the paper template

Trace around the shape of the sun lounger, deck chair or seat to be used for a soft mattress cover using the paper and pencil. Add ⅝in (1.5cm) all round for seam allowance and then cut out the paper template. Using a plate as a guide, round off the edges to create a curved edge on all four corners for the piping. To calculate all the fabric requirements, multiply these measurements by two, and then add 1yd (1m) extra for self piping if it is required.

Above *A lxurious soft mattress, covered in a stunning green and blue fabric, creates a comfortable corner in which to sit and relax in comfort.*

Cutting out

Cut one back and one front mattress piece, using the paper template. Cut the layers of wadding using the paper template, and then trim 1in (2.5cm) off all edges to ensure it fits inside the finished mattress. For fat, stuffed self piping, measure the length of all sides of the mattress, add 1¼in (3cm) seam allowance and cut a piece of fabric this length by 6in (15cm). The fabric for piping should be cut on the cross (diagonally) so it will be necessary to join the fabric sections together to create the correct piping length (see The workshop, page 211).

Making the piping

Cut the heavyweight wadding for the piping into 6in (15cm) wide strips. The total length of the strips should match the length of the piping fabric. Roll the strips up and stitch loosely to hold in place. Lay out binding fabric, wrong side up. Position the rolls of wadding along the length of the binding, butting the ends together. Wrap the fabric around the wadding so the raw edges match and baste in place along the length. This line of basting will be the seam line of the piping. Trim seam allowance to ⅝in (1.5cm).

Sewing the piping to the fabric

Lay piping along the right side of the top mattress section with the raw edges lying flush with the raw edge of the mattress section. Baste piping to the fabric edges and machine stitch in place along the line of basting stitches. Lay the wadding on the wrong side of the mattress and baste in place, making a grid of stitches across the mattress.

Joining mattress sections

With right sides together, baste the front section to the under section of the mattress. Sew together along the same stitching line as the piping, leaving an opening of approximately 8in (20cm) in one short edge. Press, turning back and pressing seam allowances along opening at the same time. Trim and notch seam allowance and turn to right side. Hand stitch opening closed.

Sewing on the buttons

Mark out positions of buttons equally on the top of the mattress. An appropriate number for an average sun lounger would be eight, four down each side. If you are using covered buttons, cut pieces of fabric and cover the buttons, following the manufacturer's instructions. Stitch the buttons on firmly through all layers of fabric and wadding. Remove the grid of basting stitches. If making the mattress for a deck chair, sew on ribbon ties at the top corners and tie onto the top of the deck chair.

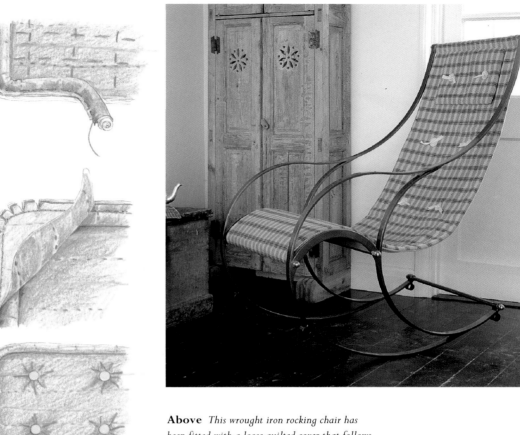

Below *A boxed garden bench in simple checked fabric provides a contrasting focal point to the floral themes in this sunny garden room.*

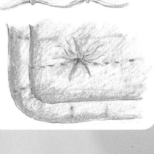

Above *This wrought iron rocking chair has been fitted with a loose quilted cover that follows its curvaceous seat. A matching head cushion in blue cotton check fabric has the same knotted effect – an effective alternative to buttoning.*

Optional Finishes

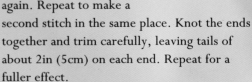

- Instead of using buttons to finish the mattress, take six strands of embroidery thread and stitch through all layers of the mattress from front to back and through to the front again. Repeat to make a second stitch in the same place. Knot the ends together and trim carefully, leaving tails of about 2in (5cm) on each end. Repeat for a fuller effect.
- For a tailored effect, use standard piping cord and 1in (2.5cm) wide bias-cut strips in place of stuffed piping.

6 Deck chair with head cushion

*T*ired or shabby looking director's chairs or deck chairs can be given a new lease of life with easy to make covers, or slings as they are often called. Narrow width deck chair fabric is available in many different patterns and colours, and its ready-finished selvedge eliminates the need for making any seams. However, it is possible to use other fabrics, of similar strength, in different patterns and colourways which can be cut and seamed to fit. Making a new cover for a deck chair from deck chair fabric actually requires no sewing at all, since the fabric is folded under at both ends and secured with rows of upholstery pins. Slings and covers for director's chairs do require sewing, but they are very simple to make.

Measurements
Size of cover This varies according to the size of the deck chair – add 20in (50cm) of fabric for the head pillow of a deck chair.

Suggested fabrics
Deck chair fabric or heavyweight canvas for both deck chairs and director's chair covers in plain colours or stripes.

Above right *A classic deck chair can be given a new lease of life with a bold cotton stripe cover with a comfortable head pillow.*

Below *You can create a striking effect by covering deck chairs in plain canvas in bold contrasting colours.*

Materials
Sufficient deck chair fabric or canvas of similar weight: standard fabric is available in a 18in (45cm) width • 25in (62.5cm) matching or contrasting fabric for pillow • Scissors and sewing equipment (see The workshop, pages 200–201) • Upholstery pins • Hammer • Matching sewing thread • Stick and sew touch-and-close fastening • Feather or foam filling for head pillow

Making deck chair cover and head pillow
To calculate the fabric length required for the deck chair, fold chair completely flat and measure the length of the chair from front lower edge of fixing bar, around bar, down to lower bar and around lower bar to front upper edge. Add approximately 8in (20cm) to this to allow for folding the fabric under the frame, and a further 25in (62.5 cm) of fabric for the head pillow.

Attaching fabric to upper fixing bar

Turn under 4in (10cm) at both ends of deck chair fabric. Position one folded edge level with front lower edge of fixing bar and tack in place with upholstery pins through folded fabric along underside of fixing bar.

Attaching fabric to lower fixing bar

Wrap fabric over bar and down the length of the chair. Check folded edge will wrap under lower fixing bar and fit tightly, then open chair out so that you can tack upholstery pins on the lower edge.

Sewing the head pillow

Fold the 20in (50cm) length of fabric with right sides together in half and sew both side seams together and for 1in (2.5cm) at each end of opening. Turn to right side and press remaining raw edges to inside of cover, then insert filling. Cut a piece of fabric the width of the pillow and 5in (12.5cm) wide. Turn under a ⅜in (1cm) wide double hem along two short edges and one long edge. Attach "sew" half of touch-and-close fastening to long hemmed edge, insert unfinished edge into opening in pillow cover and topstitch to close.

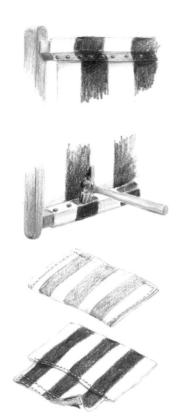

Above *Plain natural calico fabric has been used to make up this set of director's chair covers, inspired by the simple natural wood decor of this dining terrace.*

Making a director's chair cover

For a standard wooden director's chair you will need a piece of fabric measuring 25½ × 16in (65cm × 40cm) for the chair seat and another piece 25½ × 8in (65 × 20cm) for the back of the chair. Make a turning of ⅝in (1.5cm) along top and bottom (i.e. longer edges) of chair seat and repeat for chair back. Turn under 2in (5cm) at the shorter edge of each panel. Tack upholstery pins along one folded edge of fabric to hold in place under the side seat fixing bar, wrap fabric over the top of the bar, over the second fixing bar and around to underside. Tack folded edge firmly in place with upholstery pins. Repeat around side fixing bar to finish the chair back.

6 Windbreaks and rugs

*W*hen you are having a picnic on a beach you often find that you need some protection from the wind, so this windbreak is ideal to make if you regularly go to the beach. You could also make the picnic rug, with its PVC backing, and coordinate its colours with the windbreak.

Windbreak
This windbreak is simply constructed from a panel of fabric and four poles.

Measurements
Size of windbreak 40 x 42in (120 x 325cm)

Suggested fabrics
Use heavyweight canvas.

Materials
3¾yd (3.5m) of 48in-(120cm)-wide fabric plus ¾yd (70cm) of 48in-(120cm)-wide fabric for tabs • Scissors and sewing equipment (see The workshop, pages 200–201) • Matching sewing thread (bold or button-hole thread for strength) • 5 wooden poles 1in (2.5cm) diameter and 5ft (1.5m) long • 2¾yd (2.5m) of 1in-(2.5cm)-wide webbing for central pole tabs (sharpen the ends of poles a point to push them more easily into the sand. The dimensions allow for the posts to be pushed 12in (30cm) into the ground.

Sewing the top and bottom hems
Make a turning of ⅝in (1.5cm) along top and bottom edges of fabric and topstitch in place. Press flat. Lay fabric flat and divide into four equal sections and mark these on fabric.

Sewing the outside pole casings
Make a turning of ½in (12mm) then 2½in (6.5cm) down the outer edges of fabric to make a casing for the wooden poles and topstitch in place. Sew along top of casing to hold the pole in position. Then press.

Making the central pole tubes
Cut 3 strips of fabric, each 8 x 48in (20 x 120cm). Turn under and press a ⅝in (1.6cm) single hem across top and bottom of each strip. Stitch top and bottom hems in place by machine. Fold tab in half and stitch across top from the fold line, leaving 1 ¼in (3cm) free so you can turn under seam allowances.

Attaching the central pole tubes
Turn under and press a ⅝in (1.6cm) turning down each long edge of each strip and open flat. Pin the pole tubes to the windbreak down the marked lines, so that the top edge of the tube is aligned with the top edge of the windbreak. Baste in place, then stitch with a line of stitching down each seam allowance of each tube. You may have to roll up the main part of the windbreak to fit it under the arm of the sewing machine.

Right *A practical windbreak can also be covered to match outdoor furniture and picnic accessories. This windbreak cover has been made up in fresh blue check cotton to match the deck chair, while the Oxford cushion in a coordinating check features a matching border.*

Cutting out

Trim main fabric to a square 60 x 60in (150 x 150cm), removing fringe if using a ready-made rug. Cut backing fabric in half and join two side edges with a flat fell seam (see The workshop, page 205). Trim to same size as main fabric. Make up rug and check dimensions before cutting webbing. Cut two lengths of webbing measuring 22in (55cm) to go around the rolled rug, with an overlap of 2in (5cm) and turning allowance of 1in (2.5cm) at each end. Use remaining webbing for strap – it should be about 41in (105cm). Cut two pieces of touch-and-close fastening 1in (2.5cm) wide and 2in (5cm) long.

Backing the rug

With right sides together, stitch rug to backing fabric all around the edges, taking a ⅝in (1.5cm) seam. Leave an opening approximately 10in (25cm) long along one edge. Trim seam allowances and clip corners. Turn right side out and press edges. Along open edge, turn under and press seam allowance and baste. Topstitch around edge of rug, approximately ⅜in (1cm) from outer edge. Fold the rug in half with the woollen side inward, then fold it again along its length. Roll up the rug and then tie with two pieces of string to check how long the webbing carrier straps have to be.

Picnic rug and carrier

This picnic rug will brighten up any summer expedition. A practical PVC backing means that it can be used on damp ground, and it rolls up neatly so you can carry it with a custom-made strap. The carrier is fastened with touch-and-close fastening, but you can use buttons or buckles if preferred.

Measurements

The size of the rug 60 x 60in (150 x 150cm) rolling up to a bundle about 15in (37.5cm) long with a 40in (100cm) carrying strap.

Materials

1¾ yd (1.50m) of 60in-(150cm)-wide heavyweight fabric, or use a ready-made rug • 3½yd (3.20m) of 36in-(90cm)-wide waterproof backing fabric • Scissors and sewing equipment (see The workshop, pages 200–201) • 2½yd (2.3m) webbing, 1in-(2.5cm-wide) • ⅛yd (10cm) touch-and close fastening • Matching sewing thread

Suggested fabrics

Plaid or tartan check wool, blanketing, heavy-weave cotton fabric, such as waffle-effect cotton. For backing, use water-resistant cotton, PVC or thin nylon fabric. For the carrier, try making it out of some cotton or nylon webbing.

Sewing the fastening to the straps

Peel open touch-and-close fastening into two separate pieces. Turn under 1in (2.5cm) to wrong side of strap at one end of each shorter piece of webbing. Position fastening over folded end and topstitch one piece of the fastening over the turnings of both straps. At other end of straps, turn webbing to right side and stitch fastening in place.

Making the carrying strap

Turn under 1in (2.5cm) at each end of carrying strap. Stitch folded ends of carry strap to the centre of shorter straps, with wrong side of carrying strap facing right side of the shorter straps.

Above *The bright checks of this colourful picnic rug, backed with a waterproof PVC lining, are ideal for a summer picnic lunch.* **Inset** *A simple carrying strap makes transporting the rug extremely easy.*

6 Garden rooms

Garden rooms in your home can form a distinctive link between an indoor living space and the outside garden, terrace or patio. By using colours such as china blue, white and primrose yellow you can add a lovely, natural freshness and lightness to the room. This colour scheme may have been carried through from the inside rooms or hallway in the house, or be a different darker or lighter tone of a colour already used. The furnishings for this room could also be worked effectively in other colours such as apple green and white, terracottas and golds, or neutral creams and beiges, depending on the decorating style that you want to create.

Planning the layout

You can base the room's layout on the traditional arrangement of a sitting room, with a coffee table situated between the sofa and armchairs, or you can make a separate dining area. By bringing garden furniture inside the room, you keep the link with the garden. The furniture can then be painted with an oil-based matt eggshell paint or decorated with paint-effect techniques to blend with your soft furnishing scheme. Either choose colours to match and coordinate with your fabrics and furnishings, or paint the furniture in bold contrasting colours to counteract the tones and patterns already existing in the fabrics.

The focal point of this room is the large antique garden seat which has been painted in deep cobalt blue. The soft furnishings for the seat have been made up in a combination of all the prints and designs used throughout the room. The box mattress and matching bolsters are piped in primrose yellow cord echoing the tone of the curtains, while a selection of wide border and cord-edged cushions are made up in fabric to match the Roman blinds and the draped curtain. The overall effect of using soft seating with plenty of wide

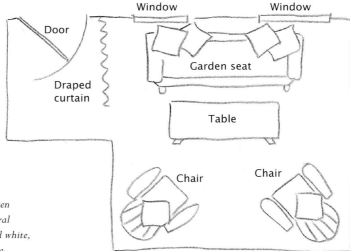

This garden room has been created using a fresh floral theme in China blue and white, highlighted with delicate touches of primrose yellow. The different tones of blue with white also give the room a subtle seaside feel. A combination of floral and striped patterns have been carried through from the wallpaper to the fabrics to give an informal yet completely coordinated look to the room. The use of two very different wall treatments — wallpaper and painted tongue and groove wood boards — also emphasize the formal and informal elements present in this scheme. The light, airy feeling of the room is then further enhanced by the white paint on the floorboards.

border and cord-edged scatter cushions and bolsters gives the room a comfortable, relaxing feel.

The floral-printed Roman blinds used here are ideal for a garden room as they allow maximum light into the room when raised, but necessary shade when lowered. Be sure to line the blinds to protect the fabric from bleaching in sunlight.

Using accessories

Accessories can also help to enhance a garden room. They can perhaps follow a favourite theme — the one used here has a seaside flavour with carved wooden seagulls. You could expand this theme by adding a display of shells, or using a group of favourite pictures or even holiday photographs, highlighting one of the fabric colours in particular.

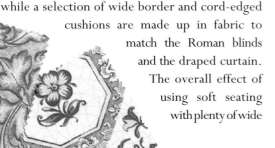

7 Linens

Linens

*L*inens – to use on both the table and the bed – have, historically, been highly prized and were handed down through generations of families, especially if these heirlooms were beautifully embroidered or very luxurious. Nowadays, people

prefer easy-care linens and choose fabrics that are simple to wash and press. But this does not limit the range of lovely fabrics, and finishings available.

Making table linens is a special opportunity for the person who sews at home. Not only can you transform a less than perfect table, but you will find they are simple to make and can be decorated and edged in a variety of ways.

Creating your own bed linen designs gives you a great opportunity to have things exactly as you want them. A bedroom is usually a personal retreat where you can indulge yourself more than in the rest of the house. The bed is usually the largest item in the room and is therefore the main focal point, so your choice of bed linen is a very important part of the room scheme.

Duvets have revolutionized bed making, but some people still prefer the full layered look and enjoy making comforters, quilts, coloured blankets, decorative sheets, throws, cushions and bolsters.

Traditional lace, hand embroidery and woven check, striped and printed fabrics all make ideal bed and table linens. Provided the fabrics are practical enough for their purpose (of all the soft furnishings, linens usually need the most frequent laundering), then a wide range of designs and effects are available for you to experiment with. Historically, needlewomen have produced fabulously creative linens, such as decorated quilts and beautifully embroidered tablecloths. Look at collections in museums and study specialist books for further inspiration.

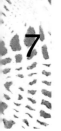

7 Table linen

The marvellous thing about tablecloths is that they can transform any old table, even a simple one made from chipboard, into a beautiful object. Tablecloths are an ideal project, even if you are new to sewing, as they are so easy to make. They can also be decorated with different edgings and trims.

Choosing fabric for table linens

Unless you want the cloth to be purely decorative, table linen fabric really needs to be washable and in a wide width to avoid joins – sheeting fabric is ideal. Washable dress fabric is an alternative but it usually only comes in narrow widths, so you will have to join it (see pages 74–75). You can also use furnishing fabric for decorative cloths if you wish it to coordinate with other soft furnishings, but again you will have to join it and it is likely to need to be dry cleaned.

Making tablecloths and napkins

If the fabric is not the full width of the cloth, you will have to join widths. Avoid a seam in the centre of the cloth as it looks rather prominent and can unbalance crockery. Instead have a whole width of fabric in the middle of the table and sew half or whole widths on either side. Ideally the seams should be in the overhang of the cloth. You will need to add ⅝in (1.5cm) seam allowance to each edge where there is a seam, and use flat fell seams for durability (see The workshop, page 205). You will also need to allow extra fabric for matching large patterns (see page 75).

Once you have made any necessary joins in the fabric, turn in ½in (1.25 cm) all round to the wrong side and then the same amount again. For napkins, turn in ⅜in (1cm) double hems. Press, then open out the corners to trim and mitre them (see The workshop, page 213). Topstitch by machine, close to the hem edge then slipstitch the mitred corners closed.

PVC-coated fabrics make great coverings for tables, both indoors and out, that get a lot of hard use. There is also the benefit that the fabric does not fray so there is no need for hemming or finishing. As PVC is not suitable for napkins, there is usually non-coated coordinating fabric available to make these from.

Measurements for tablecloths and napkins

Either measure up a tablecloth that you already have that fits your table, or measure the length and width of the table top and then decide how long you want the cloth to be. If you want it to be lap length, sit on a chair at the table and measure from the top of the table to your lap. For a long cloth measure from the table top to the floor. Add twice the length measurement plus 2in (5cm) for hem allowances to your table length and width measurements. If you want to bind the edge or add some braid you don't need to add extra for a hem.

Napkins are usually square and can be any size from 12in (30cm) square for teatime napkins to 24in (60 cm) square for dinner napkins – 16in (40cm) is a good compromise. Choose fairly absorbent fabric that is easily washable, and allow 1½in (4cm) for hems in each direction. For other ideas as to how to finish the napkins, see the box opposite.

Right *However big or small your table and whether the setting is formal or informal, table linen brings lots of extra colour and interest, and can be bought to match the room's decorative scheme. Large tables will need very wide fabric, so to avoid joins, look for wide-width fabrics such as sheeting.*

Right *Circular tables look best with a circular cloth. These are not difficult to make and the fabric can coordinate with the curtains. As curved hems can be tricky to sew, circular cloths often have trims or binding, or you can add a contrasting edge in a different fabric.*

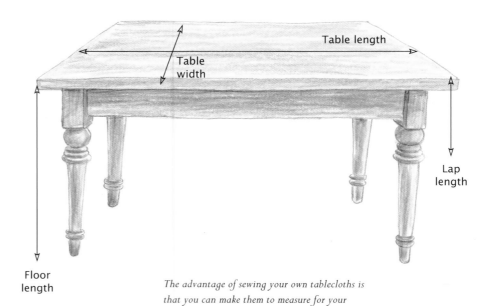

The advantage of sewing your own tablecloths is that you can make them to measure for your tables, and you can choose your fabrics and designs to suit your own decor.

Edging table linen

Tablecloths can be finished with a plain hand-sewn or machined hem, but you can also add a decorative touch at this stage, with embroidery, binding, braid or trimmings. Before you use any type of edging, check that it is pre-shrunk, colourfast and washable, if you plan to use it on a cloth that will be washed.

• Fringing is suitable for fabric with a moderately loose weave. Cut fabric to size, then machine zig-zag stitch all round the napkin about 1in (2.5cm) in from the edge. Working on one side at a time, pull out threads around 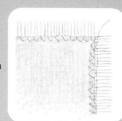 the edges until you meet the stitching. Use a pin if the threads don't come out easily at first.

• Satin stitch can be used to emphasize a hem. Make the tablecloth or napkin as described, mitring the corners and machine topstitching close to the hem edge, then set your machine on a wide, close satin stitch and, using a contrasting coloured machine embroidery cotton, centre the satin stitching along the hem line. Other fancy machine embroidery stitches can be used in this way for ornamental borders.

• Lace can add a delicate touch. You can use broderie anglaise, cotton or nylon lace, preferably flat woven with pre-finished edges. It looks better if the corners are mitred. Make a narrow hem along the tablecloth's or napkin's edge, then machine or hand stitch the lace in position, overlapping it with the edge slightly. When you reach the corners make a diagonal pleat at 45° to allow the lace to lie flat. Machine or oversew along the crease then trim off any excess. Join the pieces of lace at the corner.

7 Tablecloths and napkins

Making your own tablecloths and napkins can be very rewarding as you are creating something unique, but be careful when choosing an appropriate binding that it can washed in the same way as the main fabric: some ready-made bindings are not colourfast, and many are made from lightweight cottons that may not wear particularly well.

Rectangular tablecloth and napkins

A rectangular tablecloth is simple to make and this bound-edged version can look impressive on a dining table, and allows you to introduce a striking, contrasting colour. By sewing some matching napkins you can really make a stunning dining set.

Measurements

Size of tablecloth Follow instructions for measuring up (see pages 164–165), but add no extra fabric for hems. Fabric quantity is for six napkins, 16in (40cm) square.

Right *This tartan tablecloth and matching napkins with bound edges are perfect for an elegant dining room setting.*

Above *Binding adds a smartly tailored finish to a napkin, in matching or contrasting colours.*

Suggested fabrics

Sheeting fabric, washable dress fabric, furnishing fabric and coordinating cottons.

Materials

Sufficient fabric to make up the cloth, plus 1yd (80cm) of 48in-(120cm)-wide fabric for napkins • Scissors and sewing equipment (see The workshop, pages 200–201) • contrasting fabric for binding (enough to go round both tablecloth and napkins) • Matching sewing thread

Cutting out and joining fabric

Cut one panel of fabric for the tablecloth, omitting hem allowance. Use flat fell seams if you need to join widths. Cut six panels of fabric for napkins, each 16in (40cm) square. For the tablecloth, cut four strips of straight binding in a coordinating colour, each 2½in (6.5cm) wide and the same length as each side of the cloth, plus 1⅛in (3cm). You may need to join fabric to get a strip long enough. For each napkin, cut four lengths of binding, 2½in (6.5cm) wide and 17in (43cm) long.

Above *A pretty circular tablecloth can transform even a plain occasional table. Add a glass top to protect the cloth from dust and dirt. Your local glazier will cut it to size and polish the edges.*

Making a round tablecloth

Measure the diameter of the top of the round table and then decide how long you want the cloth to be. For lap length, sit on a chair at the table and measure from the top to your lap. For a long, cloth measure from the edge of the table to the floor (see Measurements for tablecloths and napkins, page 164). Add twice the length to the diameter of the table top, plus 1⅛in (2.8cm) for a narrow hem. Omit this if you wish to bind the edge.

Cutting out

Cut a square of fabric to this size. If you have to join widths of fabric, use a full-width panel at the centre, with narrower strips on either side, to avoid seams on the table top. Fold the square in four to form a smaller square. Cut a piece of paper to this folded size and using an improvised compass made from a drawing pin, a pencil and a length of string, hold the pencil upright and draw a quarter circle the radius of the finished cloth. Pin this pattern onto the fabric and cut through all layers. Open out to reveal a circle.

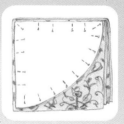

Preparing the binding

Fold binding in half lengthwise, wrong sides inward, and press. Turn in long raw edges to meet the middle.

Binding opposite edges

Apply binding along two opposite edges of the cloth, as described in The workshop, (see pages 212–213). Trim ends of the binding level with the cloth's edge.

Binding remaining edges

Apply the remaining two lengths, positioning them so they extend ⅝in (1.5cm) to either side. Before topstitching the binding in place, fold over the raw edges of the binding so that they are enclosed when you fold the fabric to the wrong side. Oversew the corners by hand for a neat finish. Alternatively, mitre the binding at the corners, (see The workshop, page 213). To make the napkins, follow the same instructions.

Finishing the hems

To finish the edge, either neaten the edge with an overlocker or a zig-zag stitch on a normal machine, then sew on braid or fringing (see page 96). Or you can edge the tablecloth with one continuous strip of bias binding (see Bed linen pages 168–169), or hem with a narrow hem. To hem, machine around the cloth ⅝in (1.5cm) from the raw edge, then turn under the fabric's edge so that the stitching is just on the wrong side. Press in place, easing the fabric as you go. Turn raw edge under a further ¼in (6mm), press then baste in place and either machine stitch close to the fold or hand hem. For a faced circular hem, see The workshop pages 206–207.

7 Bed linen

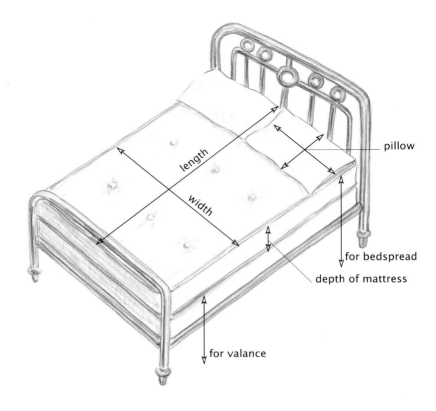

With so many beautiful ranges of bed linen in the shops it may seem that there is no need to make your own, but there are times when it makes good sense. Bed linen is very easy to make as it is all straight seams, and it does save money to make your own. Also, as the bed is the most dominant part of your bedroom scheme it can be the perfect way to make sure you get exactly the colours and fabrics you want. Making your own linen also allows you to coordinate fabrics and add your own special decorative touches. While you can embellish ready-made linen, it is much easier to do when you make your own, especially with pillowcases and duvet covers.

Choosing fabric for bed linen

Apart from bed spreads, comforters and valances, ordinary furnishing fabrics are not normally suitable for making bed linen because they feel just too coarse next to the skin.

• Pure linen is the most luxurious choice – it feels lovely and cool in summer as well as being strong and durable. To say linen will last a lifetime is not a total exaggeration, but it is expensive, creases badly, is time consuming to iron and not widely available.

• Pure cotton is the next choice for luxury and comfort, although unless it is 'easy care', it too needs pressing.

• Egyptian cotton is superior to ordinary cotton, having longer, finer fibres than average, while percale is made from very fine threads which make a delicate, more luxurious fibre.

• Cotton flannelette has a warm, fluffy surface which makes it suitable for winter sheets.

• Cotton polyester is non-shrink, hard-wearing and takes less looking after than natural fibres. It is also less expensive, but it does not have the same softness, absorbency and quality as pure cotton. Look for blends with high proportions of cotton.

Measuring up for bed linen

Sheeting fabric is very durable and is made extra-wide to avoid having to sew any unnecessary seams. Sheeting comes in a 70in (178cm) width for single beds and 90in (230cm) for double beds. Extra-wide fabric for larger beds, 104in (264cm) and 108in (275cm) is also available but can be harder to find in stores. To measure for a flat sheet, first measure the mattress in each direction and add extra for tuck-ins and hems Measure the pillows from seam to seam to find the finished cover dimensions.

Left *Patchwork (or 'pieced') quilts are often prized as works of art and some become heirlooms that are passed down through the generations. Look out for museums that have good collections of inspirational antique designs.*

Seam allowances will depend on the type of seams and opening that you choose, and whether you include a border. Duvets should also be measured from seam to seam in each direction. Standard dimensions of beds and bed linen are given on page 224.

Making pillowcases, sheets and duvets

As these items will be washed frequently, they should be sewn with French seams which encase the raw edges inside the item and prevents them fraying (see The workshop, page 205). If you have an overlocking machine you can serge or overlock seam allowances. For making pillow cases and cushion covers, see pages 120–121 and 122–123.

Making a flat sheet

Measure the length, width and depth of the mattress. To the length and width add twice the depth plus 20in (50cm) for a single sheet and 24in (60cm) for a double sheet. Make two side turnings along the long edges toward the wrong side, first turning under ¼in (5mm) then ⅜in (1cm). Machine them neatly in place. Turn the top edge ⅜in (1cm) to the wrong side, turn another 2in (5cm) then machine. You can decorate this edge with machine or hand embroidery or appliqué (see pages 166–167) if preferred. Turn the bottom edge ¼in (5mm) then 1in (2.5cm) to the wrong side and machine stitch in place.

Valance

Measure the length and the width of the bed, and also the height from the bed base to the floor. For the flat panel, cut out a piece that is 1¼ in (3.2cm) larger than the bed in each direction. For the depth of the valance side panels, add 2⅝in (6.7cm) to the height. Cut out two panels that are 1½ times the length of the bed and two panels that are 1½ times the width. Cut and join the valance strips, using French seams, to make a continuous loop. Along the lower edge, turn up a 1in (2.5cm) double hem and stitch this by machine. Then run lines of gathering stitch along the top edge of the valance and draw up so that each section fits one side of the main panel. With right sides together, position the frill for the valance around the main panel, matching the corner seams of the frill with the corners of the main panel. Press and trim the seams, then zig-zag the raw edges to make a really durable finish.

Making a duvet cover

Measure the length and width of duvet using a cloth tape. Double the length and add 6in (15cm). Add 4in (10cm) to width and cut some fabric to this size. You can decorate the cover at this point. Turn two short ends under ⅜in (1cm) toward the wrong side and machine in place. Fold fabric in half widthwise across the centre, wrong sides together. Make a French seam down each long side. Then turn to wrong side and sew in from either side parallel to the hemmed edges for 10in (25cm), 1in (2.5 cm) above lower edge. Turn cover right sides out — clip corners to make turning easier — and sew a closing in place in the gap. This can either be snap fastener tape (use a zipper foot to sew this on), individual snap fasteners, touch-and-close fastening dots, tape ties or buttons. Space them evenly and make sure they are opposite each other. If using a zip, insert it before sewing the side seams.

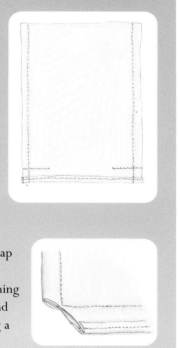

Below *Look for washable, wide-width fabric for bed linen: sheeting fabric is best as it is designed to be used against the skin. Furnishing fabrics are only suitable for comforters and bedspreads.*

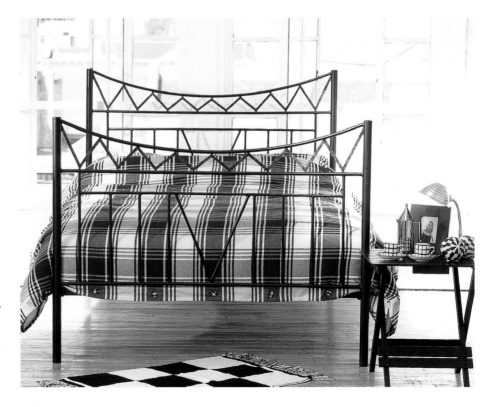

7 Decorative edging

Bed linen can be personalized simply, but very effectively, by adding an appliqué border. It is easier to do this while you are actually making the linen (see pages 168–169), but you can also add your own touch to bought sheets, pillowcases and duvet covers. Keep decoration to the turned-down edge of sheets and close to the open edge of pillowcases, as this makes it more comfortable to sleep on. The word appliqué comes from the French meaning 'to apply' and involves fixing coloured fabric shapes onto a background fabric to create a bold design.

Above *This machine appliqué rope twist pattern looks striking in deep blue, grey and red and gives a uniquely personal touch to a bought sheet and pillow case.*

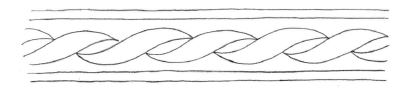

Bed linen with appliqué edging

You can make your bed linen unique and distinctive by adding an attractive appliqué design.

Measurements
Size of sheet and pillowcases Fabric quantities are given for edging a ready-made double sheet and two standard housewife-style pillowcases.

Suggested fabrics
Sheeting fabric, dressmaking polyester cotton, use a similar weight of fabric for appliqué as sheeting, plus a similar fibre content. Look for fabrics that wash well, press crisply, do not fray easily, are colourfast and pre-shrunk.

Materials
½yd (45cm) of 36in-(90cm)-wide fabric in each of three contrast colours • Tracing paper and pencil • Dressmaker's carbon paper • Thin paper or card for templates • Scissors and sewing equipment (see The workshop, pages 200–201) • Fusible webbing • Matching or contrasting sewing thread

Planning the design
Following the instructions on page 215, enlarge the template to actual size (shown here at 40 percent of actual size) and transfer onto a piece of tracing paper. Use the tracing to check how the pattern will fit onto a pillowcase or flat sheet. The edge of the blue strip should be 1¼in (3cm) from the edge of a pillowcase, and 1½in (4cm) from the turndown edge of a sheet (this may need to be adjusted on ready-made sheets according to seam positions). When satisfied, mark the pattern onto the item to be appliquéed using dressmaker's carbon paper (see The workshop, page 215).

Making templates

Transfer the main pattern shape onto thin paper or card to make a pattern. Cut three or four templates of the same size so that you do not have to cut more if the first piece becomes bent around the edges. Mark the grain lines on the shapes as these should run in the same direction as the fabric onto which it is sewn.

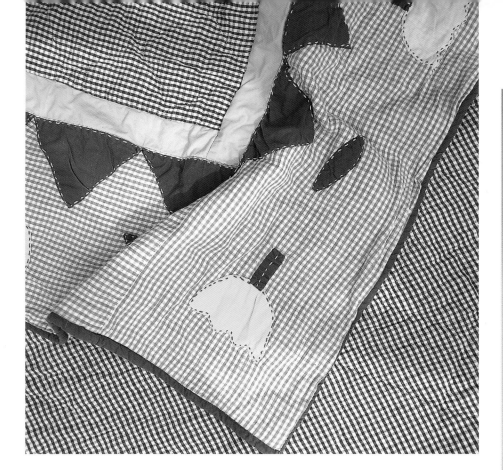

Alternative appliqué techniques

By machine – If the fabric will not fray, cut the shapes to size without fusible webbing and baste them in place. Machine around the edge with a narrow zig-zag stitch before going round again with a closer satin stitch. If the fabric frays, cut the fabric pieces slightly larger all round than the finished pattern pieces. Cut backing pieces from lightweight iron-on interfacing, omitting seam allowances. Press interfacing onto the back of the appliqué pieces. Baste in place on the main fabric, then stitch all round with narrow zig-zag stitch. Trim seam allowances from appliqué shapes close to stitching line and stitch with satin stitch.

Hand-backing motifs

For best results, cut the shapes ¼in (6mm) bigger all round than the pattern. Turning in this allowance is easier if you cut the actual shape excluding the  allowance in fine interfacing and press it onto the centre back of each shape. Test interfacing first on scrap fabric as some fabrics can pucker.

Turning under edges

Clip curves and awkward shapes by snipping almost up to the interfacing. Turn under allowance, press in place, baste if necessary, and baste the shapes in position on the backing fabric.

Stitching

Sew neatly around the shapes with tiny slipstitches or buttonhole stitch (see The workshop, pages 206 and 217).

Finishing

You can also topstitch close to the edge with some small running stitches. Remove any basting stitches.

Cutting out

Back the appliqué fabric with fusible webbing. Position a template on the paper backing and mark out the design, checking that the grain lines are straight. Repeat to mark sufficient shapes in each fabric colour to complete your design. Cut out all the shapes. For the edges of the design, cut enough strips (with fusible webbing backing) ⅜in (1cm) wide to go twice across the sheet or pillowcase opening.

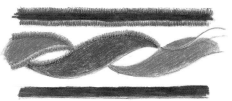

Positioning and stitching

Remove paper backing from the webbing and arrange the shapes in position on the bed linen. Iron in position, then stitch around the edges of the shapes, using a closed-up zig-zag stitch (satin stitch) or other embroidery stitch.

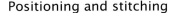

Appliqué tip

To make it easier to work the appliqué on a ready-made pillowcase, unpick the seams for 6in (15cm) on either side of the opening. When you have finished the appliqué, turn pillowcase inside out and fold in the tuck-in flap before re-stitching the seams.

Above *Hand-sewn appliqué has a wonderful folk-art quality to it, so do not worry if your stitches are not perfectly uniform as it just adds to the charm and shows that your piece of work is very unique.*

7 Quilts and comforters

Although furnishing fabric is not normally used to make bed linen such as sheets or duvets, it is ideal for making a comforter or throw for a bed. It will also give a luxurious, fully coordinated look to a bedroom scheme if you use fabric from the same range as the other soft furnishings in the room.

Making a quilted comforter

This comforter is quilted to pick out the fabric design, but the quilting is not just decorative, it also holds the fabric and wadding layers together in the quilt.

Measurements

Size of quilted comforter For a standard double bed, about 20in (50cm) high plus bedding, the overall dimensions should be 100in square (250cm). See note on measuring up below.

Suggested fabrics

Lightweight furnishing fabric, such as glazed cotton. For the lining, use curtain lining fabric. You will also need polyester wadding – light- or mediumweight is easier to work with.

Materials

6¾yd (6m) of at least 54in-(135cm)-wide main fabric (allow extra for matching patterns) • 5¾yd (5m) lining fabric • Scissors and sewing equipment (see The workshop, pages 200–201) • 8½yd (7.80m) of 36in- (90cm)-wide polyester wadding (or 5¾yd (5m) of wide wadding) • Matching and contrasting sewing thread • Large number of safety pins, preferably quilting pins • Paper pattern • Piece of string, pencil and drawing pin

Cutting out and joining widths

In the main fabric, cut a panel the length of the finished bedspread. Check the pattern match before cutting a second panel the same length. Cut the second panel in half lengthwise, and join each half width to either side of the main panel using flat fell seams. Cut the wadding into three lengths and join the panels by butting edges together and sewing them by hand with herringbone stitch. Cut remaining main fabric into 4in (10cm) wide bias strips, joining the strips to make a total of about 12yd (10.50m).

Preparing the quilt

Lay the lining fabric out on a flat surface, wrong side up, lay the wadding on top and then the main fabric right side up. Make sure all the edges align. Pin the three layers together randomly all across the quilt. Safety pins are ideal for this, especially if you can find some curved quilting pins. Make a paper pattern of a quarter circle, the radius of which is the height of the bed. To do this, make a compass from a piece of string, a pencil and a drawing pin. Use the pattern to round off the bottom two corners of all the layers of the quilt.

Basting the layers together

Baste down the centre line of the quilt and then across the middle, next go across the quarter lines and the diagonals and all round close to the edge of the quilt. Avoid basting close to where the quilting stitches will be as the machine's presser foot may get caught in the stitches. Carefully remove all the pins.

Left *A traditional bedstead provides the perfect setting for this comforter. Quilting is used to highlight the design of the floral fabric.*

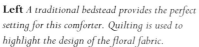

Left *Comforters are great for children's rooms as you can use bold fabric and they are really cosy. Single bed quilts are also easier to make than larger sizes.*

Alternative ideas for quilting

If you do not wish to go to the trouble of machine quilting around a design, try these other ideas for holding the layers of fabric and wadding together. Measure out the positions carefully first, marking with tailor's chalk or vanishing marker before you start sewing.

• Coloured buttons can be sewn onto the quilt through all thicknesses at intervals. They can be sewn in straight lines 8in (20cm) apart or with every other row staggered.

• Bows of coloured embroidery cotton can be sewn through the quilt with a backstitch and tied in reef knots at intervals. Stranded silk embroidery thread can also be used as the ends fray to form attractive tassels.

• Narrow embroidery ribbon, each piece measuring about 10in (25cm) long, can be threaded through a large-eyed needle and sewn through the quilt. Tie in a small bow, trim the ends if necessary and sew the knot firmly in place with small stitches in matching cotton.

• Quilting by hand is more time consuming than machine stitching, but is more manageable than trying to fit the quilt under a sewing machine and produces quite a different effect. Some people like to use a frame for quilting but if you baste the layers together well before you start your quilting you can manage without one. Use neat, small running stitches for the best effect.

Stitching the pattern

Fit a quilting foot to your machine, select a slightly longer than normal stitch and loosen the top tension slightly. Put the machine on a large table to support the quilt's weight. If your machine has dual feed, engage it. Roll up the quilt very tightly lengthwise and pull this rolled part under your sewing machine arm, so you work from left to right across the quilt, unrolling it gradually as you work. Sew around the main motifs in the design, keeping the work flat. Alternatively, make straight lines of stitching down the quilt's length. If you are doing stitch lines from top to bottom of the quilt, always work in the same direction.

Binding the edge

Press binding in half along its length and then press the raw edges in to meet the centre line, then open out flat again. Pin binding along the first crease line down the sides and across the lower edge of the quilt, right sides together with the raw edges level. Ease the binding around the bottom curved corners so it lies flat; be careful not to stretch it out of shape. Trim binding level with the top edge at the top corners. Baste binding in place close to first pressed fold. Machine along the fold, then press binding to the wrong side along the centre fold. Tuck in raw edge of the binding along the third fold and slipstitch binding in place on the back of the quilt (see The workshop, page 212).

Finishing the top edge

Repeat along top edge, except that the binding should extend beyond the quilt's edges by ⅝in (1.5cm) on either side. Machine binding in place, then tuck these extended pieces in before pressing the binding to the wrong side. Slipstitch the corners closed.

Measuring up for a quilt

Measure the bed with all the bedclothes and pillows in position. Measure the bed's length, add to this the bed's height from the top of the bedding to the floor. Measure the bed's width and add to that twice the height of the bed from the top of the bedding to the floor. This is the amount of top fabric and plain coordinating or contrast lining needed, plus extra top fabric to bind the edges.

7 Patchwork and appliqué

W*ith patchwork and appliqué you can make some stunning quilts. If one outlives its use, it can then take on a new life by converting it into a cheerful nursery wallhanging.*

Cot quilt

A decorative patchwork and appliqué quilt makes bedtime a much more exciting prospect for a young child.

Safety tip

Quilts should be hand washed, never dry cleaned. They are not suitable for babies under one year old.

Measurements

Size of finished quilt 36in (92cm) wide by 46½in (118 cm) long (seam allowances are ⅝in (1.5cm)). Always press seams open. Use either imperial or metric measurements, not both.

Suggested fabrics

Choose similar weight cotton fabrics of at least 43in (110cm) wide. Craft fabrics (from needlework shops) with a tiny pattern or small texture are ideal. Wash all fabrics to avoid later shrinkage.

Materials

⅝yd (0.50m) bright blue textured fabric • ⅝yd (0.50m) navy fabric with white stars • 3½yd (3 m) red and white spotted fabric • 1¾yd (1.50m) yellow fabric • ¼yd (15cm) blue and white spotted fabric • ⅝yd (0.50m) rusty orange fabric • ¼yd (20cm) off-white fabric with grey crackle pattern • Scraps of white fabric • 1⅜yd (1.20m) lightweight polyester wadding • Scissors and sewing equipment (see The workshop, pages 200–201) • Thin card for templates • Pencil • 1¾yd (1.50m) fusible webbing, at least 18in (45cm) wide • Sticky tape or masking tape • Machine embroidery thread in rusty orange, cherry red, grey and mid blue (for blue spotted fabric) • Skein each of bright blue and pale blue stranded embroidery cotton • Red machine thread • Large glass-headed pins or large safety pins • Red quilting thread

Right *A decorative patchwork and appliqué quilt makes bedtime a much more exciting prospect for a young child. A fun day time and night time theme inspired this colourful sun and moon cot quilt.*

Cutting out

Cut out the following fabric shapes: cut a card template of shapes A – J first and draw round it onto the fabric. The fabric's grain must run from top to bottom.

A	9 x 9in (23 x 23cm)
B	9 x 9in (23 x 23cm)
C	9 x 3½in (23 x 9cm)
D	9 x 3½in (23 x 9cm)
E	3½ x 3½in (9 x 9cm)
F	4½ x 4½in (11.5 x 11.5cm)
G	39 x 4½in (99 x 11.5cm)
H	30¾ x 4½in (77.9 x 11.5cm)
I	46¾ x 2¾in (118.9 x 7cm)
J	37¼ x 2¾in (94.5 x 7cm)

Preparing templates

Following the instructions on page 176, enlarge the templates, back the fabric with fusible webbing, and cut out the appliqué shapes for the suns and moons (you will need six of each).

Assembling the sun appliqué panels

Remove backing paper from each flame section of finished sun and iron it into position in the centre of each of the pale blue squares (A). Machine in rusty orange around edge of flame shapes with satin stitch. Near the points of the flames narrow the stitch to make turning easier. Centre the yellow sun faces on flame shapes, and press in place using a dry iron. Iron some fusible webbing onto the back of the white fabric and cut six mouth shapes, then iron in position. Machine embroider the eyebrows, nose and chin using the rusty orange, then embroider the mouth and cheeks in red. Sew eyes by hand with three strands of blue embroidery cotton in satin stitch.

Assembling the moon panels

Assemble the moon panels in the same way, stitching the face section to the blue spotty fabric (B) with white satin stitch, then adding the hat sections. Add a tiny scrap of white fabric for the mouth, fixing it in place with fusible webbing. Embroider the features by machine in dark grey and red.

Assembling the patchwork

Lay out pieces for quilt in correct order. Sew each row of suns and moons together, with a red strip (C) between each, using red machine thread. Sew the three rows of red strips (D) and yellow squares (E) together as shown. Join the four sun and moon strips together vertically, inserting a red and yellow strip between each one.

Adding the edging strips

Sew one red strip (F) onto either long side of the suns and moons rectangle. Make up two rows using a red strip (G) in the middle and sewing two blue spotty squares (H) on each end. Sew these onto the top and bottom of the rectangle.

Making up the quilt

Cut red spotted backing fabric to the same size as finished front. Lay out backing, wrong side up, place wadding on top and trim to same size as backing. Place quilt on top, right side up. Pin all layers together using large safety pins or curved quilting pins. Baste down the middle across the centre, along both diagonals and all round the edge close to raw edges. Machine with a medium-sized, straight stitch through all thicknesses along all straight seam lines using red quilting thread (engage dual feed if your machine has one).

Binding the side edges

Press I binding strips in half lengthwise (wrong sides together) and then open out again. Sew two longer strips up long sides, working on quilt's front, with right sides together and one raw edge and both ends of strip level with the raw edges of quilt. Fold strip to back of quilt along centre fold, press the raw edge under by ⅝in (1.5cm) along whole length. Pin and oversew in place on wrong side (back) of quilt.

Binding ends and finishing corners

Sew J end strips on similarly, with ⅝in (1.5cm) extending on either side. Fold in two ⅝in (1.5cm) overlaps, then fold strip to back, and sew in place as before. Oversew open corners with tiny stitches. Remove visible basting.

Above *A comforter can be quilted in straight lines, as shown here, if preferred. If your sewing machine has dual feed always engage this for quilting work, and sew parallel lines in the same direction. You can also add a frill around the edge of a comforter for extra interest.*

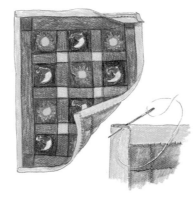

7 # Templates

H*ere are the sun and moon motifs for the cot quilt. Instructions for making up the quilt and using these patterns are on pages 174 and 175. You need to make six appliqué panels of each design.*

Cut out the shapes for the appliqué motifs and assemble each one before joining the patches together. The motifs shown here are 25 percent of the finished size of the appliqué patches.

Preparing the templates

Enlarge sun and moon pictures using a grid (see The workshop, page 215) so that the sun's finished diameter is 7in (17cm) and the moon measures 6½in (16.5cm) from top to bottom. Cut templates for the sun's flame shape, the sun's centre, the moon's face, the moon's hat, plus a circle 8in (20cm) in diameter.

Cutting out fabric for sun appliqué

Cut out six rusty orange fabric circles with the 8in (20cm) template and back them with fusible webbing. Place sun flame template wrong side up on back of each circle and draw around template onto the webbing's backing paper with pencil. Cut around the flame shapes. Iron sufficient fusible webbing onto the back of the yellow fabric then cut out six sun centres. Trace embroidery lines for the faces through the fabric with the marker pen. This is easier if you stick the fabric and pattern with sticky tape on a well-lit window.

Cutting out fabric for moon appliqué

Do the same with the moon, cutting the hat from the blue and white spotted fabric and the moon from grey crackle print fabric. Assemble the appliqué panels and complete the quilt as described on the previous page.

8 Accessories

Accessories

Finishing touches and small accessories can have a huge impact on a room, and if you make them yourself, they will give lots of lasting pleasure. It is the details that are included in a room that make it so personal and so unique.

Fabric-made accessories are a perfect way to add some dashes of colour and texture. The colour can be chosen to extend an overall decorating theme by adding a lighter or deeper tone. For a more eye-catching effect, make them in a dazzling contrasting colour. Soft furnishing accessories contrast well with the harder surfaces of wood, glass and ceramics.

Lining a basket in a cheerful gingham, making a laundry bag in an attractive fabric or attempting a pretty sprigged fabric lampshade are all excellent ways to try out your basic sewing skills. Once you have mastered the technique, you can try adding patchwork, appliqué or embroidery to these homely items. Most accessories are small and require only small pieces of fabric so they need not be costly. Inexpensive fabric remnants are normally more than enough for most projects. This way, you can also indulge in some luxurious fabrics such as silk, scraps of antique lace or why not recycle the fabric from a favourite old garment?

Accessories can have a great effect on a room. They can give it individuality and style, and they can help to emphasize a specially chosen colour scheme. Making your own will also give your home a very personal look too.

8 Laundry bag

A drawstring bag is the most straightforward of items to make up. In its smallest form it can be a scented bag to hold lavender or herbs to add a wonderful perfume to drawers. Make up a medium-sized bag and it will be ideal for keeping shoes separate from clothes in a suitcase or for carrying trainers to and from the gym. A large version is perfect for laundry. Fabrics such as gingham and ticking stripes will give a crisp country style or to add a more romantic feel, use silk, velvet or damask. Remember that light-weight fabrics will draw up better than thick ones.

Measurements
Finished bag is 17 × 27in (45 × 69cm)

Suggested fabrics
Light- or mediumweight furnishing cotton or linen; striped ticking or a fabric to coordinate with bathroom curtains or bathrobes.

Materials
1yd (1m) of 36in-(90cm)-wide fabric • Paper, pencil and ruler to make a pattern • Scissors and sewing equipment (see The workshop, pages 200–201) • Matching sewing thread • 2yd (1.90m) cord for the drawstrings

Making a pattern and cutting out
Make a paper pattern measuring 18 x 30½in (47 x 77cm) and use to cut out two pieces of fabric. 5½in (14cm) from the top edge on either side of both pieces of fabric make ½in (1cm) cuts. The fabric above this point will be used as the heading.

Preparing the casing
Make a ½in (1cm) turning to the wrong side along the top edge of one piece of the fabric and press. Turn over ½in (1cm) either side above the cuts and press.

Left *This charmingly childish matching set of drawstring bags are the perfect size for storing children's toys and accessories.*

Above *A drawstring bag can take on many guises. These robust bags, in a pretty Provençal print, are ideal for holding laundry or tidying up smaller bedroom items.*

Optional ideas

• Line the bag with a waterproof fabric so that it can be used as a soapbag or for a swimsuit. Cut out two pieces of waterproof fabric to same size as the outer fabric. Baste to the wrong side of each piece of fabric and proceed as opposite.

• Instead of sewing the casing for the cord, fix on metal eyelets and slot the cord through.

• A tiny drawstring bag made from a scrap of velvet or silk will hold precious jewellery pieces safely.

• Store bulky balls and half-made handknits of wool in a large bag to keep them orderly and looking decorative until the last stitch has been cast off.

• Add appliqué or embroidery detailing to your bag for a decorative finish.

Right *A useful laundry bag, which can be hung at the end of the bed, becomes an attractive part of the entire room scheme when it is made up in a matching type of fabric.*

Stitching the casing

Turn over the top edge again so that it is level with the cuts. Machine stitch close along this folded edge and also 1¼in (3cm) above it to make the casing for the cord. Repeat this method on the other piece of fabric.

Making up the bag

To make up the bag, take the two fabric pieces and with right sides together and edges matching, machine stitch a ½in (1cm) seam along the sides and bottom edge. Turn to the right side and press.

Threading the cords

Thread one length of cord through from the right to the left of the front casing, then back from left to right in the back casing and tie the ends. The second cord goes through in the opposite direction so that the knots are on opposite sides.

Cross stitch motif

A pretty cotton bag, with a cross stitch motif, is the perfect way to present a gift, as these sweet mice on the small bag below clearly indicate. You need to embroider the initial motif before you make up the bag. Mark the position of the initial with the marker pen in the centre of the bag. Thread the tapestry needle with embroidery thread, but do not tie a knot. Work the loose end into the back later. Work along the top row of the initial in even diagonal stitches, then stitch back across them to make the cross stitches. Work along each section making sure that the direction of the top stitches is the same throughout. Make up the bag as opposite using even-weave fabric and tape to match the embroidery thread.

8 Lined basket

An ordinary basket can be transformed with a fabric lining into an attractive and useful container. Use one to store baby changing necessities in the nursery, to organize perfume and make-up on the dressing table, to hold sewing equipment, or to serve bread on the dining table. You can add a frill around the edge, trim it with lace, or simply bind the edges with a bias-cut strip. We have used quilted fabric, which holds its shape well and adds a soft finish to the lining.

Suggested fabrics

Lightweight quilted fabric plus a small piece of matching unquilted fabric for the optional elasticated straps, or cotton fabric plus wadding and backing to quilt your own fabric.

Materials

Fabric • Basket • Paper and pencil to make a pattern • A pair of compasses • Scissors and sewing equipment (see The workshop, pages 200–201) • Matching sewing thread • ¼yd (20cm) 1in (2.5cm) wide elastic (optional) • Pre-gathered ¾in-(2cm)-wide broderie anglaise trim to match the circumference of the basket, plus ½yd (50cm) to continue the edging around the handles • 4yd (4m) of ¾in-(2cm)-wide ribbon.

Making the paper pattern

Make a paper pattern for the base by measuring its diameter. Add ½in (12mm) all around for the seam. If it is not perfectly round, stand basket on the paper and draw around it to get the basic shape. Put the paper pattern inside the basket and draw a line where the base meets the sides to indicate the stitching line.

For the side lining measure, the height of the basket and add on 3½in (9cm). Cut four matching wedge shaped sections for the sides of the basket, plus two narrower pieces for the ends of the basket, to fit through the handles. Add ½in (12mm) seams down the long sides and across the short ends of the six side pieces. Check that the pieces fit neatly inside the basket and mark the seam lines.

Preparing the elastic straps

Cut two 4in (10cm) lengths of elastic. Cut two strips of unquilted fabric, 8in (20cm) long and 3in (7.5cm) wide. Fold strips in half lengthwise, with right sides together, and stitch along the long edges of the fabric, taking ½in (12mm) seams. Centre seam along back of strip, press, then press seam open. Turn right side out, press and thread elastic through, gathering the fabric so the raw ends of the fabric match the raw ends of the elastic. Stitch across ends to hold in place.

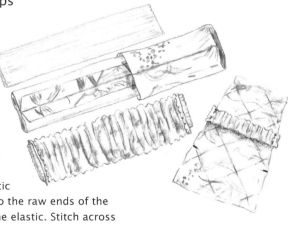

Left *This lined basket for baby accessories uses a quilted fabric edged with trimmed lace in a fun animal print to great effect. The same print, in a plain cotton, was used to make a matching laundry bag.*

Above *A very simple tie-on lining can give a traditional item a new lease of life. This wicker basket was transformed, with a simple tie-on lining, into a useful container for knitting and wool.*

Gingham bread basket with handles

For this straight-sided basket, cut one base piece, as for the baby accessory basket, and one strip for the side lining, 4in (10cm) deeper than the basket and 1¼in (3cm) longer. Join the ends of the side lining to make a ring, then join the lower edge of the lining to the base. Mark positions of handles. Cut away D-shaped sections of the fabric and edge with ½in (12mm) wide binding. Turn under ½in, then 1½in (12mm then 3.5cm) all around outer edge of lining. Stitch to make a casing and thread two 30in (75cm) lengths of tape through. Place lining in basket and tie tape in bows.

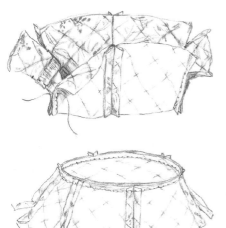

Joining the side panels

Join the six side panels together along the side edges, catching the elastic straps in the seams as you stitch. Stitch only as far as the marked point when joining the end panels. Trim wadding from seam allowance and zig-zag stitch the raw edges of the fabric to neaten.

Joining side to base

Pin the base to the lower edge of the lining, easing the edges to match neatly. Stitch in place, trim wadding from seam allowance and neaten raw edges.

Finishing outer edges

Trim wadding from ½in (12mm) seam allowance all around outer edges of basket, including the open sections of seam which go around the handles. Turn under seam allowance and zig-zag stitch in place, using a narrow stitch. Position broderie anglaise around edge of lining on the right side. Pin and topstitch in place, finishing it off neatly at the seams.

Adding the ribbon

Cut the ribbon into 8 equal pieces. Turn under one end of each and stitch to the corner of the lining at the openings.

8 Towelling mat

*W*hether your bathroom is spacious or tiny, it is easy to make a bath mat that is exactly the right shape. Towelling is available by the yard in a few popular colours, but for something different you could buy white and dye it. As towelling is made of absorbent cotton it dyes very successfully. If you cannot find the dye colour you want ready-mixed, combine two or more (as you would paint) to make the exact shade. Large items can be dyed using special machine dye in an automatic front loading washing machine. Appliqué shapes are cut from brightly coloured light- or mediumweight cotton fabric and stitched around the edge with zig-zag stitching. Iron-on adhesive webbing sticks the shapes to the towelling to hold them while you stitch.

Measurements
Finished size of bath mat: 30 x 24in (75 x 60cm)

Materials
1yd (1m) of 48in-(120cm)-wide marine blue towelling fabric • ½yd (0.5m) iron-on fleece or wadding • Fusible webbing for appliqué • Scraps of yellow towelling for appliqué motifs • Scissors and sewing equipment (see The workshop, pages 200–201) • Washable marker pen or dressmaker's chalk • Marine blue sewing thread and yellow topstitching thread

Using wadding
If you prefer, you can use wadding as an alternative to iron-on fleece. Synthetic wadding is washable and light, and is sold in different thicknesses, usually defined by weight. Light wadding – 2 or 4oz (56 or 113g) is suitable for the bath mat and would be thicker than the fleece. Cut out in the same way as you cut the fleece and attach by basting to the towelling with a grid of basting stitches running in each direction.

Cutting out
Cut out two pieces of blue towelling fabric measuring 32 x 26in (80 x 65cm). This includes 1in (2.5cm) seam allowances. To cut the corners so that they are rounded, draw around the edge of a saucer or small plate with the marker pen and cut away the excess. Cut out a panel of iron-on fleece in the same way, omitting seam allowance.

Above *A seaside theme inspired this bath mat in its sea and sand colours with starfish motifs and wavy zig-zag detail.*

Making the appliqué shapes

Lay the adhesive webbing with the backing paper uppermost onto the wrong side of the yellow fabric. Press with a dry iron. On the backing paper, draw around the templates and cut out all layers. You will need one large and three small starfishes, plus two shells. Remove backing paper. Apply the design following the diagram on page 192; arrange the appliqué shapes on the top of one piece of the blue towelling. Mark the positions of the lines of stitching at the same time. Use an iron to press the appliqué shapes in position, then stitch all around outlines and along marked decorative stitching lines using a wide satin stitch.

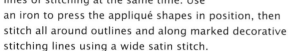

Adding fleece

Position fleece centrally on back panel of bathmat. Iron in position, following manufacturer's directions. An alternative is to place quilting wadding between the towelling pieces to the thickness you want before joining mat.

Making up the mat

With right sides together, baste and stitch the two pieces of towelling together around the edges, taking 1in (2.5cm) seams and leaving a gap of about 10in (25cm) along one side.

Finishing off

Trim the seam allowance and cut V-shaped cuts into the rounded corners (see The workshop, page 213). Turn the mat through to the right side. Hand sew the opening to close it. To give definition and help the mat to hold its shape, topstitch all around the edge of the mat close to the outer edge.

Padded Placemat

You can use the same technique to make placements. Cut out two pieces of washable beige fabric 18 × 13in (46 × 32.5cm). This includes 1in (2.5cm) seam allowances. Baste lightweight wadding or press iron-on fleece centrally to the wrong side of one piece of fabric. Then, with right sides together, baste and stitch the two pieces of fabric together around the edges taking 1in (2.5cm) seams and leaving a gap of about 6in (15cm) along one side. Trim any wadding from the seam allowance. Turn it through to the right side and hand sew the opening. With large machine or hand stitches, top stitch ⅝in (1.5cm) and 2¼in (6cm) from the outside edge. The finished placemat is 16 × 11in (40 × 28cm).

Below *The plan can be adjusted to any size, but make sure there is enough space to fit all the motifs in.*

8 Original lampshades

Lighting provides the inspiration for all kinds of creative ideas as many craftsmen and makers prove. It can be sculptural and curvy, bright and bold, elegant or pretty. Apart from the practical need to provide light, all sorts of materials are used for effect.

Shades can be made in many different sizes and shapes, and the fabric need not be flat or neatly pleated but draped, scrumpled or folded. Look for unusual fabrics such as open-weave hessian, muslin, velvet or wisps of sheer dress fabrics. They all create wildly different effects according to their density, weave and colour. Some will filter light; others will block it, so test out small pieces to judge the overall effect.

Stiffened silk shade

Bright silk fabrics arranged in folds and creases around a lampshade frame will help create an exotic glow.

Suggested fabrics

Silk or lightweight cotton or muslin

Materials

- 8in (20cm) wire pendant ring • 5yd (4.6m) $\frac{1}{16}$in (2mm) gauge galvanized wire • Reel of galvanized wire • Small pliers • 1m (1yd) silk fabric • Cotton tape to match • Needle and matching sewing thread • Washing-up bowl • Fabric stiffener • Rubber gloves

Left *Richly coloured silk fabric is held in permanent folds around a tailor-made frame creating a dramatic impact.*

To make the frame

Take the $\frac{1}{16}$in (2mm) gauge wire and, with pliers, bend into a triangle with each side measuring 14in (35cm). Make a second one and bind together with the fine wire. Attach to pendant ring with the fine wire. Repeat, making two triangles with 7in (17cm) sides and bind together. Cut three 14in (35cm) lengths of $\frac{1}{16}$in (2mm) wire to make the side struts. Using fine wire, bind the struts to the corners of the top and bottom triangles.

Binding the frame

Bind the lampshade frame with cotton tape and hand stitch the ends in place.

Cutting out

To make silk bias strips, lay fabric on a flat surface, take one corner and bring it across to selvedge side. Pin and cut fabric along diagonal fold. Cut out 4-in (10-cm) wide strips parallel to cut edge from fabric.

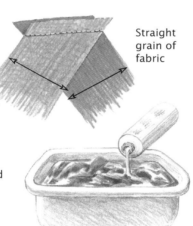

Joining the strips

Join bias strips to make a long piece. Pin short ends together so that the strips are at right angles. Machine stitch $\frac{1}{2}$in (15mm) from edge and trim close to stitching. Keep one piece to edge top of the frame.

Straight grain of fabric

Stiffening the fabric

Put fabric in washing-up bowl and add fabric stiffener. Put on rubber gloves, spreading liquid with hands until fabric is saturated; remove excess. Leave to dry flat for half an hour. It should be damp enough to hold a shape.

Wrapping the frame

Take a short strip of silk and fold in half around top edge of frame. Take main strip and work from top downward and around frame overlapping each strip. Fold over top raw edges; the lower one will be hidden by next layer. Arrange in folds and wrinkles. At lower edge, fold under fabric to inside. Dry.

Above *The bold colours of the contemporary fabric covering this card lampshade contrast with the geometric pattern on the base to create a stunningly modern look.*

Safety tip

With any homemade lampshades, for safety's sake it is advisable to use low-wattage bulbs. Try not to leave lamps turned on for long periods of time and consider the lamps as decorative features, rather than lights to work by. Always allow a clearance of 2in to 3in (5cm to 7.5cm) on all sides of the bulb inside the shade. Whenever possible, it is best to work with natural fabrics, such as cotton, silk and wool as these tend to be less flammable than synthetic ones.

8 Re-covering an old lampshade

Shop-bought lampshades are easy to find in basic colours and shapes but if you want one in a special fabric, find a shape you like and custom-make a shade. You can also look for old lampshades in car boot sales or junk shops. If the cover is beyond repair, check that it can be removed. Clean the frame and spray with metal paint, if necessary. Choose new fabrics carefully – dark colours will inhibit the light that shines through. Pale blue and green will cast a cold impression while colours such as yellow and pink will create a cheery warmth.

Soft pleated shade

A pleated shade would look pretty in a bedroom. Use fine fabric to make soft folds and let the light filter through it.

Suggested fabric

Lightweight cotton, voile or other fine fabric

Materials

Fabric to cover shade • Lampshade frame with the top bound with cotton tape • Scissors and sewing equipment (see The workshop, pages 200–201) • Matching sewing thread • Soft pencil • Ribbon (optional)

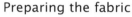

Calculating the fabric

To calculate fabric, measure the circumference of the top of the shade, then multiply by three for full pleats. Add on ¾in (2cm) for the seams. Measure the height of the shade or frame and then add on 3¼in (8cm).

Preparing the fabric

Cut out a piece of fabric to the required size. If the fabric is patterned, make sure the motifs are level. Make a double ½in (12mm) turning along one long fabric edge fabric. Press and stitch. This is the lower edge.

Neatening the top edge

Along the other long edge turn over ¼in (5mm) and press. Turn again by 1¼in (3cm). Press and stitch close to folded edge. This is the top edge.

Marking the pleats

On the wrong side of fabric ½in (12mm) down from the top edge and 1¼in (3cm) in from short edge, make a mark with a soft pencil. Then repeat every 1¼in (3cm) along the top edge.

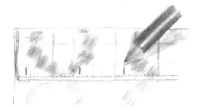

Folding the pleats

To form the pleats, make a fold in the fabric at the first mark. Bring the folded edge across to the point next but one. Pin in place. Form a fold at the next mark and repeat the folds around the top keeping pleats parallel to the seamline, the adjacent pleat and the top edges. Baste and machine stitch ¾in (2cm) from top.

Left *This simple pleated lampshade gives casual charm to an elegant and more elaborate glass base. The fabric chosen for the shade ties in with the green and red colour scheme of the tablecloth and accompanying accessories.*

Fitting the shade

Join the short edges of fabric together with ½in (1cm) seam allowance. Place fabric shade over the frame and then hand stitch to the cotton tape ¾in (2cm) from the top.

Finishing the shade

Make a tape in matching fabric or use some ribbon and tie around the top. Hand sew in position in one or two places.

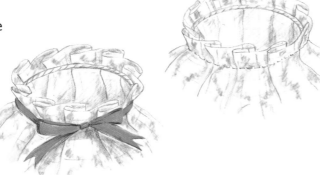

Below *Patterned fabric takes on different appearances when it is pleated or draped as these matching curtains and lampshade clearly display.*

Fabric-covered card lampshade

Drawing up a pattern

Take a large sheet of paper and draw a line equal to the bottom diameter. This is line A–B. At right angles, starting at the centre of this line, draw a line equal to the shade's height. On top of this line, centrally and at right angles draw a line the same length as the top diameter. This is the line C–D.

Draw a line from point A to join point C and extend past it. Repeat from points B to D so the two lines cross. This will be point E.

Finishing the pattern

To draw the curved outer edge of the shade, use compasses or tie together two pencils with a piece of string that equals A–E's distance. With point E as the centre, draw a curved line through points A and B, and beyond. Repeat, drawing a line through points C and D.

Along the outer curved line, mark off two points equal to the circumference of the shade plus 1in (2.5cm) for overlap. From these marks draw a straight line to point E.

Cut out pattern and use to cut out adhesive card and fabric. Add ½in (12mm) extra on all sides of the fabric for turnings.

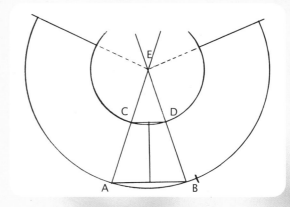

Covering the card

Lay out fabric, right side down. Remove backing from adhesive card and press down carefully onto the fabric. Snip into fabric seams and trim back to ¼in (5mm). Fold over to wrong side and fix with adhesive. Glue together with a 1in (2.5cm) overlap to make shade.

8 Desktop accessories

A home office may be for full-time work or just letter writing and paying the household bills. And whether it is a separate study or a corner of a room, it is likely to have a computer or a fax machine. Add to this files, papers, telephone and other desk items, and it may look efficient, but unhomely.

A few soft touches will alter this appearance. A notice board can hold bills, reminders and tickets, but a fabric-covered one is a decoration in its own right. Fabric-made accessories for the desk, such as a book cover and pencil pot, can also be made to match.

Notice board

A fabric-covered board in a boldly printed light- or mediumweight fabric can provide a large image that is a decoration in its own right.

Suggested fabrics

Felt, green baize, fabric to match other accessories. For the board itself, use a panel of ¾in (18mm) softboard; or ⅜in (9mm) chipboard, faced with cork. (Self-adhesive cork floor or wall tiles are convenient, but adjust board size to suit the tiles.)

Materials

Fabric 4in (10cm) larger than the board in each direction • Board about 22 × 28in (55 × 70cm), with smooth edges • Craft adhesive • Short upholstery tacks • 6yd (5.50m) decorative tape or ribbon, ½–⅝in (1–1.5cm) wide • 2 x 1in (2.5cm) gauge 8 screws with matching wallplugs and screw cups

Preparing the fabric

Press the fabric and then lay on a flat surface, right side facing down. Place the board on top of it centrally.

Fixing the fabric

Wrap the fabric over one side of the board. Starting in the centre and working outward toward the corners for about 6in (15cm), fix the fabric to the back for about 15in (37.5cm) at the centre of one edge with adhesive and upholstery tacks. Stretch the fabric over to the other side of the board and glue and tack in place. Check the fabric runs straight across the panel. Repeat for opposite two sides.

Neatening the corners

To finish each corner, pull the corner of the fabric diagonally over the corner of the board, apply adhesive and secure with a tack. Make a neat fold in the fabric either side, pull firmly around the board and pin to back. Cut off excess fabric. Turn board over and weigh down while the adhesive dries.

Fitting the tapes

To mark the position of the tapes, measure from one bottom corner and make three marks 6in (15cm) apart along the bottom and the same distance up the side from the corner. Repeat at other corner. Arrange the tapes diagonally across the board and secure on the back with a tack. When you are happy with the arrangement, weave the tapes over and under each other, and add a little glue to hold securely. Trim excess tape.

Hanging the board

Drill holes about 2in (5cm) from each top corner. Mark holes on wall, drill and plug the wall, then screw board in place.

Left *A fabric-covered noticeboard is handy for keeping important notes and cards close at hand, as well as looking decorative.*

Left *Matching desk accessories will help to make a home office more homely and friendly to use.*

Below left *Protect a well-loved book or smarten up an old desk diary with an attractive padded fabric cover.*

Cover Tips
- Make sure to pull the fabric and tapes taut before finally anchoring them to the board.
- For a softer finish cut out a piece of light wadding or flannelette the same size as the board and glue to the board before you start.
- Use plasticised fabric to cover the notebook if you require a durable finish.

Book cover

A fabric-covered diary can add style and elegance to your desk. You can also coordinate other books in the same fabric.

Suggested fabrics

Medium- or lightweight furnishing cotton with lightweight cotton lining. Binding can be cut from lining fabric, or choose ready-made binding to match or contrast with the main fabric.

Materials

Fabric for cover and lining • Scissors and sewing equipment (see The workshop, pages 200–201) • Soft flannelette, bump, lightweight wadding or interlining • Mediumweight iron-on interfacing • Matching sewing cotton • Bias binding

Calculating materials

To calculate size of fabric panels, add together the widths of the front, back and the spine of the book. Measure the height. Add 1¼in (3cm) to each measurement for seams. Cut out fabric, lining, padding and interfacing to these measurements. Cut out two flaps in main fabric, 2¾in (7cm) wide by the height plus 1¼in (3cm).

Applying interfacing

To fuse the interfacing to the outer fabric, press onto the wrong side with a warm iron.

Arranging the layers

Lay out the interfaced panel, right side facing down. Position the soft interlining on top, then the lining, right side up. Make several rows of large basting stitches across the panel in each direction, stitching through all the layers.

Adding the flaps

Make a narrow hem along one long side of each flap and press. On the wrong side of the book cover, position the flaps with their right side up and the hemmed edge toward the middle. Line up the outer raw edges and baste together, taking a seam allowance of ⅝in (1.5cm). Trim ⅜in (1cm) of fabric from all seam allowances.

Binding the edges

To bind the raw edge of the book cover with bias binding, unfold one edge of the bias binding and with the right side lined up to the fabric edge on the inside of the cover, baste the bias binding in place. Stitch using the fold of the bias binding as a guide.

Stitching the binding

Fold the bias binding over to the right side, pin in place and turn under the raw ends where they meet. Machine stitch close to the folded edge.

8 Templates

These templates are specifically to use with the bathmat project on pages 184–185 and should be cut out in brightly coloured cotton fabric. If you wanted to make a coordinated bathroom set, you could cut out some extra seashells and starfish to add to some towels of the same colour.

Enlarge the motifs using a photocopier or squared guide (see The workshop, page 215). The motifs here are about 33 percent of the actual size. Copy the shapes by tracing the outline with a pencil onto some tracing paper. You should then use the tracing paper as the pattern. Pin the pattern onto the fabric and cut the shape out of the fabric with very sharp scissors. There is no seam allowance as the fabric shapes are machine stitched to the background fabric. Use the photograph as a guide for positioning the motifs and stitching.

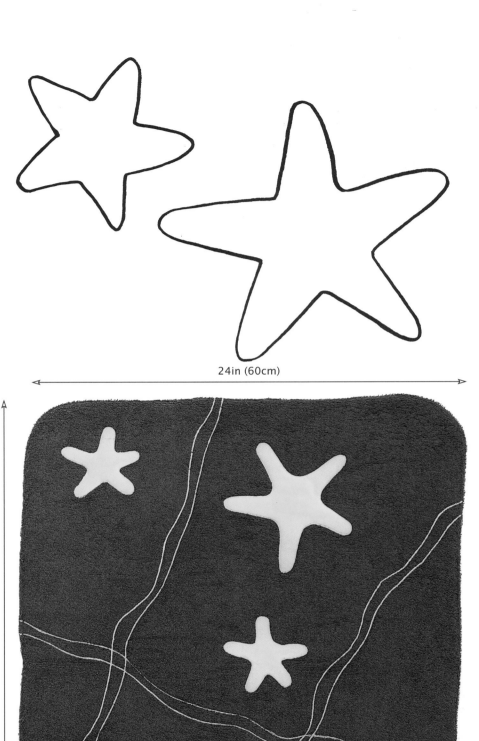

24in (60cm)

30in (75cm)

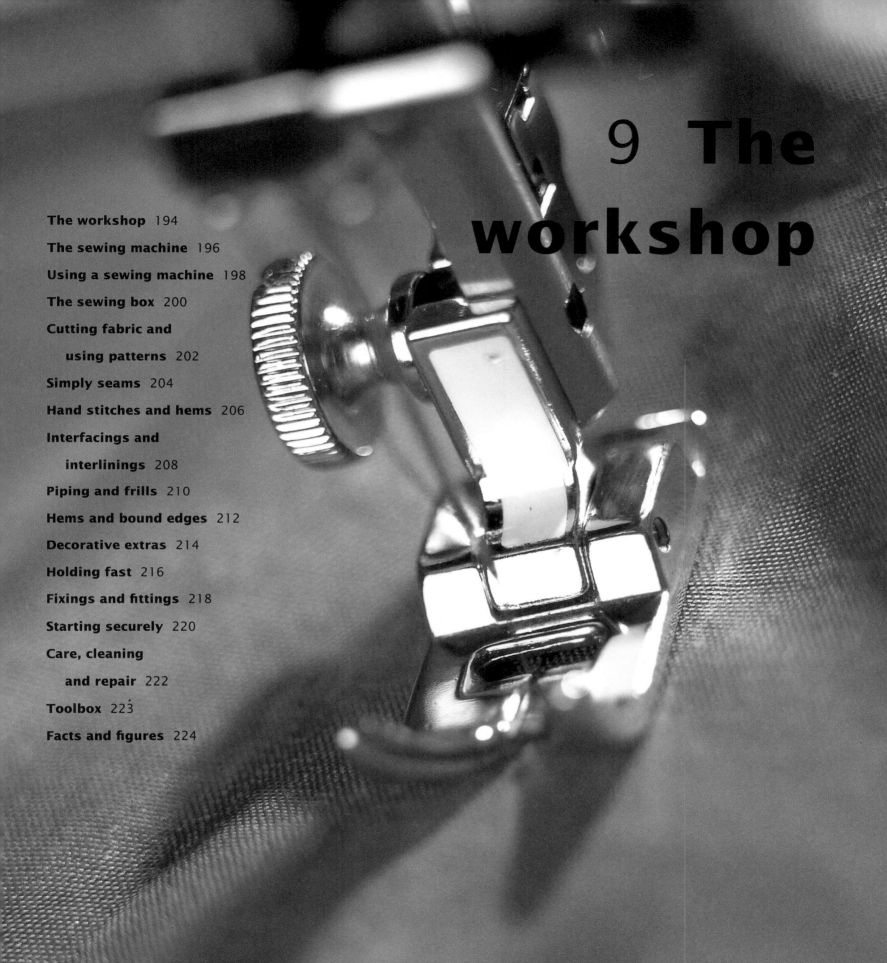

9 **The workshop**

The workshop

You do not need a separate room in your home for sewing, but if you have some space set aside it will be much easier to see projects through quickly and smoothly. You will need a large flat space to cut out fabric (if necessary, use a clean floor), a sturdy surface to hold your sewing machine, an ironing board situated nearby, carefully planned lighting, plus places to store different fabrics and accessories.

For most of us, the idea of a separate room for sewing is no more than a dream — we have to make do with the sitting room floor and the kitchen table. But do not be deterred; even people such as Laura Ashley started her business by sewing on the kitchen table. If you have a formal dining room, a dining area that you do not use very often, or a spare bedroom: these are all ideal places for a sewing area.

You will also need to allow some storage space for your sewing equipment: try to arrange convenient spaces, so that you can pack everything away quickly and easily if you need to when visitors arrive unexpectedly.

When you plan your sewing area in your home, you need to feel happy with the finished arrangement. Obviously if you have limited space you will need to plan your equipment carefully so that it can be easily stored away. If you can have the luxury of your own small sewing room, think about how you want everything laid out, and make sure that you can use your sewing machine comfortably on a sturdy table, and that all the necessary accessories are close to hand.

9 The sewing machine

The biggest investment you will make in the sewing room is your sewing machine. It is certainly the most important piece of equipment. Check out the advantages of different types of machine and get to know how your machine works before starting your first project.

For most people, the first machine is an electric machine which does straight stitch, zig-zag stitch and some more elaborate stitches. When making such an investment, go to a reputable dealer with a good range of machines and have someone demonstrate them to you, so that you can find out the advantages of each one and decide which suits your needs.

If you sew mainly curtains, plain cushions and linens, an electric machine is all you need. More sophisticated electronic machines have push button controls for

Right *A traditional sewing machine has the spool of yarn on top of the machine with a bobbin, which you have to wind with thread on the bobbin wheel, inserted into the holder beneath the plate. Some modern models have push button control so that you can do different stitches and tensions.*

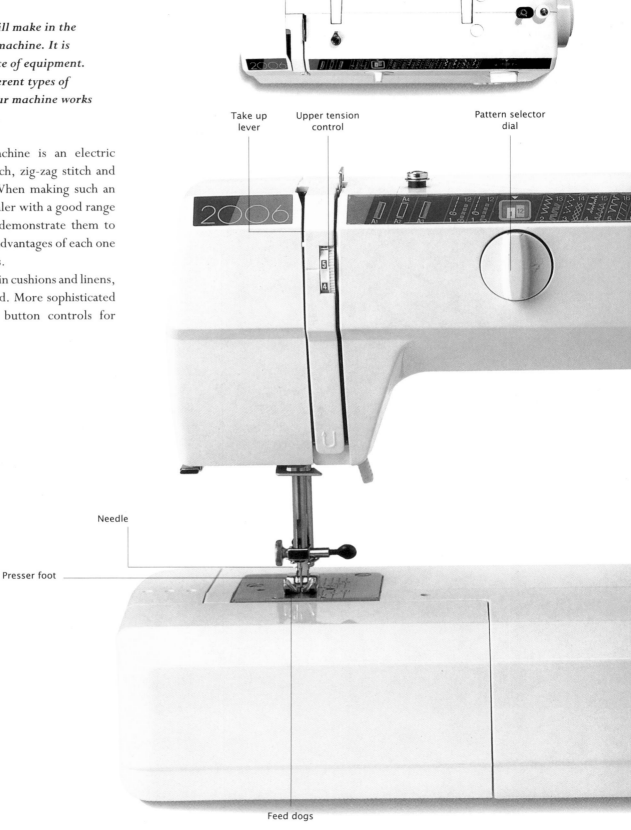

Take up lever

Upper tension control

Pattern selector dial

Needle

Presser foot

Feed dogs

different embroidery stitches and many are sensitive to fabric weights and thicknesses, with automatic adjustment of pressure and stitch depth. The top electronic machines can be programmed to produce complete embroidery motifs. Overlock machines are an expensive extra for advanced sewing: they are useful for edging linens and finishing raw edges.

Looking after your machine

When you have finished work, store your machine with a scrap of fabric under the foot to mop up any leaking oil. The foot should be down, with the needle going into the fabric. Occasionally, you may need to oil your machine to keep it running smoothly, so check the manufacturer's handbook. More frequently, you will need to brush fluff out with a stiff brush from around the base plate and feed dogs, and from the bobbin holder beneath the machine.

Spool pins

Bobbin winder

Stitch length selector

Fly wheel

Stitch width selector

Checklist for buying a sewing machine

• Are the speed control and bobbin-winding mechanisms easy to operate?

• Can you thread the machine easily? Get a proper demonstration in the shop before you buy, so you understand the threading process.

• How flexible is the machine with controlling stitch length and tension?

• How heavy is the machine?

• Is it worth buying second-hand? Check that second-hand machines have been well cared for and have them serviced if they are not running smoothly. Make sure the machine comes with its instruction manual.

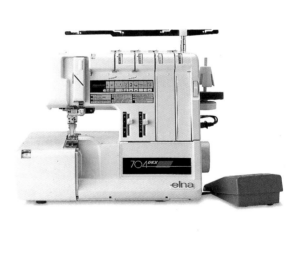

Foot control

Above *An overlock or serging machine has two, three or more spools of yarn fitted to the top of the machine, carrying thread to the needles and loopers. There is often a cutter to cut fabric as you sew, ensuring a neat edge.*

9 Using a sewing machine

When using a sewing machine, there is no substitute for experience. So the more you sew, the easier it will be to stitch. Rather like driving a car, you have to coordinate hands, eyes and feet (with a foot-operated speed control) or knee (with a knee-operated control). Try out different stitches on a variety of scrap fabrics to learn how to adjust tension and avoid snarl-ups. Here is a guide to get you started and some advice on common problems.

Start by testing stitching with the thread you plan to use on spare fabric before beginning a new project. In a conventional machine, the tension of the top spool and lower bobbin have to be balanced to form their link in

the centre of the layers of fabric you are stitching. At the same time, the foot puts pressure on the fabric and this may have to be adjusted for different fabrics. In the most advanced sewing machines, tension and pressure are adjusted automatically, but on older basic models, it can be more hit and miss. If the bobbin thread tension is set properly, just adjust the upper thread tension (usually on the dial above the needle). Adjusting the bobbin thread tension is difficult, so consult your handbook.

Correct tension
When the tension is correct, the threads link in the centre of the layers of fabric to form firm, even stitches.

Wrong tension
If the tension on the upper thread is too tight (or too loose on bobbin thread) the threads link on top of the fabric.

Wrong tension
If the tension on the upper thread is too loose (or too tight on bobbin thread) the threads link below the fabric.

Threads and needles for sewing machines
- Use synthetic thread for synthetic fabrics, and cotton or synthetic thread for natural fibres.
- Heavier-weight threads are available for heavy fabrics, such as denim and PVC, but they may not be suitable for your machine.
- Bold threads (which have a different twist to normal threads) show up more when you want a topstitched finish).
- Button thread is mainly for sewing on heavy buttons by hand.
- With a difficult-to-match colour, use a slightly darker colour that is not so dark once unwound from the spool.
- Overlock or serging machines need specially treated thread (from specialist suppliers) that comes on cones to fit straight onto the spindles.
- Buy a good selection of needles to work with different fabrics: fine needles for lightweight fabrics, all-purpose needles for general work, and heavy-duty needles for heavy fabrics and bulky items such as loose covers.
- You may need ballpoint needles for jersey fabrics and knife-point needles for sewing leather.
- Change the needle regularly as it becomes blunt during use and blunt needles will cause fabric snags.

Straight stitching
Sit in an upright chair, square to the machine, with feet firmly on floor. Before sewing, check there is enough thread on bobbin, and turn the handwheel on the right of the machine to push the needle down through the plate (just once) and draw up bobbin thread through the hole in the plate. Arrange the fabric so that the bulk is to the needle's left, with just the seam allowance (if possible) to the right of the needle. Ideally, have a small table behind you to support the fabric's weight as you sew.

Keep your hand on the fabric, about 4in (10cm) in front of the needle, to guide it through the sewing machine. Start with the take-up lever at its highest point so that the first stitch does not pucker. Always try a test seam on scraps of the fabric you are using before starting work. Start slowly at first, gradually increasing speed when the stitching is running smoothly. Make a few reverse stitches at the beginning and end of each seam, to strengthen the work.

Using zig-zag stitch

Even simple sewing machines can do a variety of stitches. These include ones for finishing edges, creating hems or working on stretch fabrics, for example. Many stitches are a variation on zig-zag stitch. When working this stitch, the needle swings from side to side. A large, open zig-zag stitch is used to finish seam allowances and other raw edges. By reducing stitch length, you can produce a closed-up zig-zag stitch, called satin stitch, which is useful for outline embroidery and appliqué. Hemstitch alternates three straight stitches with a zig-zag stitch, which just catches a couple of threads of the main fabric. Stretch stitch is a latticework of stitches, holding the fabric firmly but allowing it to stretch. Consult your sewing machine handbook for advice and other stitch details.

Zig-zag stitch

Use a wide, long zig-zag stitch to neaten the raw edges of fabric, either together, if the seam is to be enclosed, or separately if the seam has to be pressed open.

Satin stitch

With a short stitch length, zig-zag stitch becomes closed up and solid, creating a satin stitch which can be used for outline embroidery or appliqué. Adjust the width of the stitch for fine work.

Hemstitch

Press hem in place, then fold back the fabric where the hem's fold is to be stitched to main part of the work. Stitch along the folded hemline, catching a couple of threads of fabric as the needle swings to the side.

Troubleshooting guide

Problem	Cause
Fabric feeds unevenly through machine	Pressure of presser foot too light. Throat plate wrongly fitted. Teeth of feed dogs clogged with fluff. Unsuitable foot or stitch length for fabric.
Stitches are uneven	Pressure too light – fabric slips.
Fabric puckers as you stitch	Balance of upper and lower tension is wrong. Stitch length too long. Thread too thick for fabric. Thread not drawn up through plate before beginning. Take-up lever not at top before you started.
Machine skips stitches	Needle bent, dirty or not correctly fitted. Machine not correctly threaded. Presser foot and needle not suitable for fabric. Thread too coarse, too stiff or of poor quality. Thread not wound onto bobbin correctly. Bobbin wrongly inserted.
Stitching pulls to one side	Needle bent.
Fibres of fabric snag	Needle may be blunt or unsuitable for fabric.
Upper thread breaks	Needle bent, not properly fitted or wrong for fabric. Upper tension too tight. Thread too weak. Machine incorrectly threaded. Machine clogged with dust and fluff.
Lower thread breaks	Thread not wound evenly on bobbin, bobbin wrongly inserted or thread not drawn up before starting. Lower tension too tight
Needle caught in fabric	Turn off power. Free needle by turning flywheel by han, until the needle at its highest point. Ease fabric off needle, cutting threads if necessary. Check needle is not bent or blunt before stitching again.

Alternative feet

For many tasks, a transparent plastic, all-purpose foot is adequate. However, machines come with different feet, which may include the following:

- A zip or piping foot with one 'toe' for stitching close to zip or piping.
- A wide gathering foot to grip fabric loosely, gathering it as you stitch.
- A hemmer foot for rolling a fine hem as you stitch.
- A roller foot for stitching slippery fabric and PVC.
- A large button foot for machine sewing buttons.
- A quilting gauge for evenly spaced lines of quilting.

Stitching a zip or piping

Use the narrow zip/piping foot to stitch near the zip's teeth. The foot can be adjusted to stitch on each side. The narrow foot is also used to stitch binding closely in place around piping cord or to stitch the covered cord to fabric – in a seam or as an edging.

9 The sewing box

Your sewing machine will be your most-used item, but what other equipment do you need? Here is a checklist of essential items, some for more advanced projects, and some specialist items for specific tasks.

Whether or not you want to do a lot of hand sewing, you will find that there are many items you will need in your sewing corner besides the sewing machine. It is always worth buying good-quality tools and equipment – they are easier to use and will last longer.

The basic kit

1   A good pair of dressmaking shears, with angled handles and long blades, for cutting out large pieces of fabric.

2   Light trimmers for cutting out smaller items and trimming seams.

3   Embroidery scissors for cutting threads, making buttonholes and clipping into seam allowances.

4   A plastic or plastic-coated tape measure that will not stretch, for measuring curved shapes (baskets, lampshades and so on).

5   A short ruler for checking measurements of small items and marking straight lines.

6   Tailor's chalk (a), dressmaker's markers (b) or water-soluble markers for marking out shapes of pattern pieces, positions of pleats and stitching lines on fabric.

7   Pencils and paper for noting and checking measurements and calculating fabric amounts.

8   A wide variety of hand-sewing needles, use:
    Sharps for basting and hemming.
    Betweens for short, fine stitches, such as running stitch.
    Milliner's or **straws** for decorative stitches.
    Darners for carrying heavier yarns when darning.

9   Good-quality dressmaking pins with coloured heads for holding fabric together. Keep a magnet to hand for collecting dropped pins.

Other accessories

1 A thimble for wearing on the middle finger when hand sewing, to push the needle through fabric layers, particularly heavy ones.

2 A bodkin with a relatively blunt point and large eye for threading cords, elastic or ribbons through casings, and for turning tubes of fabric right side out.

3 Embroidery threads for different types of fabrics and embroidery (see pages 206–207).

4 Extra fine and sharp or broad and blunt embroidery needles for use with different yarns and different backing fabrics, such as silk, linen or canvas.

5 Tweezers for teasing out basting threads after stitching seams and hems.

6 Safety pins in different sizes for threading heavy cords through casings.

7 Beeswax for waxing heavy threads when sewing on buttons, for example. It strengthens the thread and prevents twisting.

8 Pinking shears for finishing raw edges with a non-fraying zig-zag line.

9 A stitch ripper for unpicking any seams that have gone wrong.

10 A retractable steel measure for measuring up windows and beds for home-sewing projects.

11 A yardstick or metre rule is useful for measuring and marking large fabric pieces.

Specialist tools

1 Embroidery hoops and frames for major embroidery or needlepoint projects. Hoops can be used for hand sewing and with the sewing machine.

2 Custom-made hole punches and gadgets (available at department stores) for inserting eyelets, or heavy-duty press studs can be bought for specific projects.

3 A tracing wheel and dressmaker's carbon paper for transferring embroidery or appliqué patterns and other detailed outlines.

4 Upholstery needles for specialist work. These are curved for stitching the fabric seams and pleats from right side after the fabric is fixed in place. Some can be used to sew buttons onto upholstered furniture.

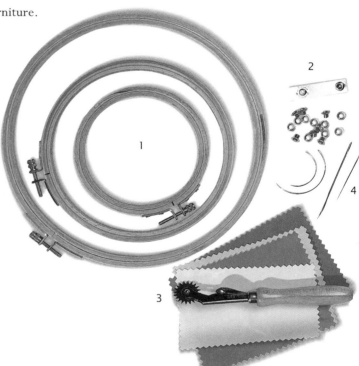

Sewing notions

You will find that, over time, you collect all kinds of extras and remnants. For example, ready-made bias binding tape, zippers, hook-and-eye fastenings, press studs, touch-and-close fastening, buttons, elastic, curtain stiffening and heading tape, cords, decorative braids, ribbons and lace, as well as short lengths of fabric, are all useful. Whenever you have items left over from a project, store them carefully, preferably in plastic bags so that you can see exactly what you have.

9 Cutting fabric and using patterns

Whatever type of project you embark on, you will need to cut out panels of fabric, cut on the straight grain for curtains, square cushions or linens, or cut to shape for irregular items like shaped chair cushions or lined baskets. You will also need to press seams and panels of fabric for a professional finish.

Cutting out curtains

You will need a large, clean and clear surface so you can lay fabric out flat for cutting. This can be a sturdy table or even the floor if you do not have a large table. If you are using a table, it should be at least as wide as the fabric you are using.

• For details of how to calculate the size of the panels of fabric for a curtain, see Curtains and drapes, pages 74–75.

• Work out your calculations on paper and draw a diagram to show how curtain lengths fit together.

• Measure out the first drop and draw a cutting line with tailor's chalk exactly at right angles to the selvedge.

• Cut the length and write "TOP" on the back of the top edge with tailor's chalk. Repeat for the number of drops you require.

• If you are working with a patterned fabric, check that you always position the same part of the pattern at the top of the panel of fabric. If the patterned fabric has a half drop, check that the pattern matches down the side edges which are to be joined.

• Trim off the selvedges, or at least clip them every 4in (10cm). The selvedges are woven more tightly than the rest of the fabric, so if you do not do this the fabric may pucker and the curtains may not hang properly.

• Lay out the drops so that you have two curtains of equal width. If you have an odd number of drops, cut one in half lengthwise. Position these halves on the outer edges of the whole drops.

The first stage in a sewing project is marking out cutting lines and other features, and then cutting the fabric. Whether your pattern pieces are full widths of fabric for floor length curtains or small panels for appliqué, you must mark and cut accurately. Lay the fabric out flat before starting to mark cutting lines, and ensure that it remains flat as you cut it. When cutting rectangular panels, you will get a much better finish if you are using good-quality fabric with a straight weave. If you are using patterned fabric, it should be accurately printed so the pattern is aligned with the grain for the fabric.

Never use the selvedge as the edge of a panel of fabric when sewing: the selvedge may be tightly woven, preventing the fabric from draping correctly, and the unprinted selvedge area may not be the width of the seam allowance.

Pattern pieces

For some projects, you may want to mark a pattern shape on the fabric – a shaped chair seat or the base of a lined basket, for example. For shaped pieces of fabric, cut a paper pattern as a guide before you cut. Brown parcel paper is good for large pattern pieces, as it does not tear easily. If you are making a set of circular seat cushions or need to cut a set of other matching shapes, you will ensure all the pieces are the same if you draw the shape on brown paper, cut out the paper pattern, then pin the paper pattern onto the fabric so that you can cut around it. When cutting a pattern piece, make a note of whether or not you have included a seam allowance. It is sometimes easier to add the seam allowance when you cut out, by cutting ⅝in (1.5cm) away from the edge of the paper pattern. If you want to cut several layers of fabric at once, pin them together to prevent them slipping (which would distort the shape of the fabric pieces).

Cutting out through several thicknesses

If you have to cut several pieces the same shape (for a set of chair seat cushions, for example), pin the fabric layers together and mark the pattern shape on the top piece. Cut out with the fabric laid as flat as possible. The pins will stop the layers from slipping.

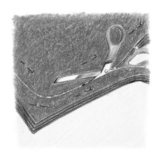

For some shapes and motifs it is easier to use tracing paper for the pattern. You can mark a detailed pattern shape onto the tracing paper and then transfer the pattern with a tracing wheel and carbon paper.

Using a tracing wheel and carbon paper

Lay some carbon paper on the fabric, position the pattern you are using (for example, a shaped seat cushion, drawn on paper) over the carbon paper, and use the tracing wheel to run around the outline of the pattern, so that the carbon paper marks the fabric. This method can also be used to transfer appliqué shapes and embroidery patterns to the surface of a panel of fabric.

Pattern matching

Before stitching seams, panels of fabric must be pinned together to hold them in place. In some projects, you will have to be careful to match the pattern along seam lines. This is particularly important with bold patterns on large items, such as curtains, bedspreads or sofa covers. When cutting out the fabric, allow a slight margin of error, then join the widths of fabric before cutting the fabric accurately.

Matching patterns

To join the widths of fabric, press under seam allowance of one fabric piece, then position it on the second piece to see the right side of both pieces to be joined. Move folded edge over other piece until pattern matches. Pin seam allowances together from beneath the fabric.

Pressing and ironing

Do not regard the iron as something you use just to tidy up cushion covers and curtains after you have made them. Pressing is an integral part of good seamstressing.

Ironing helps to remove wrinkles and creases; pressing, however, is a more precise technique: working on a small area at a time, you use the heat and steam from an iron to flatten details, lifting the iron up and down. Use the point of the iron to get into corners.

If you press your seams as you work, you will get much better results and you can attack the corners that you will not be able to get at once an item is made up. After stitching a straight seam, press along the line of stitching, to set the stitches into the fabric, then open out the seam and press the seam allowance open from the wrong side. A steam iron is one of the best to use: flatbed and roller irons take up a lot of space. Small hand-held steamers can be used to steam curtains once hung.

Tips for pressing

• Test the iron on a scrap of fabric before starting a project to ensure that it does not mark the fabric.

• In most cases, you should press on the wrong side of the fabric.

• For extra protection, to prevent the iron making the fabric shiny, use a dry pressing cloth (a double thickness of material such as muslin for lightweight fabrics or a firmer weave, such as sheeting, for heavier fabrics). Put the cloth between the iron and the fabric.

• Stubborn creases (particularly in cotton and linen) may come out more easily if the fabric is damp. If your iron does not have a spray feature, use a hand-held mist spray.

• Some silks mark very easily with steam or water, so do not use steam or a hand-held spray if this is the case.

• Velvets are difficult to press: for best results, just steam them. Lay them pile side down, set the iron to steam and hold it over the fabric without actually putting the weight of the iron on the fabric. Alternatively, use a steamer. However, you can press seam allowances, which will help to flatten them and make them less bulky.

• Always press embroidery and appliqué from the back of the fabric. To avoid crushing the decorative work, cover the ironing board with extra layers of soft fabric (such as interlining) so that the raised stitching can sink into it.

Cool iron
220°F (110°C)
For acrylic, nylon, acetate, polyester and other synthetic fibres

Warm iron
300°F (150°C)
For polyester/cotton mixes, wool, silk

Hot iron
390°F (200°C)
For cotton, linen and viscose

NOTE: The iron's temperature is at least 70°F (40°C) higher than the temperature that the fabric reaches during pressing.

9 Simply seams

M ost sewing will involve seams – long straight seams down curtains and bedspreads, short curved seams in basket linings and other accessories or bulky piped seams in cushions and upholstery. Some seams are decorative; others need to be invisible. For strength, most seams are stitched by machine, but in some cases you may prefer to sew by hand, using a fine running stitch or backstitch.

Before machine stitching a seam, you must match seam allowances carefully. On plain or striped fabrics, match the edges to be joined, with right sides together, and pin the layers together close to the stitching line. Position pins at right angles to stitching lines, so that points just reach the seam line. If you are not very experienced, join the layers with a row of basting stitches before stitching the seam.

Flat seams

A flat seam is commonly used for joining fabric widths such as curtains. The same method is used for joining fabric panels for cushion covers and padded panels, but here the seams are enclosed and seam allowances can be pressed together (or in one direction).

Stitching a flat seam

Stitch seam with right sides together and raw edges matching. Normally a ⅝in (1.5cm) seam allowance is used. Reinforce ends of seamline by reverse stitching.

Finishing flat seams

To make a seam lie flat and prevent unsightly lumps on right side of fabric, you may need to trim and layer the seam allowance, particularly if there are several layers of fabric, as in seams. Each layer is trimmed a different amount, so that the edges do not all fall together when the seam is pressed. Also trim, notch and clip the seam allowances of curved seams and at corners. When the piece is turned right side out, you will have a smooth unpuckered curve or a crisp corner. You can also neaten

the edges of a seam allowance, by trimming with pinking shears, with zig-zag or overlock stitch, by turning under and stitching the raw edges or, with a heavy fabric, you may prefer to bind the raw edges with bias binding.

Layering seam allowances

Trim each seam allowance in a seam of a different amount to reduce bulk. This technique is particularly important for a smooth fit on items with bulky, piped seams, such as slip covers for armchairs and sofas.

Clipping corners

On a corner, such as the corner of a cushion cover, clip away the seam allowance diagonally across the corner. For particularly bulky and sharply angled corners, you can taper the seam allowances further, to reduce the thickness of the fabric in the corner when the cover is turned right side out.

Clipping and notching curved seams

On an outer curve, on a circular cushion cover, for example, cut little notches out of the seam allowances every 1–2in (3–5cm) so that when the cover is turned right side out the fabric lies flat. On inner curves, clip into the seam allowance, so when the item is right side out the outer edges of the seam allowance lie flat.

Cornering tip

When stitching around corners in bulky fabrics, such as heavyweight cushion covers, it may be difficult to create a neat corner. A couple of extra stitches, diagonally across the corner, will allow for the fabric's bulk. Stitch to just before the corner's point, stopping with the needle in the fabric. Lift presser foot and pivot the fabric 45° around the needle. Lower the foot and make two stitches diagonally across the corner, stopping again with needle in the fabric. Lift foot, pivot again, then continue stitching seam.

French seam

With a French seam, the seam allowances are closed together, but make an unsightly bulge on the fabric's reverse side. It is useful when joining fine fabrics, when making pillowslips that have to be laundered frequently, and when making items such as drawstring bags (see pages 180–181), which are subject to wear and tear on the inside as well as the outside. This type of seam is difficult to work around curves and corners. The two layers are first joined with wrong sides together, taking only a very narrow seam, and then the seam allowance is trimmed and the fabric turned so that you can finish the seam from the wrong side.

French seam

Join fabric layers with wrong sides together, stitching about ¼in (6mm) outside seam line. Trim seam allowance to ⅛in (3mm) of first line of stitching. Press first stitching line, pressing seam allowances together.

Turn the fabric to bring right sides together, folding the fabric along first stitching line. Stitch on seam line, enclosing the fabric's raw edges.

Flat fell seam

A flat fell or run-and-fell seam is a flat seam which encloses the fabric's raw edges without creating too much of a ridge in the fabric along the seam line. The seam is highlighted with a line of stitching running down beside it. On the back of the seam, you can see two parallel lines of stitching. It is useful for joining seams that will get strain, such as a lined picnic rug, and for seams which may be seen from either side – on a reversible throw or unlined curtains, for example.

Flat fell seam

Stitch a normal seam, with right sides of fabric together. Press seam, press it open, then press both seam allowances to one side. Trim under seam allowance to ⅜in (1cm) then turn under ¼in (6mm) down the opposite seam allowance. Pin and baste upper seam allowance in place, enclosing fabric's raw edges. Topstitch close to the folded edge.

Mock French seam

A mock French seam gives a similar result to a French seam, but is only suitable for lightweight fabrics. The technique makes it easier to position the main seamline accurately, and it has the advantage that it can be used around corners. After stitching an ordinary seam, the raw edges are turned inward and stitched together.

Stitch an ordinary seam, with right sides of fabric together. Press along line of stitching. Turn up and press a narrow ¼in (6mm) turning down each seam allowance, so that the turned-in edges can be neatened together. Make a line of stitching close to the folded edges of the seam allowance, through all layers of fabric. On curved seams, clip into the seam allowance before pressing and stitching turnings.

Lapped and butt seams

Lapped seams are simple seams, used to join fabric widths that will not fray, or will be enclosed in the item. The seams create minimal bulk, and are useful for joining widths of interlining that will be enclosed in a curtain, bedspread or thick tablecloth, or for joining non-fray fabrics such as PVC or felt. The seam allowances can be trimmed after stitching. If the layers of fabric are particularly bulky; for example, when joining widths of wadding in large, quilted panels, they can be joined with a butt seam: the edges of the fabric are joined by hand without overlapping them at all.

Lapped seam for non-fray fabrics

When joining PVC or felt, for minimal bulk, overlap the two edges to be joined by a total of 1¼in (3cm) and, with right sides upward, make a row of stitching along the seam line. If the seam is subject to wear and tear, make a second row of stitching ½in (12mm) from the first. Trim the seam allowances close to the rows of stitching.

Joining interlining or wadding

To join layers of wadding or interlining with minimal bulk, use a wide or multi-zig-zag stitch. Overlap the seam allowances, stitch with zig-zag stitch and then trim away excess fabric. For bulky layers of wadding or very thick interlining, butt together the edges that are to be joined, and stitch by hand with herringbone stitch (see page 207), taking stitches across the join on alternate sides.

9 Hand stitches and hems

Careful attention to detail turns an ordinary sewing project into something special, and it is often hand-sewn details that make all the difference. Some stitches are essential, practical tasks, while others are purely decorative.

When sewing practical stitches, such as basting, running stitch or back stitch, use ordinary sewing threads. Finer thread is available for basting, which is less likely to mark the fabric and is easier to remove after stitching seams. The embroidery yarn chosen for a project will depend on the fabric used and the effect wanted. For example, stranded embroidery cotton is used for working on cottons and linens, pearled cotton gives a heavier stitch, suitable for loosely woven, mediumweight fabric and wool embroidery threads are used for canvaswork.

Practical stitches

• Running stitch was the most common stitch before the advent of sewing machines. It is used to join fabric pieces to make an ordinary seam. Two lines of running stitch are used to gather fabrics for frills or to ease fullness around curved corners. Work from right to left, with the seam allowances away from you so that the fabric is supported on your lap. Make several stitches at a time, by running the needle up and down the fabric along the seam's line. Basting is done in the same way as running stitch, but has longer stitches.

• Backstitch is used similarly to running stitch, but produces a more solid line of stitching and a firmer seam. It is also used for topstitching because the stitches make a continuous line.

• Slipstitch is a useful hand stitch for stitching up openings in covers and reversible items, or for joining patterned fabric from the right side by hand.

Backstitch

Working from right to left, or toward you, take a stitch at least ¼in (6mm) long through the fabric and up to the right side. Draw the needle through, then insert it in the fabric again, halfway along the previous stitch. Pull through, then repeat, inserting the needle right next to the previous stitch.

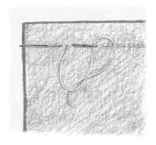

Slipstitch

Working from right to left, with folded edge and fabric it is to be joined to in your left hand, bring needle out through the folded edge. Take a stitch across into the other fabric panel, then bring the needle up about ¼in (6mm) along, and stitch across folded edge again. Repeat along the fabric's length.

Hems and edges

• Hemming stitch gives a firm finish to the edge of a tablecloth or bedspread. The stitches are sewn close together, but should not show on the fabric's right side.
• Slip hemming or blind hemming (often used with curtains) makes a stitch that is less visible from the fabric's wrong side. Work from right to left, or toward you, with lower edge of hem away from you.
• Herringbone stitch is both decorative and useful for a firm hem. Use it for hems where you want a minimal bulk, for example, with very thick fabrics. Do not make an extra fold in the hem – simply neaten the fabric's raw edge with zig-zag stitch before making a herringbone-stitch hem.
• Blanket stitch can be used to finish the edge of heavier fabrics such as a picnic mat. Try and turn under raw edges before finishing with blanket stitch. Use the folded edge as a guide to make even stitches.

Running stitch

Take four or five even stitches, which are about ⅛–½in (3–12mm) long, according to the thickness of the fabric. Do not pull the thread too tight, to avoid any puckering of the material.

Hemming stitch

Working from right to left, or toward you, bring the needle out through the hem's fold and make a diagonal stitch into the fabric. Try to pick up only a single fabric thread, then stitch back under hem. Repeat this stitch all along the hem's length.

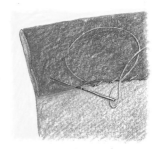

Slip hemming

Bring the needle up through the fabric fold, then take a tiny stitch in the main fabric, picking up only one or two threads as you do so. Angle the needle diagonally and bring it up through the fabric's fold about ¼in (6mm) along the hemline. Take a tiny stitch in the fold, then take the needle down and back through the main fabric, as before.

Herringbone stitch

Working from left to right, bring the needle up through the hem, then insert it in the main fabric diagonally up to the right. Take a tiny stitch in the main fabric, then move the needle down diagonally to the right and take a stitch right through the hem. Then repeat this stitch all along the hem.

Blanket stitch

With the edge to be finished toward you, and working from left to right, push the needle through the fabric and under the edge, so it is pointing toward you. Loop thread over needle, then make the next stitch about ⅛–¼in (3–6mm) further on. The looped thread should run along fabric edge.

Button loops

You can easily make button loops by hand, using blanket stitch to strengthen the thread loops. Use a double strand of button thread to make the loop. Anchor the end of the thread with a couple of backstitches. Take two stitches across the point where the button is to be fixed to make a secure foundation of four threads for the loops.

Work blanket stitch over the foundation threads, pulling the stitches tight. Finish with a couple of backstitches.

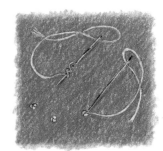

Decorative stitches

Hand embroidery stitches are always worked from the right side of the fabric to see the finished effect. With most fabrics, you need to stretch the area you are working on over an embroidery hoop. With an even tension on the fabric, you can keep an even stitch tension.

• Cross stitch forms the basis of canvaswork embroidery, and is also used on linens and cottons.

• For embroidering a design with large colour areas, use satin stitch or long and short stitch for very large areas, where the satin stitch might pull into loops with wear.

• French knots can create spot details – the eyes on a face or the pollen in a flower, for example.

Cross stitch

Make a row of diagonal stitches along the pattern line, taking stitches straight down behind the fabric. The top stitches must lie at a 45˚ angle to the fabric weave.

Work back along fabric in the same way, taking diagonal stitches over previous row of stitches. Again, on back of fabric the stitches will run straight with the fabric grain.

Satin stitch

Mark the area to be filled in with a dressmaker's marker or fine basting stitches. Working from right side of fabric, bring the needle up at one end or corner of the shape you are embroidering. Take a stitch across the area, then bring needle out again on the marked line next to the beginning of the previous stitch. Over large areas, adjust stitch length, staggering them to prevent a line forming across the embroidery.

French knots

Bring the needle up through the fabric at the point where you want to make the knot. Take a tiny stitch at the point where the thread comes out of the fabric and, leaving needle in fabric, wrap thread around the point twice. Hold the knot close to fabric, pull needle through, then take the needle back through the fabric at the same point, to anchor the knot.

9 Interfacings and interlinings

Interfacings and interlinings give home sewing a professional finish. Although many types are intended for dressmaking and tailoring, there are many useful tips when it comes to home sewing.

From heavy pinch-pleated curtain headings to delicate, appliqué accessories, there are many ways you can improve a finished project by adding extra hidden layers as you make up the item. Interfacings can stiffen fabrics and give a crisp finish, while interlinings are soft fabrics, which give extra body to soft furnishings.

Choosing and using interfacings

Interfacings are ideal to stiffen fabrics such as curtain headings and pelmets. Interfacings can be used similarly to stiffen items such as tailored tiebacks and to give extra weight to home furnishing accessories, such as book covers. Traditional interfacings are woven, but modern non-woven interfacings, which are often available with a special backing so you can iron them onto the main fabric, are easier to work with.

• Buckram is a traditional, very stiff interfacing. It is available in narrow strips – convenient for giving a crisp finish along the top of a curtain. Buckram can also back pelmets to give a tailored look to the top of a window.

• Purpose-made stiffening for curtain headings is available in convenient widths.

• When working appliqué or embroidery, use lightweight fabrics such as silk organdie, marquisette, bastiste or fine lawn interfacings to back the main fabric.

• Purpose-made, non-woven interfacings in different weights, with or without an iron-on backing, can also be used instead of traditional interfacings. The advantage of these interfacings is that because they have no grain, they do not have to be aligned with the fabric to match the weave when cutting out. The interfacing is usually trimmed away close to the stitching before finishing the project, to reduce the seam bulk.

Delicate fabrics hold their shape while you sew, if backed with a lightweight iron-on interfacing, and double-sided iron-on interfacing makes an appliqué project easier (see pages 170–171 [bedlinen project]).

Most interfacings are only available in black, white or neutral colours.

Using iron-on interfacing

Always press fabric to be interfaced carefully before fusing interfacing, and apply interfacing to the fabric's wrong side. To protect the sole plate of the iron and to ensure the iron does not over-heat fusible (iron-on) interfacing, use a pressing cloth between the iron and the interfacing.

Lightweight sew-in interfacing

Cut interfacing to the same size as the main fabric piece to be faced, and baste the interfacing to the wrong side. Use the two fabric layers as though they were a single layer. Trim away all the interfacing from the seam allowances, close to the seam line, after finishing the seam.

Using sew-in interfacing

With very heavy, stiff interfacing, trim all seam allowances, plus an extra ⅛–¼in (3–6mm) from outer edge of interfacing. Position the interfacing on the wrong side of fabric and hold it in place with herringbone stitch, picking up only a single thread from the main fabric as you stitch over the edge of the facing.

1

2

3

4

5

6

7

Below left *Interfacings and stiffenings give a crisp finish to soft furnishing projects: 1. Non-woven, iron-on, lightweight interfacing; 2. Marquisette; 3. Non-woven sew-in mediumweight interfacing; 4. Stiffening for curtain headings; 5. Organdie; 6. Buckram; 7. Double-sided, iron-on interfacing.*

Above *Interlining and wadding add a touch of luxury: 1. Bleached bump; 2. Natural domette; 3. Lining fabric; 4. Lightweight, iron-on fleece; 5. Synthetic interlining; 6. Heavyweight wadding or fleece.*

Interlinings

Interlining is a layer of soft fabric, caught between the main fabric and lining, which gives a luxurious finish and helps to improve a curtain's drape. Traditional interlinings include bump and domette, which are used under decorative, lined circular tablecloths or in curtains. Flannelette and synthetic wadding (available with iron-on backing for quilted projects) can also be used. When choosing interlinings, check whether it will wash (or dry clean) with the fabric used. The colour choice is often even more restricted than with interfacing.

Interlining is a bulky fabric, so join widths by machine with lapped seams, or by hand with herringbone stitch to prevent any stiffness at the join. Once made up, the interlining is enclosed by fabric and lining, so raw edges are protected from fraying.

What's beneath the fabric?

The example on the right shows how you might position various types of stiffening and softening layers behind the fabric in a single project.

When stitching appliqué to fine fabric, iron non-woven interfacing (a) to the wrong side of the fabric motif. Do not cut out the motif. Stabilize the main fabric by basting interfacing (b) to the back if required. Pin motif in place, stitch around outline, and trim away excess fabric. On the back of the fabric, remove basting and trim interfacing close to stitching. To give a decorative table cover a luxurious finish, position a layer of interlining (c) beneath the main fabric, and finish the cloth with a lining (d), turning under a hem and slipstitching the lining to the turning of the top fabric.

Locking in interlining

Thick interlining can slip around inside curtains or heavy, lined tablecloths, so lock it to the wrong side of the main fabric before making up the curtains. Lockstitch is a long, looped stitch, worked down the length of the curtain on a fold in the interlining. Pick up only a single thread of the curtain fabric and do not pull the thread taut.

Heavy self-adhesive stiffening

Projects such as shaped pelmets, tie-backs and lampshades are made easier with self-adhesive stiffening. The card can be cut to the shape required, then the backing is removed and the adhesive side covered with fabric. When sticking fabric to self-adhesive card, work from one end to the other, smoothing the fabric to remove wrinkles.

9 Piping and frills

Straight seams and hems should be as invisible as possible in many soft furnishings. However, you can make a feature of seams with piping and frills which outline an item to emphasize its shape. Even if a pattern does not give instructions for including piping or frills and flounces, they can be fitted into almost any flat seam.

Bold piping or generous flounces set into seams can make a real style statement. Piping is ideal for outlining the shape of a cushion or sofa cover, for example, while frills of gathered fabric can be used to give a soft finish to bedroom pillows and linens.

For many projects, you will need fabric strips, cut on the bias so that they can be eased around corners and curves, known as bias strips or bias binding. Shop-bought bias binding is often of poor quality, so it is better to cut binding yourself. Always choose the same weight of fabric as the main fabric. For covering piping cord, you will need 1½–2in-(4–5cm)-wide strips, depending on fabric weight and the size of the piping cord to be covered. This gives a ⅝in (1.5cm) seam allowance, plus fabric to wrap around the cord. The same strips can be used for binding edges (see overleaf). For large projects (loose covers, binding the edge of a bedspread), join all bias strips and cover lengths of piping before starting.

Marking and cutting bias strips

Take a rectangle of fabric and mark a diagonal, at a 45° angle to the selvedge, from one corner across to the opposite edge. Measure width of binding at right angles to this first line, then mark in the bias strips parallel to the first line. Cut out along marked lines.

Joining bias strips

Position two strips at right angles, right sides together. If they were cut across the same rectangle, the raw edges can be positioned together. Overlap the pieces so that the corners extend on either side and you can make a seam line running from edge to edge and ⅜in (1cm) from the raw edges. Press the stitching, then press seam open and trim away corners.

Ruched piping

Ruched or gathered piping gives a sumptuous finish to seams. Use the heaviest piping you can find. Fabric for binding the piping can be cut on the straight grain or the bias, and the width should be at least eight times the diameter of the cord. Cut cord and binding one and a half times the finished length of the seam to be piped. Wrap the binding around the cord and baste in place. Stitch ⅛ – ¼in (3–6 mm) from the cord. Stitch across one end of

the piping, through cord and binding. Slide the binding down the cord. When sufficiently gathered, stitch across the open end of the binding to hold the cord in place, and trim away the extra cord.

Working with piping

Piping cord is usually cotton and should be pre-shrunk (or wash before use) if you are inserting it in an item that is washable. Attach piping to the seam in three separate steps, rather than trying to combine all stages. First wrap bias strips around the cord (open out pre-folded binding first). Then stitch as close as possible to the cord, through both fabric layers.

Use a piping foot on the sewing machine, adjusted so that the needle is between the foot and the piping cord. When piping is fitted around a pattern piece, such as a cushion, join the piping ends when pinned in position.

Stitching piping in place

Position covered piping on right side of one fabric panel, so that the piping stitching line matches the fabric's seam line and the raw edge of the piping covering is towards the raw edge of the fabric. Stitch in place, then position the second panel of fabric on top of the piping, right side inward, and stitch again.

Turning corners

Where the piping goes around a corner, stitch in place as far as the corner, then snip into the seam allowance of the piping covering at the corner point, so that you can turn it around the corner. If the corner is gently curved, make several cuts into the seam allowance so that you can ease it into position.

Setting in the frill

Start by stitching the frill to the right side of one of the fabric panels, with raw edges matching, making sure that the fullness is distributed evenly. Position the second fabric layer (the back of a cushion cover or lining of a

curtain), right side inward, over the frill and stitch seam. Press, trim seam allowances and turn to right side. Allow extra fullness at corners if the frill extends around the corner – on a curtain or a cushion cover, for example.

Joining ends of piping

After pinning piping in place, trim ends of fabric diagonally (following the fabric's grain) and cut off piping cord, leaving a ⅝in (1.5cm) seam allowance at each end. Unravel piping cord at the overlap and twine loose ends together. Turn under seam allowance of binding and slipstitch together by hand.

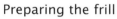

Frills and flounces

Frills of matching or contrasting fabric can be inserted into seams – around the edge of a cushion or between the main fabric and lining of a simple curtain, or topstitched to fabric – across the top of a duvet or around the edge of a lined basket, for example. For an inserted frill, a folded fabric strip is usually used (to save hemming); for a topstitched frill, the edges of the frill must be finished before you gather and stitch the frill. Decide how wide you want the frill to be before you cut the fabric: for a medium-sized cushion, 16in (40cm) square, you will need a finished frill at least 2in (5cm) wide. Other ideas for adding frills to cushions and covers are given in Cushions (see pages 97–128).

Piped and frilled finish

For extra detail, combine piping with a frill in a seam. Position piping along the raw edge of the top panel, and stitch in place. Then position gathered frill and stitch. Finally position back panel of fabric, so that the piping and frill are sandwiched in place. Stitch seam. Trim seam allowances, press and turn to right side.

Preparing the frill

Cut a fabric strip equal in width to twice the width of the finished frill, plus seam allowances. The length should be 1½–2 times the finished seam's length. Neaten the ends of the frill by folding the strip in half lengthwise, wrong sides inward. Stitch short seams at each end, press, trim seam allowances and turn right side out. Press for neat corners.

Topstitched frill

Cut frill to width of finished frill, plus turning or serging allowance. The length should be 1½–2 times the gathered length of the frill. Turn under hems all round and stitch down (use a fine zig-zag stitch or make a double hem) or serge and trim the outer edge. Gather the frill along stitching line, then topstitch in place, distributing the fullness evenly.

Gathering the frill

Gather the frill with machine or running stitch. If you are using running stitch, make two rows of stitches, quite close to each other, staggering the positions of the stitches to prevent pleats from forming. Draw up the gathers so that the gathered length matches the seam. Anchor the gathering threads around a pin at each end. Check that the fullness is evenly distributed and pin or baste before stitching the frill in place.

9 Hems and bound edges

The edges of many items of soft furnishings – curtains, bedspreads, table linen – have to be carefully finished to ensure that they look good and do not fray when they are laundered. The alternatives here are to hem the edge or to bind it with matching or contrasting fabric.

Hems are generally intended to provide an almost invisible finish to the edge of an item. The traditional dressmaker's hem involves a narrow turning, and then a deeper turning which can be adjusted at the final fitting stage. Most hems or edges in home sewing, however, are double hems, with two equal turnings, to give a crisper finish.

Finishing hems

Hems can be stitched in place by hand for an invisible finish (see page 207), by machine using a special hemming stitch (see page 199) or they can be topstitched by machine – or emphasized with satin stitch for a decorative finish.

Two major problem areas with hems are getting a neat finish at corners on square items, and creating a flat hem around circular items, such as round tablecloths. To finish corners neatly, the hems have to be folded to create a diagonal pleat – a procedure known as mitring. At the same time, excess fabric is trimmed away so that the corners are not lumpy.

The easiest way to deal with a circular hem is to edge it with a bias strip, positioned inside the cloth, known as a faced hem. The bias strip can be eased into shape around the curved edge of the cloth. Choose a binding to match the fabric as closely as possible, or cut a bias strip from matching remnants.

Mitring hems

If the hem goes around a corner, whether stitching the hem by hand or machine, you must reduce the fabric's bulk by mitring for a neat finish. First press the turning allowance and the hem all round the edge of the item and baste in place.

Trimming the fabric

Trim off fabric across corner, cutting ⅛in (3mm) diagonally outward from the point where the fold lines cross. Press under a ⅛in (3mm) turning across the corner.

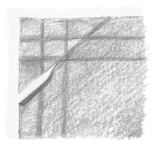

Folding the mitre

Re-fold the first turning of the hem, keeping the diagonal turning in place. When you turn under the second fold of the hem, the edges of the diagonal turning should meet neatly at the corner. Baste in place then stitch by hand or machine.

Faced hem

Stitch binding to the cloth, with right sides together and the fold line of the binding positioned just outside the fold of the cloth's hem. Trim seam allowances and press. Turn the binding to the inside of the cloth, folding and pressing hem in place. Slipstitch folded edge of binding to cloth, keeping it flat as you stitch.

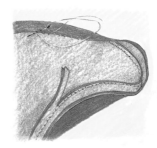

Binding edges

Ready-made bias binding comes pre-folded, but if cutting it yourself, press in turnings down each long edge before sewing. The turnings should be just under half the width of the finished binding. Turn over and press. The fold lines become stitching lines when using the binding. To bind the edge of a piece of fabric, you open out one half of the binding, position it along the edge to be bound, then fold it over the raw edge and stitch the folded edge down.

You can either attach the binding to the right side of the fabric with a straight machine stitch, then turn it to the wrong side and slipstitch the remaining folded edge by hand, or you can attach the binding to the wrong side of the item, then fold it over and topstitch the folded edge in place by machine. Either way, the first stitching line should follow the seam line. Trim and layer seam allowances (see pages 204–205) after making the first row of stitching along the binding.

Stitching binding in place

Open out the binding and position it on the main fabric, with right sides of the binding facing the fabric's wrong side, and with the fold line of the binding on the fabric's seam line. Stitch along the fold line. Trim seam allowances and press stitching.

Topstitched finish

This finish is added from the right side of the finished item. Fold binding over raw edges to right side of fabric. Press. Baste binding in place, then from the right side of main fabric, topstitch binding in place through all fabric layers close to inner fold lines of binding.

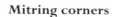

Handstitched finish

Stitch the binding to fabric along the first fold line with the right sides together. Trim the seam allowances, press, and then turn binding to fabric's wrong side. Press again. Slipstitch the fold of the binding in place close to the previous stitch line.

Square-bound corners

If you do not want to mitre the binding around a corner, you can use a neat, square finish instead. Cut a length of binding for each edge to be finished, adding a seam allowance of ⅝in (1.5cm) at each end. Starting with two opposite edges, apply binding as usual and trim away seam allowances level with remaining unbound edges. On the remaining two strips, turn under and press the seam allowance. Bind the edges, then slipstitch folded ends of binding together to enclose the corners.

Mitring corners

When binding square corners; for example, around a tablecloth and napkins, you have to mitre the binding at the corners by folding it and making a short, diagonal hand-sewn seam at the corner. Mitre each corner in turn as you reach it, rather than trying to make the mitres after stitching the binding in place. The technique is a little tricky, but worth the effort.

Pin the binding in place along the first edge of the item to be bound. Mark the corner point on the main fabric with a pin. Baste the binding in place to ensure it is accurately positioned before stitching it in place.

Stitch to marked point

Mark the corner of the main fabric where the stitching lines (seam allowances) cross. Open out the binding and, with right sides facing, stitch binding to the fabric by machine, stopping at the marked point.

Fold back the binding

Fold the binding back on itself, so that it forms a little tuck with a double fabric layer, equal in width to the finished binding, extending beyond the point where you stopped stitching.

Stitch the mitre

Fold this extension back diagonally so that you can see to stitch along the next side of the panel. Use a needle to make a short, diagonal seam from the point where you finished stitching to the folded centre point of the binding. Continue stitching the binding in place along the next edge.

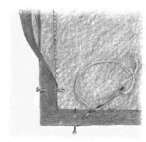

Finish the mitre

Fold the binding over the edge and stitch a second short diagonal seam across the binding before finishing the remaining edge of the binding.

9 Decorative extras

Many different braids, fringing, cord and ribbon are available to add detail to soft furnishings without having to cut and prepare custom-made piping and frills. A look round a haberdashery department will bring you many ideas for ready-made finishes. Some are intended for setting into seams in the fabric, others are topstitched in place before making up an item. You can also add a personal touch to home-sewn or shop-bought soft furnishing accessories with hand-embroidered details.

You can add silky, rope-twist insertion cord (which has a flange woven into it to stitch into the seam) giving a luxurious touch to scatter cushions; you can gather up delicate frills of broderie anglaise to add a feminine touch to bed linens; or you can add lacy trims to accessories such as washbags and bedroom accessories.

Woven braids add style to curtains and swags, or can be stitched to the top panel of a cushion, while fringing can emphasize the edges of both cushions and curtains. For Victorian-style finishes on linens, you can topstitch ribbons and lace to bed linens and tablecloths for special effects. You can also make your own fabric strips to topstitch in place a simple decoration for a textured or patterned fabric – try placing them along a towel's edge, for example.

Finishes for seams and hems

Insertion cord is used in the same way as piping cord, to emphasize seamlines. Position it along the seamline of the main panel of fabric, and stitch in place with a piping foot, taking care to stitch only the flange, not the cord itself. Position the second panel of fabric before completing the seam.

Using insertion cord

Stitch the cord in place to one panel of fabric before completing the seam.

Coping with corners

If the insertion cord has to fit around a corner, first clip it into the flange so you can then more easily manoeuvre the cord into place.

Topstitched finishes

When applying a topstitched finish, such as braid, fringing, ribbon or lace, it is important to measure and mark accurately. The decoration should be applied before making up an item. This makes it easier to work and, where the trim runs to the item's edge, you can be sure that the raw edges will be stitched into the seam as you make up the curtain or cushion.

Marking the position

Mark the trim's position on the panel with chalk. Decide whether to align the trim centrally, or to one side of the marked line. Cut lengths of braid, lace or ribbon to match the marked line, allowing at least ½in (1.25cm) for turning under at each end.

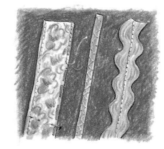

Topstitching

Pin and baste the trim in place, then topstitch by machine. Wide trims should be topstitched close to each edge with straight stitch, or use a narrow zig-zag stitch worked over the trim's edge. If you are making two lines of stitching, work them both in the same direction to avoid twisting and distorting the trim. Very narrow trims can be held in place with a single line of stitching (straight or zig-zag) down the trim's centre.

Turning a corner

On bed linens and cushions, you may want to add a square or rectangle of ribbon or braid, topstitched in place, which involves mitring the corners. Mark outer line of rectangle as a guide for positioning the trim. Topstitch trim in place along outer edge, stopping at the corner. Reverse stitch to strengthen the stitching, then remove the panel from the machine. Fold trim back on itself at the corner and stitch a short, diagonal seam by machine across the trim, from the outer corner down to the trim's inner edge. Clip away seam allowance, if necessary. Press flat. Continue stitching to the next corner. When complete, topstitch the inner edge of trim in place.

Embroidered touches

Embroidered details can turn an ordinary accessory into a personalized heirloom. An initial on the corner of a towel, a floral motif on napkins and table linen, or an appropriate motif on a book cover or laundry bag turn everyday items into something special. If you have an electronic sewing machine, complete with embroidery programs, you will have no difficulty in finding suitable motifs and letters. However, if you would like to hand-embroider an item, you will have to select a suitable motif and then select colours and stitches to suit the pattern. For example, you might want to copy an outline from a patterned bathroom blind onto plain towels, or you could pick out a child's favourite cartoon character on a floor cushion or laundry bag.

Motifs and materials

If you cannot copy an image freehand, you can always trace it. And if you need to change the size, you can do this on a photocopier which has a reduce/enlarge facility. If you do not have access to such a copier, follow the instructions on the right for enlarging an image.

The weight of the fabric dictates the weight of embroidery thread you choose. For most purposes, stranded embroidery cotton is the ideal choice: it can be used on fine-to mediumweight cottons and linens, and is available in a very wide range of colours. Pearled cotton thread can be used on heavier fabrics and fine wool embroidery yarn is suitable for more coarse, open-weave fabrics.

Mark the outline of the embroidery pattern directly onto the fabric you are working on. You can do this by using pins (for beaded patterns), dressmaker's marking pencils (for freehand outlines) or dressmaker's carbon paper (for copying an outline by tracing over it). For the best results, stretch the area that you are working on tautly across an embroidery hoop, so that it is easy to keep the stitching even without worrying about distorting the fabric.

Using stranded embroidery cotton

Stranded embroidery cotton comes in six strands, loosely twisted together. Cut off a short working length – 12in (30cm) is ample for most purposes – and divide the thread into two sets of three strands, unless you are working with a very chunky fabric.

Enlarging an image

If you are working from a specific pattern, suitable motifs may be provided, but you might want to add your own touches with motifs taken from other printed material, such as magazines and wallpaper. This is a particularly useful source for simple letter outlines. More decorative alphabets are available in embroidery books. If the motif you are copying is not the right size for the piece you are making, you can adjust the size using graph paper, and then transfer the pattern with dressmaker's carbon paper.

On tracing paper, draw a grid of ½in (1.25cm) squares to fit over the item to be copied. Decide on the size of the motif: for a motif twice the height, draw a grid of 1in (2.5cm) squares, drawing the same number of larger squares as you had on the tracing paper; for a motif 2½ times the height of the original, make the squares 1¼in (3cm). Working freehand, carefully copy each part of the motif's outline, working on one square at a time.

Right Combine your favourite colours, or highlight colours from a room scheme, when you select threads for embroidery.

9 Holding fast

Many soft furnishings and accessories need openings (for easy removal for cleaning, for example) and openings need fastenings to keep them closed while in use. Zips have been used for years, but touch-and-close fastenings are useful on some heavy-duty items, while hooks and eyes, press studs and buttons are often more economical.

If you use a pattern for soft furnishings, the size and position of the fastening is usually explained there. But you can also develop your own methods of finishing covers. For example, you can make a simple cushion cover with a button-down flap, or set some eyelets into the edge of a cover and lace them together with ribbon of your choice. Fastening by the yard (touch-and-close, hook-and-eye or press-stud tape) is often used for slip covers, but zips are much more often used for cushion covers. Closures are often fitted in the seam lines of cushions and loose covers, but it can be easier to set them across the back panel to give the finished cover a neatly piped outline, for example. Many linens are finished with stylish buttons or ties, but for duvet covers you may prefer to use lightweight zips or some light, plastic press-stud tape.

Fastening by the yard

Nylon touch-and-close fastening comes in long strips made up of a double layer: one half has tiny hooks and the other has a soft mesh of nylon loops. When joining two fabric pieces, allow an overlap equal to the width of the fastening you are using. Also allow for a turning down each of the edges to be joined. Topstitch the fastening in place to the wrong side of the overlap and the right side of the underlap. Fix with glue, while you stitch them down, because the backing is difficult to pin in place. Use the mesh of loops on the overlap and the crisper hooks ontheunderlapping fabric.

Position hook-and-eye and press-stud tapes in the seam allowance or along overlap. The eyes of the hook-and-eye tape, and the studs of the press-stud tape, should be on the right side of the underlap; the hooks and the sockets should be on the underside of the overlap. Topstitch in place. Do not stitch close to the metal or plastic inserts in the tapes.

Setting a zip into a cushion panel

Set a zip between two flat panels, close to the seam line to be less intrusive. On boxed cushions, set the zip into a side panel before making up the cushion.

Joining the panels

Decide which cushion panel should have the zip and where it should be. Make a paper pattern of the panel's finished dimensions and cut it along the zip line. Then use the two patterns to cut out two fabric pieces, adding 1in (2.5cm) seam allowances along the edges where the zip is to be. Baste the two pieces together along the position of the zip, taking care to match patterns, if appropriate. Stitch the two fabric pieces along the seam line leaving the seam unstitched where the zip will be. Leave the seam basted along the zip line.

Positioning the zip

Press the seam, then press seam allowances open (including along basted section). Position the zip behind the seam, so that it is central to the basted seam line. Pin and baste in place, then, from the right side, topstitch the zip in place, across ends and down both sides. Use a zip or piping foot to avoid damaging the zip, but do not stitch close to the zip or the fabric will gape and the zip will be difficult to operate.

Hand-sewn fastenings

Individual hooks and eyes, and press studs are sewn on by hand; and buttons are best sewn by hand for a secure finish. Mark the position of these closures carefully, and check both halves are aligned before stitching in place.

Hooks and eyes

Stitch hooks and eyes on with several stitches around the link of each eye. Check the positions carefully before stitching. On an overlapped closure, the hardwear should not show when the fastening is closed. The eye (or bar) should be on the underlap.

Press studs

Align the two halves of the studs by pushing a needle through the central hole, and through both fabric layers to be joined. Stitch in place with stud on overlap and socket on underlapping edge of item.

Holes and loops

You can stitch buttonholes by machine, and bound buttonholes are particularly effective on simple fabrics of Shaker-style furnishings. Hand-stitched button loops (see page 207) are a foolproof method of finishing fastenings that do not take up too much time and effort.

Rather more elaborate to make are rouleau button loops, which are put together from a long fabric tube which is stitched into loops down the overlapping edge of a closure. These can either be spaced apart on the soft furnishing item, or alternatively butted together to make a more dramatic effect. The loops have to be set into a seam that is down the opening edge of the item, created by a facing of fabric.

Machine stitched buttonholes

Buttonholes are best worked through more than one fabric layer, so allow a generous turning on the overlapping edge where you wish to stitch the buttonhole. Measure the button's diameter and mark the position and length of the buttonhole. Use the settings on your machine (some are automatic) to work the outline of the buttonhole. Use fine embroidery scissors to cut the fabric between the stitches, without cutting into them.

Rouleau loops

Rouleau loops are made from long fabric strips. Each loop should be long enough to go over the button's diameter, plus seam allowances to stitch into the opening's edge. Work out each loop's length, including seam allowances, and cut a single strip of fabric the total length required and about 1in (2.5cm) wide. Turn under ¼in (6mm) down each long edge, then fold in half, right sides outward. Stitch down middle to enclose raw edges.

Attaching rouleau loops

Set rouleau loops into a faced opening, so that the raw loop ends are enclosed. Position the loops next to each other for a traditional "buttoned dress" finish, or space them apart down the opening for less work! Pin loops along the raw edge on the right side of the overlap, with raw edges matching. Stitch in place, then position facing over the loops, right side down, and stitch seam. Press, turn facing to inside and press again.

Covered buttons

Covered buttons provide a subtle finish to a buttoned opening. They look particularly effective in combination with rouleau loops – small buttons for tightly spaced buttons, and larger buttons for a more casual effect. Use fabric to match the cover you are making, or add plain-covered buttons to a patterned item. For extra detail, coordinate the buttons with rouleau loops.

Button forms are available from haberdashery departments in a range of sizes, complete with instructions. If you are using very fine or slippery fabric, use iron-on interfacing to give the fabric a firmer finish before covering the button.

Covering a button

Simply cut a circle of fabric a little larger than the diameter of the button (you will find a precise guide in the instructions) and tuck it over the front portion of the button before fixing the back in place.

Modern touch

Simple fabric ties and metal eyelets are ideal for today's soft furnishings. They can be used to tie cushions to stylish metal furniture and to sling curtains from slim, shiny rods. Fabric ties are the simplest fastenings, needing only fabric remnants to make up. For metal eyelets, you need a special gadget to insert the eyelet.

Making ties

Make these in the same way as rouleau loops, or make a tube of fabric and pull it through. Cut each half of tie at least 10in (25cm) long, or make a double length to attach to an edge or insert in a seam – 4in (10cm) is a good width. Fold the strip in half lengthwise, inside out, and run some tape or cord along the length, close to the fold. Stitch across one end, catching the end of the tape or cord into the seam. Then stitch along the long edge of the tie, taking a ⅝in (1.5 cm) seam allowance, taking care not to catch in tape or cord. Trim the seam allowance and pull the tape or cord to turn the tie right side out. Trim away tape or cord, then turn in raw ends and slipstitch the opening.

9 Fixings and fittings

*Y*ou cannot hang curtains, blinds and drapes *without some sort of track or pole running across the window. The actual fixing method depends on the surface you are fixing into and the brackets supplied with the track, rod or pole. If you are fitting ready-made blinds, these are usally supplied complete with a heading box which is held in place at each end.*

How will the tracks be fixed?

Start by taking a good look at the wall or ceiling above the window you are dressing. The window may be in an alcove, you may want to fit a track to the wall above the window, or it may be easier to fit the track to the ceiling. Many American homes and modern European houses are built from a timber frame construction. This means that the walls are hollow, with a plasterboard surface supported on upright studs every 12–15in (30–37.5cm) across the wall. You can make a safer fixing if you drill into one of these studs, or into the wooden framework surrounding the window. Then you can use wood screws to screw the brackets in place. It may be easier to fit a wooden batten above the window, painted or papered to match the wall, so that you can fit the brackets supporting the rods at any point across the top of the window. This also applies if the walls are uneven, or the plaster is old.

Blocks for plastic tracks

Plastic blocks for some tracks can be screwed either into the wall or alternatively be fixed directly into the ceiling.

Lightweight ceiling tracks

This simple track can be screwed into the ceiling. Runners slot into the track, but they are only ever suitable to be used with lightweight drapes.

Wooden poles and brackets

Brackets for wooden poles are available in different lengths, to adjust the curtain depth from the window. The brackets should be fitted about 2in (5cm) from the end of the pole (excluding the finial) so that there is room for a single ring between the bracket and the finial. This anchors the curtain when you pull it closed. The brackets can also be slung from the ceiling. Wooden sockets are available if the pole is fitted in a recess.

Metal poles

For most systems, there are only limited brackets available to support the poles. The chosen finials and brackets make a style statement. Check whether you need a central bracket to fit a long pole, and that there is a suitable point on the wall or window frame where you can fit it.

Rods and sockets

Brass and other lightweight rods are suitable to be placed inside a recess. Sockets can be fitted on each end, which are then screwed into the side of the recess. Or if you prefer you can buy surface-mounted sockets if the rod is to be fitted on the wall surface or attached to the window surround.

Telescopic rods

Some shower curtain fittings and lightweight curtain rods are telescopic. Buy them slightly longer than the recess they are to fit into, and put them in position: a spring inside pushes the ends against the sides of the recess and there is no drilling or screwing required. Common finishes include plain white plastic, aluminium and brass.

Curtain wires

Plastic-covered sprung curtain wires, which are again only suitable to hold lightweight curtains, are looped onto screw eyes fitted at either end of a surface or recess. The screw eyes are only suitable for fixing into a wooden surround.

Screws and wall plugs

Most systems come with suitable screws, and sometimes even wall plugs.

• If you are fixing to a hollow wall away from a stud position, use special expanding plugs that have flanges to grip the inside of the wall as you tighten the screw.

• Solid walls, of brick or other building blocks, have to be drilled so that you can fit plastic wall plugs to grip the screw in place.

• If you need to drill into concrete (many windows have a concrete lintel above them) use an electric drill which has a hammerhead action to make a neat hole to take the wall plug.

• Most brackets are easier to screw into wood than directly into a wall. The solution, often, is to fit a wooden batten to the wall above the window – particularly if the walls are timber-frame, or the plasterwork is uneven.

Fitting a wooden batten

A wooden batten above the window makes it easy to fit curtain tracks as you simply screw the plastic brackets into the batten. Use a batten if you have hollow (stud) walls, if you have a concrete lintel above the window, or if the plaster is unsound in places. Avoid battens if you are fitting poles or rods, as the raised wooden strip will detract from the clean lines of this style – even if the batten is decorated to match the wall.

Use a batten of planed (par – planed all round) softwood, ½ x 2in (12 x 50mm). It should be 2in (5cm) shorter than the track, so that it is hidden behind the curtain heading.

Marking the position

Decide on the track's position (for example, halfway between the top of the window and the ceiling) and hold the batten in place. Use a spirit level to check that it is horizontal, and measure carefully to ensure it is centred on the window. Make a pencil line along the wall to indicate the position of the top of the batten.

Making good

You may need to fill cracks and holes in plasterwork where old tracks have been taken down. Smooth filler into cracks and when dry, sand with fine-grade glasspaper. Paint over to match existing paint or wallpaper. Use the following tools and equipment to fill holes:

• A shave-hook or narrow filling knife to scrape out any damaged plaster.

• Use powdered or ready-mixed filler to fill cracks and holes. With powdered filler, mix it in a suitable container (such as an old pudding basin). Add water slowly until the paste is smooth.

• A filling knife will smooth the paste into the cracks. Alternatively, you can try using an old, bendy knife.

• Glasspaper (fine grade for plasterwork) is essential for getting a good finish after making good.

Fitting the batten

Remove the batten and drill a hole at each point (using a masonry bit or hammer-head drill). The hole's size depends on the wall plugs/screw sizes used. Knock wall plugs into the holes, and fit a screw into each pilot hole in the batten. Re-position the batten and fix each screw into the wall plugs. Finally, position brackets to hold the track along the length of the batten.

Marking fixing points

Take the batten down and drill pilot holes through the batten every 10–15in (25–37.5cm) along its length. The diameter of the pilot holes should match the shank of the screws used. Re-position the batten, and with a long, pointed tool (such as a bradawl) mark the wall by inserting it into each hole.

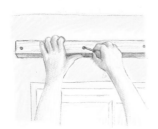

9 Starting securely

Careful marking and secure fixing are essential for long-lasting, good-looking tracks and poles. Get the right tools for the job, and measure and mark carefully before screwing the supports in place.

Do not spend hours planning window dressing and making up drapes and blinds, only to find that they collapse as soon as you hang them from the track. After doing any making good, ensure that the tracks are accurately and securely fixed.

Measuring and marking

When buying curtain tracks, you may be able to order them to measure, or you may have to trim them to fit once home.

• Measure accurately with a retractable metal tape measure before cutting.

Pelmet shelves

Wooden pelmet shelves give a secure fixing point for curtain tracks and the pelmet or valance itself. You can also attach elaborate swags and tails to the front of a shelf.

Use planed timber (par, planed all round), about ½in (12mm) thick and 4in (10cm) deep, according to window's size and the weight of the curtains. The shelf should extend about 2½in (6.5cm) beyond the window at either end. Angle irons are a convenient way to fix the shelf in place: these are L-shaped metal plates, with two holes in each leg. One side is screwed into the underside of the shelf, then the shelf can be held in position so that you can mark drilling points through the remaining holes on the wall above the window. Position them every 8in (20cm) along the shelf's length. If the shelf is flush with the top of the window recess, angle irons may be fitted above the shelf. Once the pelmet shelf is up, attach a pelmet, valance or swag to the front, and fit a track for curtains to the underside.

• Once tracks are the right length, make sure they are level and central to the window. This job is easier with more than one person. Hold the track itself up against the wall and measure how far it extends on each side of the window. Move it from side to side until it is central, and use a spirit level to check it is level and mark the track's position.

• Next, remove the track and lay it on the floor. Check the brackets, and see how the system fits together. The brackets may protrude above the track or pole, so judge where the top of the bracket should be relative to the line drawn on the wall to mark the top of the track.

• With decorative brackets, check how far from the outer edge of the window they should be, allowing for the finials and also a single ring between the finial and the bracket.

Marking bracket positions

Hold bracket up to the wall and mark fixing holes, with a pencil or fine-pointed bradawl to make a mark through the screw holes. Then take down the bracket. If fixing into a wall, drill holes to take the wall plugs that fit the screws supplied with the track. If fixing into wood, use a bradawl to make a pilot hole.

Rest the spirit level on top of the track or pole to check that it is flat. Now mark the position lightly in pencil every 10in (25cm) or so along the length.

Fitting the track and hanging the curtains

With the brackets in place, fit the track, runners, hooks and curtains. You will need enough hooks and runners to position them 2–3in (5–7.5cm) apart across the width of the curtain, with one at each end. The heavier the curtains, the more hooks and runners you will need. Pinch pleated curtains should be hung from a hook positioned at each pleat.

• Plastic tracks usually clip onto block supports, but you may have to slide the track onto the supports before you screw them in place with some systems.

• Rods and poles usually slot through the brackets.

• Ensure you have enough runners or rings slotted in place before fixing (to save stretching into awkward corners). With rods and poles, leave two runners off, fit the pole so the rings are between the brackets, then add two reserved rings between end brackets and the finials.

• With the curtains laid out flat, insert hooks into the curtain tape, positioning one at each end and the remaining ones spaced evenly across the curtain width.

• Hook a curtain hook onto each runner or ring. You may need someone to support the bulk of the curtains while doing this.

• Finally, for a really professional finish, steam the curtains with a hand-held steamer to help the fabric to drape well.

Positioning tie-backs and hold-backs

Once the pole is up, you can measure up for the curtains. If you want to add tie-backs and hold-backs (either hooks to hold fabric tie-backs in place, or decorative brackets that you can loop the curtains around), use some tape or string to check the proportions. Tie tape to the centre of the pole (or the point where the leading edge of the curtain will hang during the day) and hold the tape to the side of the window to see where the curtain will hang. A second tape down the outer edge of the curtain can act as a further guide. If the pole or track has long brackets, so that the curtains hang well clear of the window, you can mount tie-back fixtures on a wooden block so the tie-backs do not pull the curtains in toward the wall. Generally, the tie-back should be below the finial of a pole, or be level with the end of a track.

Tie-backs hold curtains clear of the window. The height depends on curtains you have, and the amount of light you want to let in. This is particularly important if you hang the curtains so that they do not draw away from the window, but are only held by tie-backs. When you are sure of the position, mark drilling holes amd fix the tie-back with screws. Use wall plugs if you are screwing into the wall rather than a wood surround.

Wide windows

Tie-backs are useful at either end of wide windows, or curtains across bay or bow windows. They hold the bulk of the fabric out of the way during the day. Most of the bulk is in the curtain heading. Check how bulky the curtains are when drawn back and make the tie-back short enough to pull them in and drape attractively.

High ties

To allow maximum light through a window, position the tie-back as high as possible – particularly if there is only a single curtain.

Elegant drape

To give a window a more elegant look, position the tie-backs lower down the window, (two-thirds of the way down, or level with a chair rail, for example). Bear in mind that the curtains may cut out some daylight.

9 Care, cleaning and repair

If you look after your soft furnishings carefully, clean them regularly and deal with spills and marks as soon as possible, you can extend their life and ensure that your home looks as smart as possible. Here is a guide to some day-by-day and emergency treatments for fabrics.

There is no substitute for regular, day-to-day care of soft furnishings. Plumping up pillows and keeping dust at bay can help to prolong life as well as improving the look of a room. The amount of cleaning will depend on where you live and the type of home you have: a draughty, city terraced house attracts grimy dirt, while a well insulated country cottage will need considerably less cleaning; of course, children seem to bring their own dirt and dust with them!

Regular cleaning

Start by including care of soft furnishings as part of your cleaning routine: you should plump up pillows every day, particularly if they are feather and down, so that they keep their shape and look good. Use the nozzle of a vacuum cleaner to clean out the dust from the cracks between the seat and the back of upholstered furniture every week, and vacuum curtains and drapes at least once a month, paying particular attention to fixed headings and swags, where the dust cannot be shaken out.

Of course, table and bed linens should be washed regularly, and loose covers should be removed for laundering or dry cleaning every six months or so, depending on how much wear and tear they get.

Emergency treatments

It is impossible to avoid some accidental spills, but dealing with them promptly can help to prevent them from becoming a permanent feature! The following treatments are mainly for cotton and linen fibres. Some may cause the colour to fade, so check the effect on a discreet corner before applying to the centre of an item. Always check the effect before using cleaners on synthetic fibres. Act as quickly as possible, and launder the item normally after stain removal. If cleaning fixed fabrics (such as upholstered chair seats) try to use dry cleaners, as water may bring through colours from the natural fibres used in the stuffing. If an item is dry clean only, take it to a specialist with as much information about the fabric and stain as possible.

Blood Applying salt to the surface helps to soak up initial staining. Soak the item in cold, salty water.

Chewing gum Not so much a stain as a problem of sticking. Pick off as much gum as you can by hand, then get the gum as cold as possible (by putting the item in the freezer or applying ice cubes to the affected area). Once chilled, the gum becomes much more brittle and is easier to pick off.

Ink stains If you have children who are careless with ball-points and felt tips, invest in proprietary stain removers to suit the type of pens they use. Methylated spirit is often effective on ball-point marks. Petrol or white spirit are effective on some ink stains.

Mildew Grey spots of mildew sometimes develop on furnishings if your home is damp or has problems with condensation and is not properly ventilated. They can be removed by soaking an item in bleach and water (the concentration of bleach depends on the strength of the bleach you are using – check the manufacturer's instructions). Warning: The bleach may cause coloured fabrics to fade.

Oil and grease Cooking and salad oil, and greasy marks from hair oils, are among the commonest stains. Place a clean cloth under the fabric, and dab the surface with a little proprietary stain remover or petrol for stubborn, tarry marks.

Wax Once the hot wax has set, pick off as much as possible by hand. To remove any remaining wax, sandwich the fabric between two layers of blotting paper or clean, absorbent rags and press with a hot iron.

Wine Red wine responds well to being dabbed with white wine, which 'thins' the wine and makes it easier to wash out. Alternatively, cover the red wine stain with salt while it is still wet. Vacuum up the salt at the end of the evening, and much of the stain will disappear. The best solution, however, is to launder the item while the stain is still wet.

Curry/turmeric If you are serving a curry meal, then try to use white or pastel coloured linen on the table. Then you can soak it in bleach without fear of having any problems with the material fading.

Toolbox

If you have to embark on any DIY tasks, collect a kit of good-quality tools to make the job easier.

Measuring and marking tools

• A retractable metal rule for measuring up rooms and windows; use a small steel rule for finer measurements.
• Keep pencils sharp: use hard ones for marking walls and soft ones for marking wood. Also use a notebook and pen for jotting down any measurements and for making calculations.

Drilling and fixing tools

• Use a sturdy stepladder to stand on, so that you can drill squarely into the wall above the window.
• An electric drill is ideal to fix a lot of brackets in place. Keep a selection of drill bits – fine wood drills for window frames and boards; bits with reinforced tips for masonry and concrete.
• Wall plugs hold screws in place. For solid walls, use tapered or finned plastic plugs, with woodscrews. The plugs expand as you screw into them. The size of the screws supplied with tracks varies, so keep some different plugs. For hollow walls, use special plastic toggles with ordinary wood screws. You may also need gravity or spring toggles for fixing items like angle irons and tie-backs. These come with their own screws, so check that it is the right size for the item you are fixing.

• Screws are normally supplied with tracks, but keep some screws for other jobs. For example, chrome screws with matching metal cups give a neat finish when hanging notice-boards; ordinary woodscrews are needed for fixing battens in place above a window so that curtain tracks or Roman blinds can be fitted.
• Screwdrivers – use a stout one to screw up pelmet shelves and metal brackets, and smaller ones for plastic brackets. Also a long, fine screwdriver can reach into the brackets if the screws are deeply recessed. You may also need cross-headed screwdrivers. An electric screwdriver is worth considering.

Cutting and shaping tools

• Cut metal and plastic tracks with a hacksaw. For wooden poles, a tenon saw gives a neat, straight cut. Use a mitring block to check that you are cutting at right angles to the pole, and a vice or workbench is useful for holding the work steady as you cut.
• A sharp craft knife with interchangeable blades is another useful item in your tool kit.

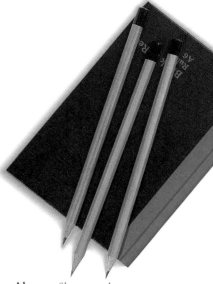

Above *Sharp pencils are essential for accurate marking. Keep a notebook for jotting down measurements and calculations for fabrics as well as tracks and poles.*

Below *Keep a basic toolkit for DIY tasks such as fitting curtain tracks: 1. Electric drill; 2. Selection of drill bits; 3. Variety of wallplugs to suit your needs; 4. Selection of screws; 5. Long, short and cross-headed screwdrivers; 6. Hacksaw; 7. Tenon saw; 8. Vice; 9. Craft knife and blades.*

9 Facts and figures

Both imperial and metric measurements have been given in the instructions throughout this book. You should choose to work in either imperial or metric, but do not mix the measurements. For quick reference, a series of conversion charts is given below: detailed conversions of small amounts, fabric yardage/metrage and common fabric widths. These last two charts are for use in stores that sell by the metre when you have worked out quantities in yards.

Fabric lengths

⅛yd	=	10cm	3¾yd	=	3.5m	
¼yd	=	20cm	4yd	=	3.7m	
⅜yd	=	40cm	4⅜yd	=	4m	
½yd	=	45cm	4½yd	=	4.2m	
⅝yd	=	60cm	5⅞yd	=	4.5m	
¾yd	=	70cm	5yd	=	4.6m	
⅞yd	=	80cm	5½yd	=	5m	
1yd	=	1m	10yd	=	9.2m	
1½yd	=	1.4m	10⅞yd	=	10m	
2yd	=	1.9m	20yd	=	18.5m	
2¼yd	=	2m	21⅓yd	=	20m	
2½yd	=	2.3m				

Fabric widths

2¾yd	=	2.5m	36in	=	90cm
3yd	=	2.7m	44/45in	=	115cm
3¼yd	=	3m	48in	=	120cm
3½yd	=	3.2m	60in	=	150cm

Type	Size	Duvet size	Flat sheet size
Small single	2ft 6in x 6ft (75 x 190cm)	4ft x 6ft 3in (120 x 195cm)	66in x 99in (165 x 250cm)
Single	3ft x 6ft 3in (90 x 200cm)	4ft 6in x 6ft 6in (135 x 200cm)	70 x 102in (180 x 260cm)
Double	4ft 6in x 6ft 3in (135 x 200cm)	4ft 6in x 6ft 6in (200 x 200cm)	90 x 102in (230 x 260cm)
King size	5ft x 6ft 6in (150 x 210cm)	7ft 4in x 7ft 2 in (225 x 220cm)	108 x 108in (275 x 275cm)
Super king size	6ft x 6ft 6in (190 x 210cm)	8ft 6in x 7ft 2in (260 x 220cm)	130 x 108in (290 x 275cm)
Standard pillow	19 x 29 in (48 x 74cm)	**Square pillow** 26in square (65cm square)	

Always check measurements of beds and bedding before making up bedlinen as precise dimensions vary from manufacturer to manufacturer.

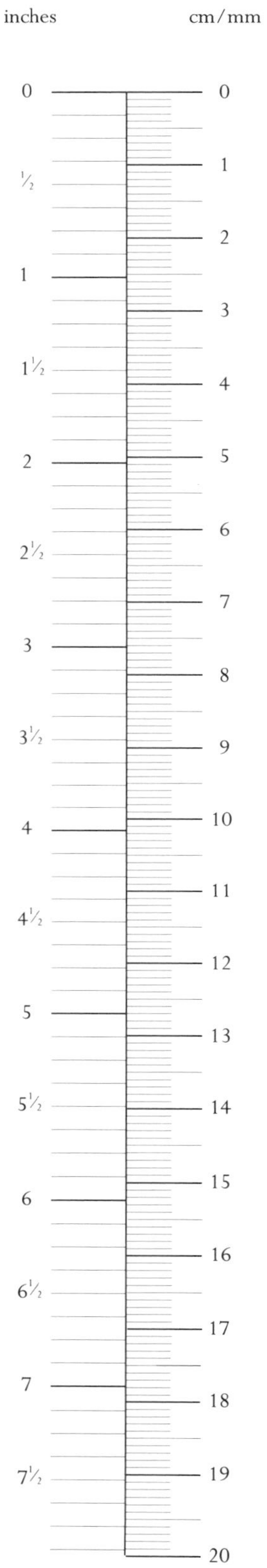

inches / cm/mm scale:
0 — 0
½ — 1
 — 2
1 — 3
 — 4
1½ — 4
2 — 5
 — 6
2½ — 7
3 — 8
3½ — 9
4 — 10
 — 11
4½ — 12
5 — 13
5½ — 14
 — 15
6 — 15
 — 16
6½ — 17
7 — 18
7½ — 19
 — 20

1in = 2.54cm
(2.5cm approx)

1cm = 0.3937in
(⅜in approx)

1ft = 0.3048m

3ft = 1yd = 1m
(approx)

1m = 3.281ft

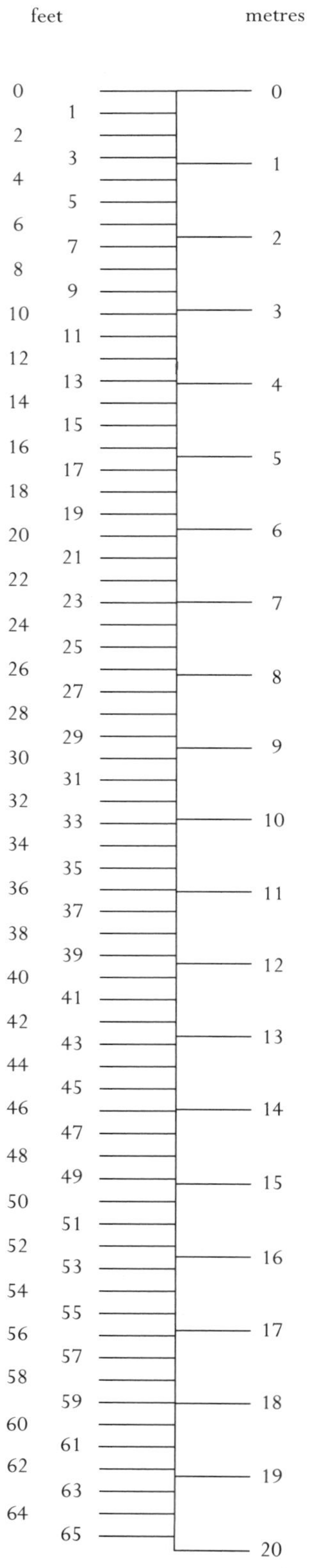

feet / metres scale:
0 — 0
1, 2, 3, 4, 5 — 1
6, 7 — 2
8, 9, 10, 11 — 3
12, 13, 14, 15 — 4
16, 17, 18, 19 — 5
20, 21, 22, 23 — 7
24, 25, 26, 27, 28 — 8
29, 30, 31 — 9
32, 33, 34 — 10
35, 36, 37, 38 — 11
39, 40, 41 — 12
42, 43, 44, 45 — 13
46, 47, 48, 49 — 14
50, 51, 52, 53 — 16
54, 55, 56, 57 — 17
58, 59, 60, 61 — 18
62, 63, 64, 65 — 19
— 20

Glossary

Acrylic Synthetic fibre used to make fabric that has similar properties to wool.

Appliqué Method of decorating fabric by stitching on shapes cut from other fabrics.

Austrian blind Elaborate blind made like a curtain, with the addition of rings and cords on the back so that the panel can be pulled upward during the day.

Axminster Particular weave used to make carpets; several colours are woven into the backing as the carpet is made, so that quite elaborate patterns are possible.

Basket weave Woven effect in fabric with several strands of warp and weft threads running together to create a small block effect.

Batten Strip of wood: fine battens are fitted into casings at the bottom of Roman blinds and roller blinds, to keep the fabric taut; more substantial battens are fixed to the wall above a window to provide an even surface for curtain tracks.

Berber A breed of sheep from north African; the term is used to describe carpet with a fairly chunky weave, usually in a natural, oatmeal colour.

Binding (bias and straight cut) Narrow strips of fabric used to cover the edge of a larger panel of fabric; bias binding is cut diagonally across the fabric (on the bias) so that it can be eased around curves without pleats and puckers.

Bouclé Yarn spun with a loose, looped finish; fabric woven or knitted from boucle yarn.

Bound button holes Tailored buttonholes finished with strips of fabric binding, rather than machine or hand-sewn buttonhole stitch.

Bradawl Small pointed tool, rather like a screwdriver, used to make holes in wooden surfaces before screwing in screws, hooks, etc.

Braid Woven trim, used in upholstery or for topstitched decorations; braids are more substantial, and often more elaborately woven, than ribbons.

Brocade Medium to heavy weight fabric woven in two colours to create a satin background with a relief pattern.

Broderie anglaise Cotton fabric that has been pierced and embroidered to create a decorative effect; available as a full-width fabric and as a narrow trim; usually white or cream in colour.

Bump Thick fabric, traditionally a loosely woven brushed cotton, that is used to improve wear of curtains and to give curtains and other furnishings a soft and luxurious feel.

Button loops Fabric or hand-stitched loops that act as button holes. Fabric button loops are also known as rouleau loops.

Calico Medium-weight cotton cloth, usually white or unbleached; its low price makes it suitable for making cushion pads with foam or polyester stuffing.

Canopy Fabric suspended over a bed or other feature in a room.

Canvas Heavy weight cotton fabric, often used for deck chair covers.

Canvaswork Embroidery, usually in wool, on special even-weave, holey canvas.

Cased heading A simple curtain heading made by stitching a casing which is slotted onto a curtain wire, rod or pole.

Casing A channel in a piece of fabric made by folding over the top and making two lines of stitching; used to make drawstring bags, curtain headings, etc.

Check A grid pattern, usually woven but may be printed onto fabric.

Chenille Subtly ribbed, velvety fabric, softer in texture than velvet or corduroy.

Chintz From a Hindu word, chintz is a printed cotton fabric, usually glazed (glossy), but the term is now used to denote any glazed cotton fabric.

Chisel Woodworking tool with sharp cutting edges, used to shape wood; edges must be protected and kept sharp.

Clip Cut into fabric at right angles to the raw edge, or diagonally across corners, to prevent distortion of curved seams and bulk in corners when an item is turned right side out.

Complementary colours Colours on opposite sides of the colour wheel: red and green; blue and orange; yellow and purple.

Corduroy Heavy weight fabric with pile woven into the fabric to form narrow ribs.

Covered buttons Buttons covered with fabric; you can make them with special button forms, available from haberdashery departments and shops.

Crewel work Flowing style of embroidery, developed in 16th century Europe, usually in wool on linen,

Damask Fabric (usually silk or linen) with a pattern woven into it; often woven in a single colour, so that the pattern only shows as the light catches the fabric.

Denim Originally from the city of Nîmes in France, a twill weave fabric traditionally woven using indigo warp and white weft threads.

Dobby weave Fabric woven with small, repeating pattern, such as a small diamond or raised star.

Domette Soft fabric, often synthetic, used as a layer of padding in curtains or under table-cloths.

Dowel Length of round wood which can be fitted in casing to keep Roman blinds hanging crisply.

Dress curtains Permanently fixed curtains that are not intended to be drawn closed. Often used in combination with a roller or Roman blind.

Dressmaker's carbon paper Paper with coloured coating on the back, so that when you trace an outline on it the motif is transferred to a layer of fabric placed beneath the carbon paper.

Drop-in chair seat An upholstered panel that can be lifted out of (or dropped into) the frame of an upright chair.

Duck Originally used for sails and outerwear, this plain weave fabric in cotton or linen is hardwearing, and can be used for loose covers and other furnishings.

Easy-care fabrics Usually woven from a mix of fibres, easy-care fabrics need minimal ironing.

Electronic machine Electric sewing machine with microchips to make it easy to adjust the type, size and tension of the stitch.

Facing Panel of fabric used to back the main fabric of a cushion or other item around the opening, giving a neat finish.

Faille Silk fabric with a ribbed weave

Felt Non-woven, non-fray textile, traditionally in wool, with many craft applications.

Festoon blind Blind with a gathered heading and vertical tapes to gather the fabric into festoons. The blind is be raised with a system or rings and cords.

Field The background colour of a printed or embroidered piece of fabric.

Finials Decorative knobs, loops and twirls supplied to fit to the end of curtain tracks or poles.

Fitted sheets Bottom sheets for beds which are tailored to fit the mattress, with elasticated corners to hold the sheet taut in place.

Flat seam A simple seam used to join two pieces of fabric with a single line of stitching.

Flat sheet Bedlinen that is not fitted at the corners. Often made with a deep hem across the top edge.

French seam Double seam in which the raw edges are completely enclosed.

Geometric print Regular print, of abstract shapes arranged in a regular pattern.

Gingham Lightweight woven fabric, usually white and one other colour, originally a striped fabric, but now used to describe check.

Grain of fabric The lengthwise grain is the direction in which the warp threads of the fabric run, parallel to the selvedges.

Ground The 'background' fabric that is used in embroidery, appliqué etc.

Gusset A narrow panel, sometimes shaped or gathered to give fullness; the side panels of a box-shaped cushion.

Heading tape A specially manufactured tape which is stitched across the top of a curtain; it has an arrangement of cords so you can gather up the curtain and loops and slot curtain hooks through the tape.

Herringbone A fine, hand-sewn stitch, which can be used to join panels of wadding or to hold hems in place; may also be used as an embroidery stitch.

Hold-backs Metal or wooden knobs or hooks, fitted at the sides of windows, so that you can loop curtains clear of the window.

Housewife pillowcase Pillowcase made with an internal flap at the opening end so that the pillow can be tucked in place.

Ikat Fabric woven from pre-dyed yarn; the yarn is coloured in sections so that pre-dyed patches are woven in next to each other to create a pattern.

Interfacing Layer of fabric, often synthetic, non-woven and iron-on, used to stiffen lightweight fabrics and make them easier to handle. In soft furnishings it may be used to stiffen curtain headings or fabrics used for appliqué motifs.

Interlining Soft fabric (usually bump or domette) caught inside curtains between the main fabric and the lining to give added weight and luxury.

Jacquard Fabric with colour-woven pattern, similar to brocade or damask, taking its name from the inventor of the loom on which it is woven.

Lambrequin Fabric covered pelmet, shaped to frame the window. Usually used with a blind rather than curtains.

Lapped seam Seam made by overlapping the edges of the panels of fabric to be joined.

Lawn Fine plain-weave cotton fabric.

Layer To trim the seam allowances within a seam to different lengths, eliminating bulk.

Linen union Plain weave fabric made from a mixture of linen and cotton threads.

Lining Layer of fabric added to give improved wear; curtain lining fabric is usually a satin weave cotton fabric.

Liséré Embroidered and beribboned or elaborately woven fabrics and trims.

London blind A fabric blind, usually lined, with an arrangement of cord and two rows of rings to draw up the blind in soft scoops; similar to a Roman blind, but without the stiffening dowels.

Lycra Brand name for a stretch fibre (elastane).

Matelasse Padded cushion or mattress.

Mercerized cotton thread Sewing thread that has been specially treated to improve wear and look more lustrous.

Monochromatic scheme A colour scheme that uses only one colour (plus white) in varying tones.

Monotones A scheme using only one tone of a colour.

Motif Abstract or figurative outline or pattern on printed or woven fabric, or pattern for embroidery or appliqué etc.

Muslin Fine, loosely woven cotton fabric, usually in white or natural.

Nets Translucent curtains, hung to give privacy to windows.

Notch To cut a V-shaped wedge out of the seam allowance; this is done to enable you to re-match seams after preparing panels of fabric, and to reduce bulk in curved seams when an item is turned right side out.

Organdie Fine stiff cotton open-weave fabric, now often available in synthetic fibres.

Organza Finely woven stiff silk, made from a particular type of twisted silk yarn.

Ottoman Heavy, twill-weave fabric, in silk, cotton, linen or synthetic fibre.

Overlock machine Advanced sewing machine that forms stitches in a more elaborate way than a traditional sewing machine; particularly useful for stretch fabric.

Oxford pillowcase Housewife pillowcase with a wide, flat border extending all around the edge.

Paisley An intricate pattern with elongated and curved oval motifs, originating in India but taking its name from the Scottish town renowned for its textile industry.

Pelmet A wooden or fabric covered box fixed over the heading of a curtain to cover tracks and protect from dust.

Pelmet shelf A wooden shelf fitted above a window; the front of the pelmet box or a valance is normally fitted to the front of the pelmet shelf.

Petersham ribbon Hard-wearing, ribbed ribbon, traditionally made of silk.

Petit point Fine cross stitch, worked in wool on needlepoint canvas.

Pile The 'fur' of a carpet or of a velvety fabric.

Pincers Scissor-like tool used to lift nailheads and tacks.

Piqué Light or medium-weight cotton fabric woven in a single colour with an fine, embossed effect.

Plaid Colour-woven fabric (check).

Plumb line A tool used to check vertical lines: it consists of a length of cord with a weight hung at the bottom.

Polyester wadding Thick, soft, lightweight padding available in standard widths and thicknesses.

Primary colours The three basic colours, from which all other colours can be mixed (with the addition of black and white): red, blue and yellow.

Provençal print A small, geometric interpretation of paisley patterns, printed in strong colours on lightweight plain-weave cotton.

Pucker Unsightly gathering along a seamline, caused by a blunt needle or a bulky seam.

PVC A plastic coating applied to fabrics to make them waterproof and wipeable.

Rayon A synthetic fibre – the first one to be developed – that imitates silk.

Roller blind A simple window blind consisting of a sprung roller, a sheet of stiffened fabric and a batten to stiffen the lower edge.

Roman blind A fabric blind, often lined, stiffened with dowels and a batten, that can be drawn by a system of cords and rings.

Rouleau A fine tube of fabric, used to make button loops.

Ruching Gathering fabric to create a panel of luxurious folds.

Sateen Cotton fabric woven to produce a glossy effect on the right side.

Satin A type of weave in which warp threads run over the surface of the fabric to give a glossy finish; a silk fabric with a satin weave.

Satin stitch A closely worked stitch that gives a satin effect: may be worked in lines by machine or over larger areas by hand.

Screw-eye Metal loop with a tail that has a screw thread for fixing into wood fittings.

Scrim Stiff, loosely woven lightweight linen fabric.

Seam allowance The allowance for making a seam around the edge of a panel of fabric. Add a seam allowance to the finished dimensions before cutting out.

Seam line The marked or imaginary line around the edge of a panel of fabric where the stitching runs when you make a seam.

Seam tape Firmly woven narrow cotton tape used to prevent seams from distorting; the seam tape is positioned along the seam line on the wrong side of the fabric, and stitched into the seam as you join layers of fabric.

Secondary colour The three colours obtained by mixing any two primary colours: purple, green and orange.

Seersucker Plain woven fabric, often with woven stripes or checks, in which groups of warp and/or weft threads are drawn tighter, creating rows of ruching down or across the fabric.

Selvedge The woven, non-fraying edges of a length of fabric.

Serging machine See overlock machine.

Sheers See nets.

Shot silk Silk fabric woven with different colours for the warp and weft, creating a fabric that reflects different shades as it catches the light.

Silk dupion Fabric made from silk spun by a particular type of silkworm: two silkworms spin a double cocoon producing a double thread that can be unravelled for weaving.

Squab Small cushion tied to the seat of an upright chair.

Stuffed-over seat Upright chair or stool with upholstery that extends right over the top of the seat and a short way down the chair frame.

Swag Length of fabric draped across the top of a window.

Taffeta Plain fabric, usually silk, with a glossy, stiff finish.

Tail A length of fabric, decoratively draped at the side of a window; may require accurate tailoring for even a casual effect.

Take-up lever A lever on a sewing machine that moves up and down to allow the thread to loop through the fabric as you stitch.

Tarlatan Stiffened fabric, similar in weight to muslin.

Tartan Originating in Scotland, tartan is wool fabric woven to create a checked design; each clan or family had its own particular tartan.

Template A pattern; when cutting repeated identical shapes, for appliqué or patchwork, the pattern is cut out in card so that it can be used over and over again.

Tenting Fabric used to cover the ceiling of a room, usually gathered up and stretched from a central point.

Tertiary colours Colours containing all of the three primary colours.

Tester A canopy over a bed head.

Thread count The number of threads in a specified area (a square inch) of a woven fabric.

Ticking Tightly woven fabric with a distinctive woven stripe; traditionally featherproof with black and off-white stripes, but now available in a range of natural and muted colours.

Tie-backs Bands of fabric or lengths of cord used to hold drapes clear of a window or bedhead.

Toile de Jouy Cotton fabric, originating in 18th century France, with figurative scenes printed in a single colour onto a neutral background.

Topstitching A bold line of stitches used to emphasize seams or finish hems.

Touch-and-close fastening Synthetic fastening, made with plastic loops on one half which link into a furry pile stitched to the opposite side of the opening.

Towelling Woven fabric with a looped pile on both sides.

Trim Cut away excess fabric.

Trompe l'oeil Literally, deceive the eye; used to describe painted effects which create a false impression – such as fake panelling, a window painted on to a wall or imitation marble.

Tufted A type of carpet made by fitting tufts of pile into a canvas backing frame.

Tussah Silk spun from the cocoons of a particular type of silkworm that feeds on oak leaves.

Twill (weave) A weave in which the warp threads form a diagonal rib over the surface of the cloth.

Valance A 'skirt' around a bed which hides the bed base and legs; a gathered fabric strip across the top of a window treatment which hides tracks and poles.

Velvet Woven fabric with a pile; it may be made from a wide range of fibres.

Venetian blind Manufactured blind, traditionally made with wooden slats, although modern Venetians may have aluminium slats; the slats may be adjusted open or closed, or the blind can be raised.

Vertical blind Manufactured blinds that are made up from strips of stiffened fabric, hung from a track. The strips can be adjusted to hang parallel to the window for privacy, opened out, or drawn to one side of the window.

Voile Translucent fabric used mainly for drapes. It may be made of cotton or synthetic fibre.

Walling Fabric stretched across walls as a form of wallcovering.

Wallplugs Plastic or fibre tubes (which may be straight or tapered) that are fitted into holes drilled in walls to secure screws.

Warp The threads running up and down a woven piece of cloth.

Webbing A broad, woven braid. Traditional hessian webbing or modern rubber webbing is used in upholstery; webbing from synthetic fibres or cotton may be used for straps and ties.

Weft The threads running across a woven piece of cloth.

Welt A name given to the gusset or side panel of a boxed cushion.

Wild silk Silk fabric made from natural silk fibre, but not from the bombyx mori (mulberry silk worm) native to China.

Wilton A carpet woven by a traditional method, so the pile is an integral part of the backing.

Yarn Thread (natural or man-made fibre) which has been spun or twisted so that it can be woven or used for embroidery or knitting.

Index

Acknowledgements

The Publishers would like to thank the following sources for their permission to reproduce the photographs in this book:

Far-flung fabrics gatefold: 1 *Robert Harding Picture Library/Adam Woolfit*; 2 background *Robert Harding Picture Library/Tony Gervis*; 2 top inset *Robert Harding Picture Library/JHC Wilson*; 2 bottom inset *Robert Harding Picture Library/Chris Rennie*; 3, 4, 5, 6 *Debi Treloar*; 7 background *Robert Harding Picture Library/Tony Gervis*; 7 inset *Robert Harding Picture Library/G Corrigan*; 8 *Robert Harding/Walter Rawlings*;

Dramatic drapes gatefold: 1 *David Parmitter*; 2 top left and bottom left *David Parmitter*; 2 right *Rupert Horrox*; 3 bottom left *David Parmitter*; 3 top left *Debi Treloar*; 3–4 bottom *Debi Treloar*; 3–4 top *David Parmitter*; 4–5 *The Interior Archive Ltd/Fritz von der Schulenburg*; 5–6 *Paul Ryan*; 6 *David Parmitter*; 6 bottom right *Paul Ryan*; 7 left *Rupert Horrox*; 7 bottom right *David Parmitter*; 7 inset *Lelievre*; 8 *Paul Ryan, design Raymond Waites*;

Outdoor living gatefold: 1 *The Interior Archive Ltd/Fritz von der Schulenburg*; 2 top left and right *Rupert Horrox*; 3 *Robert Harding Picrture Library*; 3–4 *Lara Grylls PR/Firifiss*; 4–5 *Laura Ashley*; 5 right *Rupert Horrox*; 5–6 top *Robert Harding Picture Library/Elizabeth Zeschin*; 6 right *Anna French Ltd*; 7 left *Rupert Horrox*; 7 right *Robert Harding Picture Library/Polly Wreford*; 8 *The Interior Archive/Fritz von der Schulenburg*;

Anna French Ltd 70 left, 71 top right, 84 left, 88, 122–123, 126 bottom, 127 top, 136 left, 172; *Belinda Coote* 194 inset; *Camron PR/Coloroll* 180 bottom left; *Chelsea Textiles* 51 bottom; *Ciel Decor/Les Olivades* 165 top; *Designers Guild* 32; *Elizabeth Whiting & Associates* 17 bottom right, 44, 45 top, 47 bottom right/ *Andreas von Einsiedel* 13 top, 46–47, 49 top and bottom; *Foster Berry Associates/ Lloyd Loom* 10 left; *GP&J Baker* 118 left; *Habitat* 20–21 top, 42 bottom left, 156 bottom left; *Halpern Associates/Andrew Martin* 45 bottom right; *Robert Harding Picture Library* 18/*Simon Upton* 121;

Harlequin 82 left, 83 bottom, 90 top, 94 bottom left, 165 bottom, 181 top; *Heather Tilbury Associates/Nimbus* 162–163; *Hickman & Associates/Jab* 40 top right; *Hill and Knowles* 83 top, 93 bottom; *Ikea Ltd* 148–149; *The Interior Archive Ltd* 35 bottom right, 70 top right, 123 bottom, 148 left, 150–151 top/*Tim Beddow* 110 top right, 115 bottom right/*Henry Bourne* 13 bottom/*Simon Brown* 22 left, 107 bottom right/*James Mortimer* 31 right, 63 top/*C Simon Sykes* 30/*Fritz von der Schulenburg* 10, 11, 22–2, 23, 24 left, 26–7, 27 right, 28–9, 29 right, 35 bottom inset, 42–3, 78 top right, 93 top left, 99 right, 146–147/ *Henry Wilson* 28 left, 52 top right, 53, 55 right; *International Interiors* 12 design Jo Nahem, 24–25, 38 top right design Sandra Nunnerly, 39 bottom right, 41 top right, 54 top right, 54–5 design Sasha Waddell, 63 bottom left, 67 bottom right, 72 bottom left, 80 top right, 84 right design Frances Halliday, 98–9 main, 100, 101 top left, 119 right design Kristiina Ratia, 130 left inset, 157 top right, 168 bottom left; *Key Interiors* 79 bottom, 86 left, 86–7; *Lara Grylls PR* 120 bottom left/*Design Archives* 59 bottom right, 68, 91 bottom, 67 top right, 155 top right/*The Iron Bed Company*. 163 right, 169/*Firifiss* 158–159; *Laura Ashley* 156 top right, 157 bottom left, 183 top left; *Lelievre* 154; *Liberty* 20 bottom right, 30 left, 38 bottom left, 60, 69 bottom; *Mary Fox Linton* 61 bottom right; *Melin Tregwynt* 36 bottom left, 146 inset left; *Next* 43 bottom, 46 left, 94 top right, 95 bottom right, 101 top right, 103 top left, 137 bottom, 142 bottom left; *The Nursery Window* 131 top right and bottom, 173 top left, 175 top right; *The O'Shea Gallery* 19, 20 bottom left, 69 top; *Peter Dudgeon* 34–35, 135 right; *Pierre Frey* 11 right; *Reed International Books Ltd* 15 bottom right/*Paul Barker* 15 top left/*Bill Batten* 62/*Simon Brown* 14 top/*Joe Cornish* 14 bottom right/*Rupert Horrox* 35 top inset, 37 top left, 72 top, 73 left and bottom right, 75, 76 top right, 78 bottom, 95 top, 98–9 bottom, 106 top, 108 left, 110 bottom left, 120 top right, 130–1, 132 left, 146 inset right, 147 top and bottom inset, 149 right, 152, 153 top and bottom left, 159 top and inset, 166 bottom left, 166–7, 178 left inset, 178–9, 182 top, 187 top right, 221 left and centre/*Di Lewis*

138, 139 top/*Jason Lowe* 14 bottom left/*David Parmitter* 6, 7, 17 top, 40 bottom, 47 top right, 66 inset left, 71 bottom right, 76 bottom, 77 bottom right, 81 left and right, 85 left, 87 right, 89 top, 90 bottom, 92, 93 right, 98 left, 102 bottom, 103 top right, 108–9, 112 left, 113 bottom left, 114–5, 117, 124 left, 125 right, 126 top, 128, 130 bottom right, 133 right, 134, 140 top and bottom, 141 left and right, 142 top, 143 bottom, 144 bottom, 150 centre and bottom left, 167, 170, 174 , 175 bottom right, 179 right inset, 180 top, 182 bottom, 184, 185, 186, 190, 191 top and bottom, 221 right/*Paul Ryan* 34 inset, 57 bottom, 63 bottom right, 73 top right, 89 bottom, 102 top, above centre and below centre, 104 left, 116, 130 left, 137 top, 143 top, 162 left inset, 171, 189/*Debi Treloar* 1, 2, 3, 4–5, 8, 9 ,10–11 background, 16, 33, 36 top and bottom right, 37 bottom right, 39 top left, 41 bottom, 50, 51 top, 52 bottom, 56 bottom, 57 top, 58 left, 59 top, 61 top, 65, 66–7 background, 76 top left, 77 top, 80 left, 96 top, 97, 98–9 background, 104–5 top & bottom, 105 bottom right, 112–3 top, 113 top right, 115 top right, 124 top right, 124–5, 129, 130–1 background, 144 top, 145, 146–7 background, 160 bottom, 161 , 162–3 background, 177, 178–9, 181 bottom right, 183 bottom, 193, 194–5, 194–5 background, 196 top and bottom, 197 right, 200, 201 left and right, 208–9, 215, 223 top right and bottom/*Steve Wooster* 15 top right/*Roger Oates* 56 top right; *Sahco Hesslein* 109 top right, 111 top; *Sanderson* 71 left, 79 top, 82 right, 106 bottom, 118–119, 132–133, 135 top left, 136 right,139 bottom, 155 bottom left, 188; *Timney Fowler* 61 bottom, 101 bottom right; *Today Interiors* 96 bottom left, 160 top right, 195 right; *Warner Fabrics* plc 58 right, 91 top;

Thanks is also due to those individuals and companies who generously loaned materials and props for studio and location photography: Arthur Sanderson & Sons, Middlesex/Alberta Ferretti, London/Altfield, London/The American Country Collection, Surrey/Artisan, London/The Bead Shop, London/Brunschwig & Fils,

London/Candle Maker Supplies, London/ Celia Birtwell, London/Ciel Decor, London/Colefax and Fowler, London/ Cologne&Cotton, London/Cope&Timmins, London/Designers Guild, London/Elna Sewing Machines, London/H A Percheron, London/Helen Green at Lifestyles, Interiors Ltd, London/Hobby Horse Ltd, London/The Iron Bed Company, West Sussex/JAB, London/Jane Churchill, London/Java Cotton Company, London/ Jerry's Home Store/Jim Thompson, London/Judy Greenwood, London/Lee Jofa, London/Liberty, London/Leyland Paints, London/The Malabar Cotton Company, London/Manuel Conovas Ltd, London/Material World, London/Nelson Morrow, Nelson Reis Design, London/ Nobilis Fontan, London/Nordic Style at Moussie, London/The OldCinema Antiques, London/Osborne & Little, London/Pallu & Lake and Charles Hammond at Chelsea of London, London/Paperchase, London/ Piecemakers, Surrey/Prêt a Vivre, London/ Sacho Hesslein UK, London/Sew'n'Sew, Gloucestershire/Shaker, London/Timney Fowler, London/Titley and Marr, Hamphshire/Tumi Latin American Crafts, London/V V Rouleaux Ltd, London/Vision Drapes, London/Warner Fabrics, Milton Keynes, Buckinghamshire/Wendy Cushing Trimmings, London/Wild Ones, London

In addition the publishers would like to thank the following house-owners and interior designers for their permission to photograph their homes and work:
Harriet Anstruther, Charlotte Aiviolo and Ralph James, Donna Bell, Audrey Bryant, Rachel and Tim Carson, Sarah and Nick Cheadle, Maria and Jonathan Duff, Audrey and Ron Edwards, Myra Frost, Frances Halliday, Emily Hedges, Maureen and Keith Horrox, Lauren Irwin, Catherine Lewis and Christopher Moss, Milly Lonsdale, Penny and Oliver McFarlane, Kate Malone and Graham Inglefield, Nelson Morrow FIDDA, Paul Passman, Michael Trapp, Karen White FIDDA ASID, Karin Verzariu FIDDA;

Finally, special thanks to Beryl Miller for her sewing expertise and Claudia Bryant for her tireless prop hunting and styling.